Class Tells

On Social Inequality in Canada

Alfred A. Hunter
University of Waterloo

Butterworths
Toronto

Class Tells

Printed and bound in Canada

The Butterworth Group of Companies

Canada:
Butterworth & Co. (Canada) Ltd., Toronto and Vancouver

United Kingdom:
Butterworth & Co. (Publishers) Ltd., London

Australia:
Butterworths Pty. Ltd., Sydney

New Zealand:
Butterworths of New Zealand Ltd., Wellington

South Africa:
Butterworth & Co. (South Africa) Ltd., Durban

United States:
Butterworth (Publishers) Inc., Boston
Butterworth (Legal Publishers) Inc., Seattle
Mason Publishing Company, St. Paul

Canadian Cataloguing in Publication Data

Hunter, Alfred A.
  Class tells

Bibliography: p.
Includes index.
ISBN 0-409-83770-9

1. Social classes – Canada.
2. Canada – Social conditions.
I. Title.

HN110.Z9S64   305.5'0971   C81-094403-0

Printed by Hunter Rose

To Mona and Gordon
and Margaret, Jamie, and Alexander.

Acknowledgements

Many students, colleagues, and friends (not at all mutually exclusive categories) have read at least parts of this manuscript and commented most usefully on them, or have engaged me in discussion and debate on issues of structured social inequality more generally. Although they are not responsible for what I have done with their contributions, I could not have written this book without them. Among those who have commented on the manuscript directly are Ben Agger, Roy T. Bowles, Carl Cuneo, Margaret Denton, Sue Dier, John Goyder, Neil Guppy, Ron Lambert, and Mike Manley. Finally, Ursula Ortmann and Beverly Taylor spent many hours on the University of Waterloo's interactive terminal system preparing successive drafts of this document. I marvel at their talent and tenacity, and I cannot thank them enough.

Contents

PART IV: ON CLASS IN CANADIAN SOCIETY

PART V: CLASS TELLS

Chapter 1

Introduction

"What is the answer? But what is the question?" (Dying words attributed to Gertrude Stein.)

When asked about the remarkable absence of lines on his forehead, the elderly Spencer replied, "I suppose it is because I am never puzzled" (told of the nineteenth-century social thinker Herbert Spencer).

Hundreds of years before the emergence of sociology as a recognized branch of scholarship in the nineteenth century, thoughtful observers had noted the social inequalities about them, inquired as to their origins, and debated whether or not they were just. Concern with "who gets what, when, and how," as Lasswell and Kaplan (1950:67-68) frame the issue, or with "the question of classes and class conflict," as Giddens (1973:19) characterizes it, was an important impetus to the initial development of sociology, and it continues to provide the motivation behind much modern theory and research. Many historians of the discipline would concur in Dahrendorf's judgment of "the problem of inequality as a key to the history of sociology" (1969:17). And some contemporary sociologists would even see it as "*the* problem in sociology" (Giddens, 1973:19, emphasis in the original). But sociology is not the kind of activity, at least at present, whose practitioners can agree on much for long. Not all sociologists would accept Dahrendorf's assessment — much less Giddens's — and, even among those who would, there remain important disagreements as to what aspects of "the problem" are most crucial and, even, how the problem itself is best defined. It is beyond the confines of this book, however, to chart in detail the role inequality has played in the evolution of social thought or to fix its ultimate importance for sociology. Rather, the book will attempt the more modest task of suggesting some of the likely reasons why inequality has been and remains a significant issue, and then of concentrating on an analysis of theories and facts of inequality, especially as these help us better understand modern Canadian society.

The Importance of Inequality as a Problem

How is it that the question of inequality has enjoyed such a lengthy and lively intellectual history? One probable reason is that social inequalities have been characteristic of every society and historical epoch we know about, although they have been more pronounced in some places and periods than others, and they have displayed a remarkable variety of forms (Lenski, 1965, Chapters 5–12; Bendix and Lipset, 1966: Part II; Heller, 1969: Parts II and III). The apparent universality of social inequality, though, has not meant that it has everywhere and always been analysed and questioned. Just as inequalities have varied widely in degree and type over time and from place to place, people have also varied in how conscious and accepting they have been of them. Too, reactions to social inequality are seldom determined in any simple way by the character of the inequalities people experience in their lives. This variable connection between the observable facts of inequality and individuals' reactions to them is not, however, just a curiosity in the history of inequality as a problem. It is also a theoretical and empirical issue of major importance to be discussed at length below.

Another likely reason for the continuing interest in social inequality lies in the fact that it seeps into and shapes so many aspects of our experience, even if we are not always (or even often) aware of its presence and effects. It is not something which affects only some people or touches only some isolated corner of our lives. Whenever something is both scarce and valued, individuals and groups will compete for it, and some will possess more of it than others. And inequality is the usual state of our relationships with others and of the relations among groups, and equality the rare and limiting case. A phenomenon as pervasive as this is almost synonymous with social life itself, and any thorough-going theory of inequality, then, will necessarily represent a considerable feat of mental labour, tying together the full gamut of our life's activities from home to work to play.

The apparent universality and pervasiveness of social inequality have, moreover, given rise to as yet unresolved debates as to its inevitability, necessity, and justice which touch upon such fundamental questions of group life as: By what means do societies survive and continue? And according to what principles do they change? To some (e.g., Marx and Engels, 1959), social inequality can best be seen as the historical product of group struggles under different systems of economic production, in which a few are able to benefit at the expense of many. Social order is maintained largely through the coercion of the weak by the powerful, and major social changes come about as the result of alterations in existing relations of power and authority. To others (e.g., Davis and Moore, 1945), differential rewards appear as a necessary and (perhaps even) just means whereby individuals are induced to move into positions in the division of labour of a society and motivated to perform the tasks which attach to these positions. In this way, functions important to the survival of the group as a whole (and of the individuals who make it up) are fulfilled. Debates over these and related issues have long divided social commentators (Lenski, 1965: Chapter 1), and they shall inform this chapter, as well as the rest of this book.

Finally, although this does not at all exhaust the important reasons one might point to, the longevity and vitality of inequality as a problem are likely due in part to the character of the period and place in which many of those often regarded as the founders of modern sociology lived and wrote. The nature and effects of the shift from medieval to modern Europe were questions which occupied the intellectual attentions of a great many nineteenth- and early twentieth-century scholars. These include, most notably for contemporary sociology, Marx, Weber, and Durkheim, whose major writings can be viewed as attempts to describe and account for this massive social transformation.

Marx essentially saw in it the displacement of feudalism, and the aristocracy which presided over it, by capitalism, with a dominant entrepreneurial class and a distinctive set of class relations. Weber emphasized the importance in capitalism of the processes of rationalization and bureaucratization for the erosion of loyalty to, and the authority of, such traditional forms of organization as the family, the village, the guild, and the church, coupled with the development of impersonal authority structures in business and the state (Weber, 1946, 1964). And Durkheim took as his special concern the growth of individualism and the destruction of long-established social institutions and ties as consequences of a burgeoning technology and an ever more finely differentiated division of labour (Durkheim, 1964, 1966).

While their individual visions remain very much distinct, they do share in common a number of dominant themes including, most importantly for the present analysis, the notion that "of all conflicts in European history, the most fundamental have been those relating to the location of social function and the administration of authority in human lives" (Nisbet, 1962:88). If these men did not locate these conflicts in quite the same place, it is nevertheless true that all three saw the unrest and upheaval which followed in the wake of the Industrial Revolution as brought about by, and resulting in, profound dislocations and rearrangements in existing hierarchies of power and authority. Unlike many disciplines in which the work of their pioneers has been quickly superseded and effectively forgotten, sociology has not made rapid progress, and the scholarly stamp which Marx, Weber, and Durkheim placed on it seventy-five to one hundred years ago may be faded, but it is still clearly legible today.

Elements in a Theory of Inequality

If social inequality is a feature of all human societies past and present as we know them, it is idle to speculate as to what its causes and effects might be. It is a basic axiom of logic and the scientific method that, for some phenomenon to be shown to have causes and effects, it must be known to have been present in some times and places and absent in others. Without sufficient contemporary or historical examples of societies both with and without inequality, no plausible theory of inequality as such can even be formulated, much less tested.

A theory of the origins and effects of inequality per se, then, may be an unreachable goal, at least in the present state of knowledge. But it may also be a trivial goal, since the important variations in systems of inequality probably lie in magnitude and type, which a theory of inequality as such would leave untouched. The basic task for a theory of social inequality, then, seems not to be to provide an explanation for its presence at some times and in some places and its absence at other times and elsewhere. More likely, it is to make sense of the changing process of "who gets what, when, and how," or of class formation and conflict, and to find meaning in variations in this process among different societies.

Just what, then, is intended in the term "social inequality," or "structured social inequality?" The concept of "inequality" carries with it an ambiguity alluded to, but not specifically identified, in the opening quotations from Lasswell and Kaplan and Giddens. Following Goldthorpe (1972) and Coser (1975), we can point to two analytically separate but empirically related kinds of things normally lumped together under the single label of inequality: the *distributive* and the *relational*. Lasswell and Kaplan, on the one hand, alert us particularly to consider issues in the *distribution* of scarce and valued resources among individuals and social groups. Who, for example, is well-educated, well-placed in an occupation, or wealthy? How did they become so? And with what consequences for them? These are questions with a long and reputable history in sociology, especially North American sociology, as exemplified in the work of W. Lloyd Warner and his associates in the Yankee City series (e.g., Warner et al., 1960; Warner et al., 1964). Perhaps the latter-day classic in this genre is Blau and Duncan's *The American Occupational Structure* (1967), which has provided a model for more than a decade of studies of "status attainment." Giddens, on the other hand, is more concerned with the *relational* aspects of inequality, where the salient issues involve inequalities in social relationships. Approaching the problem of inequality in its relational aspect, we are prompted to address questions involving relationships or exchanges among individuals and groups from the point of view of their reciprocity or symmetry. Relational inequalities refer to asymmetries in exchanges between units such that, for example, one person gives more of something to another than he or she receives in exchange, or one social class benefits at another's expense. The pioneering studies of Marx and Weber are major contributions to our understanding of the relational aspects of inequality. There are few modern studies to match them, although Mills's *The Power Elite* (1956) and Porter's *The Vertical Mosaic* (1965) are two impor;tant contemporary works which follow in this tradition.

The "true" study of inequality would seem not to lie in the analysis of either distributive or relational phenomena to the exclusion of the other. Quite clearly, they intersect with one another in a number of ways, and it is more than possible that one cannot be understood without reference to the other. It is not likely, for example, that we will ever know all that is important in the processes by which individuals find their way into niches in the occupational structure (e.g., physician), if we do not also apprehend the manner and means by which certain social groups (e.g., Canadian Medical Association) control access to avenues of training and use this control to their members' advantage. The one set of problems is necessarily bound up with the other, and so it may well be with a multitude of other distributive and relational questions.

The relational aspect of inequalities highlights their inherently social character. The rich, for example, can only be studied to real effect in the context of their relations with the less rich or with the poor, and the converse is no less true. But inequalities are social in the sense that they are often recognized in and given legitimation (i.e., justification) through systems of norms, attitudes, beliefs, and values which are learned in a process of socialization and passed on in some form from generation to generation. These cultural systems typically represent the interests of those groups in society powerful enough to impose them generally. And they provide definitions of positions in the division of labour, specifications as to what rights and duties come along with these positions, and rules which identify who is an appropriate candidate for a particular position and who is not. "Housewife," for example, is a position in the sexual division of labour; housewives are expected to do certain kinds of things (e.g., cooking, cleaning, and caring for the children), and not others (such as running for elected federal office or playing professional sport); and only certain kinds of people (e.g., adult females) are eligible to be housewives.

Too, the inequalities of concern here are also structured, in the sense that they are relatively organized and fairly stable. This is true both of distributive and of relational inequalities. We know, for example, that women whose labour market qualifications are in every way equivalent to those of men do not, even when they work in what seem to be identical jobs, earn as much on the average as men do. This is the case today; it was the case ten years ago; and it was the case fifty years before that. Moreover, there is little evidence that this distributive sex inequality has diminished much over time. But there is much more to it. It is also organized and maintained to some extent by the fact that men tend overwhelmingly to occupy the command posts of the occupational world, and systematically (although not always consciously) use their favoured positions to the advantage of other men. The system of occupational sex inequality is thus relational as well as distributive, and its relational aspect is no less important than its distributive one.

Whether relational or distributive, structured social inequalities can be seen to involve matters of material resources and matters of cultural belief or value. Relational inequalities of the material kind refer to circumstances in which one individual or group of individuals has material resources (e.g., wealth) which are superior to those of another and uses this advantage to receive more of something than it gives. This is the phenomenon of *power*. Relational inequalities of the cultural variety are those in which one individual or group receives benefits of some kind from another because this is generally thought to be right. This is the phenomenon of *status*. Or, as Kemper describes them, "power and ... status are ... alternative modes of social relationships by which actors obtain benefits and rewards from each other" (1974:847). As for distributive inequalities, the material involve some units having more of some scarce resource (e.g., education) than other units do, while the cultural involve the ranking of units in terms of value. As Parsons observes, "stratification in its valuational aspects ... is the ranking of units in a social system in accordance with ... standards" (1953:83). The first of these two might be termed inequalities in *possessions,* while the second can be referred to as inequalities in *prestige.*

Also, it will prove useful in our subsequent analyses to distinguish between the *macrostructural* and the *microstructural* levels of analysis in a way which is quite similar to the corresponding distinction in economics between macro- and microeconomics. Briefly, the difference between these two is essentially the difference between theoretical propositions and empirical observations which deal with the properties and performances of *aggregates* of people or organized *groups,* on the one hand, and those which describe *individual* or *family* attributes and activities, on the other. Social classes and status groups, for example, are collective phenomena, and theories and observations about them are, by this definition, macrostructural, while theories and observations which refer to the qualities of individual people (e.g., their levels of educational attainment or amounts of annual income) are microstructural. Thus, Marx and Weber (and Mills and Porter) were primarily concerned with macrostructural inequalities, while Warner and Blau and Duncan concentrated mainly on microstructural ones.

As in the case of relational and distributive inequalities, it seems likely that the macro- and microstructural phenomena of social inequality cannot be wholly understood in isolation from one another. It is often argued, for example, that North America is characterized by relatively low levels of class conflict, and that one of the reasons for this is that there is so much movement or mobility across class boundaries on the part of individuals. Or, for another example, it is clear that the overall distribution of incomes in a society necessarily places limits on the income attainment of individuals. In the first instance, the suggestion is that a microstructural phenomenon (individual mobility) influences a macrostructural one (class conflict) while, in the second, a macrostructural attribute (the distribution of incomes) is pointed to as setting limits to a microstructural one (individual income attainment).

We have, then, identified the topic to be dealt with as one of structured social inequality, and we have attempted to elaborate some basic distinctions which might assist us in studying it. First, we have distinguished between relational and distributive inequalities, in that the former refer to the character of the relationships between individuals or groups and the latter to differences between individuals or groups in their possession of whatever is both scarce and valued. Second, we have distinguished between inequalities deriving from differences in material resources and inequalities originating in cultural values or beliefs. And third, we have distinguished between aggregates and groups as the unit of analysis (the macrostructural) and individuals as the unit of analysis (the microstructural). These distinctions are summarized and illustrated in Figure 1-1.

A complete enumeration of all of the aspects of social inequality which have been identified in the sociological literature would be an exhausting and, probably, fruitless exercise. For one thing, it would be an enormous list and,

Figure 1-1 SOME BASIC DISTINCTIONS IN THE STUDY OF SOCIAL INEQUALITY

	Macrostructural		Microstructural	
	Relational	Distributive	Relational	Distributive
Material Resources	e.g., one group gains at the expense of another through coercion	e.g., one group is wealthier than another	e.g., one person gains at the expense of another through coercion	e.g., one family earns more income than another
Cultural Values	e.g., one group gains at the expense of another through voluntary means, because this is thought to be proper	e.g., one group is regarded as socially superior to another	e.g., one family gains at the expense of another through voluntary means, because this is thought to be proper	e.g., one person is regarded as socially superior to another

for another, it would reveal nothing of the *relationships* among the elements in the list. Whatever else may be involved in scientific endeavours, it is the isolation and identification of the relationships among things which is of first concern. And these relationships are essentially of three types: *empirical, epistemic,* and *theoretical* — of which only the first are directly accessible to investigation. Empirical relationships are those observed associations among the measurements which scientists make, such as the actual correlation between level of education attained and amount of annual income earned as calculated for a sample of people (as in "those persons with less than twelve years of education earned, on the average, $5,236 less per year than did those persons with twelve or more years of education"). Epistemic relationships are those which are inferred to obtain between one or more observed attributes and a theoretical variable which is only abstractly defined, such as the associations between level of educational attainment and amount of annual income, on the one hand, and prestige, on the other (as in "prestige is measured in terms of education and income"). And theoretical relationships are associations which are thought to hold between two or more theoretical variables, such as power and status (as in "inequalities in status originate in inequalities in power").[1]

---

[1]   This is a selectively simplified statement, but otherwise not a bad example of the character of theoretical propositions in sociology. Moreover, it hypothesizes a particular connection between what Kemper (1974) calls the "fundamental dimensions of social relationships," that is that voluntary relations of status *originate in* differences in power.

These three kinds of relationships can be illustrated in Figure 1–2, where i refers to the empirical association between two observed measures of a single theoretical variable, 1 and 2 denote the epistemic associations between these two measures and the theoretical variables, and I indicates the relationship between the two theoretical variables. In fact, however, all we ever observe directly are relationships of the type i, from which we attempt to infer relationships of the types 1 and I, of which 1 describes the *measurement model* and I the *theoretical model*. And the ultimate value of the inferences which we make about epistemic and theoretical relationships is judged against such criteria as: How well do they permit us to make predictions in the real world? And do they seem to suggest that the real world is a systematic and orderly place?

Figure 1-2   RELATIONSHIPS IN A SCIENTIFIC THEORY

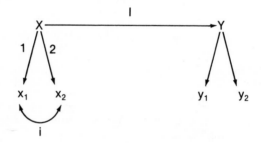

As Figure 1–2 suggests, the principal purpose of theoretical variables is to summarize and describe the associations among the empirical observations which are taken to measure them. Scientific theories are beliefs scientists hold which order and make sensible to them otherwise unrelated and ambiguous observations (Nagel, 1961; Rudner, 1966). Minimally, these theories contain a set of abstractly defined concepts or variables in terms of which the objects or events studied can be described (e.g., "power" and "status"). In addition, these concepts are tied together in a set of (at least potentially) testable, law-like propositions specifying how they are related to one another. In its essentials, then, a theory of social inequality would involve a set of general, theoretical variables yielding summary descriptions of distributive and relational aspects of inequality, along with a number of statements linking these variables together in some systematic fashion. These variables and propositions should not only provide summary descriptions and explanations of distributive inequalities and inequalities in social relationships, they should also be grounded in existing theories wherever possible. As a point of entry to the study of social inequality in Canada, a critical review of certain theories should not be an empty exercise in the analysis of dead ideas or an attempt to force foreign abstractions upon obdurate Canadian facts. Rather, it should demonstrate the life there is in sociological analyses, and how

Canadian patterns of inequality might be potentially understood. The vitality of an enterprise such as sociology is in its theory.

Part I

Concepts, Theories, and Issues

Chapter 2

On Marxism
and Some of Its Critics

*"It is alien... to the Canadian political tradition and to the
tradition of Canadian scholarship" (pioneer Canadian sociologist S. D. Clark (1976:144) speaking of Marxism).*

Despite the antiquity of structured social inequality as a problem, Marx and
Engels have good claim to have been the first to propose a theory of inequality
which is still very much with us today. In a voluminous series of letters, articles,
pamphlets, and books, including, perhaps most importantly, the compact and
immensely influential *Manifesto of the Communist Party* and the massive,
three-volume work, *Capital*, these two men developed and elaborated an
ambitious analysis of society and history animated by an evolutionary theory of
economics. Long held in disrepute by North American academics, Marxism has
enjoyed a remarkable resurgence since the mid-1960s in Canada, the U.S., and
elsewhere in the West, although little Marxist scholarship has as yet found its
way into mainstream, North American sociological journals, such as the
American Sociological Review and *The Canadian Review of Sociology and
Anthropology*.

Contemporary Marxism is a growing and several-headed beast which
defies simple, summary description (Burawoy, 1978; Agger, 1979). There remain
those orthodox true believers whom Mills (1963) denigrated as "Dead Marxists"
who think of Marxism as a comprehensive and closed system of truths. There are
those whom he labelled "Sophisticated Marxists" whose elaborations on the
themes of the founders are so detailed and complex that their origins are
obscured and their meaning obscure. There are the "Plain Marxists," among
whom Mills (arguably) counted himself, who remain true to the basic principles
of Marxism while freely adapting them to circumstance. And, within each of
these three broad categories, there are still finer distinctions of Marxism and
Marxist. The account which follows cross-cuts this simple typology, although it
is probably closer to some version of Plain Marxism than to any other.

Basic Concepts and Principles of Marxism
Marx and Engels drew many disparate strands of thought together in a social
and economic theory which turns on the belief that the substance of social life
inheres in the networks of relations which obtain among people, not in either the

isolated individual or such rarefied abstractions as "society" or "history". Society is individuals *in* their relations with others. History is the evolution of the totality of these relations over time which, if "lawful," is not strictly predetermined. And social change occurs in a *dialectical* process, whereby each material condition (e.g., the bourgeoisie) brings forth its opposite (in this case, the proletariat), and out of the interaction between them comes a wholly new material condition (e.g., a new era in social production). Marx and Engels, following Feuerbach, argued that ideas — consciousness, the mental states of people — originate in historically specific networks of social relations, and derive their basic form and content from this source. At the same time, people are not mere marionettes of their society and a set of impersonal, iron laws governing the direction of its development.

> Men make their own history, but they do not make it just as they please; they do not make it under circumstances chosen by themselves, but under circumstances directly encountered, given and transmitted from the past. The tradition of all the dead generations weighs like a nightmare on the brain of the living (Marx, 1969:398).

If what we study are people acting in relation to one another, those networks of social relations forged out of economic activities are the most decisive. They constitute, in the parlance of Marxism, the *infrastructure* which ultimately determines the structure, organization, and course of change of the political, legal and other *superstructures* of a society. To contradict Collins and others who have seen in this a straightforward economic determinism, however, Marx and Engels do not appear to have "ultimately assumed a monocausal explanation for a multicausal world" (Collins, 1975:49). It would probably be accurate to assert that, of all the many causes in a multicausal world, economic relations stand first in importance in the Marxian model, and reveal their priority in the long run. If this leaves good room for argument and specification, it is also more faithful to the original formulation.

To Marx and Engels, history could be seen as a series of epochs: the isolated primitive family, the tribe, ancient society, feudalism, and capitalism — each characterized by a distinctive *mode of production*. This mode involves certain *productive forces* — a division and organization of work and workers, knowledge and skills, and a technology — anchored in a set of *relations of production,* especially property relations. Except in the era of the family — the first productive unit in history, and the only one with no form of private property — the mode of production of an epoch is embedded in a set of *private property* arrangements, be this property slaves (as in tribal and ancient society), land (as in feudalism), or capital (as in more recent times). In the era of the isolated primitive family, the family itself was the basic productive unit, and the division of labour within it was largely organized around distinctions of age and sex. Social relations were productive relations, since labour enabled individual family members to survive and the family unit to cohere. But the satisfaction of sustenance needs generates additional needs which can only be satisfied through participation in productive units other and larger than the family. And all such units are inextricably bound up with the institution of private property.

A *social class,* in the Marxian lexicon, is an aggregate of persons similarly situated in the relations of production. The crucial element in this situation is not education or specialized training, occupation or income. It is, rather, how these people stand with regard to ownership of the means of production. Where there is private ownership of the means of production, those who partake of ownership are by that fact members of the dominant class, while the remainder belong to one or another subordinate class. Thus, though two people might otherwise have similar levels of skill, like occupations, and equivalent amounts of income, if one owns some part of the means of production of a society and the other does not, they belong to different classes, and the consequences of this difference touch upon every aspect of their lives. Where there is private ownership of the means of production, ownership becomes the single most important determinant of one's social relations, actions, beliefs, and share of the available material wealth.

The property relations within each mode of production provide, then, the foundation for a class structure and a complex of superstructures or social institutions. Members of the dominant class hold some rein on these institutions and direct them in their own interest. The systems of private property upon which dominant classes depend, for example, are typically maintained by the state (Miliband, 1969), which retains a monopoly over the means of legitimate violence (i.e., the police and the military). The state normally does this, moreover, not out of any accidental coincidence of interest between itself and the dominant class, but *on behalf of* the dominant class. Since members of the dominant class possess a disproportionate share of the wealth in any society, and since power and authority issue from wealth more than from anything else, it is to be expected that the state will usually play this kind of role. For these reasons, Marx and Engels were moved to characterize the modern state as "nothing more than the form of organization which the bourgeois necessarily adopt for the mutual guarantee of their property and interests" (1965:78). But the modern state does not invariably follow this model and, where it does, it does not follow it all of the time. There is no paucity of historical examples to show, for instance, that the state has even sometimes acted on its own behalf to expropriate the wealth of a propertied class.

A class in ascent to dominance is a creative force — developing and exploiting new technological forms, promoting innovative ideas, and liberating people from traditional and oppressive relations of production. Once in place however, it inclines toward the reactionary, since it is in the interest of a dominant class to maintain a status quo in which it occupies the most favoured position. Such, of course, is not in the interest of the various subordinate classes. As the mode of production of an era matures, then, it becomes inconsistent with the property relations and class structure within which it originally developed. Conflicts between dominant and subordinate classes breed more generalized conflicts between them, which can lead eventually to the radical transformation of society and the advent of a new era in social production. Thus, private property in ancient society began to emerge when the more affluent and powerful citizens began to demand their own personal slaves. With the establishment of this practice came conflicts between owners and nonowners of slaves — the first class conflict in history. This, coupled with simultaneous animosities pitting master vs. slave, industry vs. maritime trade, and rural populace vs. urban, rent apart the fabric of ancient society. Out of its remnants came feudalism. In tribal and ancient society, commerce created surpluses which made possible the institution of slavery and the consequent internal contradictions which brought these systems to ruin. In feudal society, these surpluses generated productive forces much too powerful to be contained within feudal property relations which "became so many fetters. They had to be burst asunder; they were burst asunder" (Marx and Engels, 1959:12).

In every historical period, social classes have done battle over the distribution of material wealth, power, and authority, and class conflict has been a potent progenitor of (often cataclysmic) social change. As Marx and Engels, in the opening phrases and characteristic prose of the *Manifesto,* express it:

> The history of all hitherto existing society is the history of class struggles. Free man and slave, patrician and plebeian, lord and serf, guild master and journeyman, in a word, oppressor and oppressed, stood in constant opposition to one another, carried on an uninterrupted, now hidden, now open fight, a fight that each time ended in a revolutionary reconstitution of society at large or in the common ruin of the contending classes (1959:7).

Class and Class Conflict in Capitalist Society

Capitalism emerged from the tatters of feudalism in nineteenth-century Europe. Its distinctive mode of production involves fixed, circulating, and variable capital (i.e., machines, raw and auxiliary materials, and money for wages, respectively), wage labour, and the relationships among these. In capitalism, capital is activated for the purpose of generating *surplus value.* The notion of surplus value comes out of what was known to nineteenth-century economists as the *labour theory of value.* Briefly, commodities are produced for the market by human labour. These have a capacity to satisfy some human want — a use-value — and they have, as well, an exchange-value determined by the average amount of labour congealed in them under normal production conditions. Machines, materials, and money become capital when exchanged among members of the bourgeoisie and between bourgeoisie and proletariat. Members of the proletariat, with only their capacity to be put to work to sell, exchange their labour power for a wage with those who own the means of production. The cost of labour power is determined by the socially necessary labour time required for labourers to maintain themselves and their families at a particular standard of living.

Those who own capital can require workers to labour longer than socially necessary, (i.e., than required for workers to produce commodities of sufficient value to maintain themselves and their families). To the extent that this occurs, these workers put in surplus labour time to produce surplus commodities whose value is surplus value. The rate of surplus value (i.e., the ratio of surplus value to wages) is equal to the rate of worker exploitation (i.e., the ratio of surplus labour time to socially necessary labour time). Surplus value, then, derives from reducing the period of time each day in which workers work for themselves. It is generated primarily through some combination of lengthening the working day, reducing wages, speeding up the process of production, rationalizing the social organization of work, and/or introducing new and more efficient machinery.

Capitalists whose enterprises generate no surplus value have no source of livelihood. Simply to maintain themselves, therefore, capitalists must require their workers to put in surplus labour time. But capitalists face the (Hobson's) choice of simply consuming each year the surplus value available to them (i.e., "simple reproduction"), eventually going bankrupt, and sinking into the masses of the proletariat, or of using a certain proportion of it to invest in their businesses and make them grow (i.e., "accumulation"). Typically, then, they seek to increase the rate of surplus value for investment purposes. So, it is part of the very logic of capitalism itself that surplus labour time be put in, surplus commodities produced, surplus value created, and workers exploited. As Marx observed:

> This boundless greed after riches, this passionate chase after exchange-value, is common to the capitalist and the miser; but while the miser is merely a capitalist gone mad, the capitalist is a rational miser (1967:153).

Capitalism does not, of course, first appear in full form, and it exists in a permanent state of transformation (Mandel, 1968). In order for capitalism to develop, it is first necessary for ownership and control of the means of production to be wrested away from a number of workers who are then gathered together in the employ of individual entrepreneurs concerned to increase the value of their holdings. These dual phenomena of the "alienation of workers from the means of production" and "primitive accumulation" tend initially to appear in the guise of a collection of artisans pursuing their traditional crafts, but doing so in exchange for a wage and under conditions where they do not control the work process or participate, as they once did, in the distribution or sale of the commodities they produce. The entrepreneur fixes the exchange-value of these commodities at a rate determined by the wages which must be paid to maintain the workers and their families at a particular level, requirements for surplus value, and what the traffic will bear. Although many artisans are able to remain self-employed in this period, they find it progressively more difficult to retain their independence in the face of competition from these growing enterprises. But the productivity of these enterprises themselves is relatively low and the possibilities for the expropriation of surplus value correspondingly limited. In time, they are replaced by more sophisticated productive units.

Alienation and accumulation are further intensified with the introduction of a division of labour (Braverman, 1974; Rinehart, 1975). Where the limits to surplus value were previously constrained by the pace of workers and the length, of the working day, they can now be raised without any necessary change in either of these. A division of labour can increase productivity through the rational articulation of the several skills of a number of individual workers, all of which are required to produce a single manufactured article. If these workers still retain their knowledge and practice their skills in the old-fashioned way, their alienation is heightened by their no longer being able in any very clear or direct way to identify with the products of their labours, for these are now collective products. With the further elaboration of the division of labour, however, the integrity of individual crafts becomes more and more compromised as workers are required to carry out in repetitive fashion only some segment of a traditional craft activity. Now the work process consists increasingly of a multiplicity of specialized tasks marshalled together and applied to the raw materials of manufacture for the purpose of creating a single article. Individual workers need only a readily-acquired competence in a relatively narrow range of activities which, due to its ease of acquisition, renders them increasingly replaceable by large numbers of potential competitors. Whatever claims to creativity workers might earlier have had become increasingly difficult to make as knowledge and skill requirements are levelled through specialization. Weakened before, identification with the product becomes weaker still.

As the increments to surplus value added through refinements in the division of labour progressively diminish, the focus tends to shift from the social organization of work to the machinery of production as a source of surplus value. The hand-operated tools of the individual worker more and more give way to power-driven equipment in the interest of still greater efficiency. Workers increasingly become appendages to machines, their control over the work process even more diminished, and their alienation from the process and products of work heightened again. In the long run, as well, the importation of increasingly sophisticated machinery into the workplace has the effect of further diluting the skill requirements of jobs and, thereby, of making workers even more replaceable than before.

These developments in the historical evolution of capitalism do not appear in any very strict sequence, even within a single country and domain of economic activity. Some countries develop earlier, at a faster rate, and in a somewhat different manner than others (Frank, 1969). Within a single country, too, different regions exhibit different rates and patterns of development than others. And, while the analysis above has thus far been couched in the vocabulary of the industrial sector and, in particular, of the shop floor, the same principles can be applied to what might otherwise appear to be very diverse kinds of work, such as white-collar clerical tasks (e.g., Braverman, 1974:Chapter 15) and systems analysis in electronic data processing (Greenbaum, 1976).

As capital accumulates, it tends also to become centralized, as the larger and wealthier capitalists become better able to consume or bankrupt the smaller and poorer of their kind. Accumulation and centralization operating together stimulate technological advance, since well-capitalized businesses can carry out programs of research and development beyond the reach of their less well-capitalized competitors — and do so in the interest of still further accumulation and centralization. Consequently, the greater the concentration of wealth in the hands of fewer and fewer people, the wealthier a nation tends to be. But, if centralization increases the wealth of nations, the wages of workers, while they can and often do increase in absolute value, do not increase in direct proportion. The greater the rate of increase in capitalization for machinery, the smaller the rate of increase in capitalization for wages, since both must come from increases in surplus value. Although some Marxists hold that accumulation and centralization of capital lead ultimately to *absolute* decreases in wages, this is open to some interpretation. Anderson (1974:22–24) argues, for example, that this was an early notion which Marx later abandoned in favour of the idea of relative poverty. Insofar as there is a disparity between the rate of increase in the wealth of nations and the rate of increase in the wages of their workers, these workers become *relatively* impoverished — if, perhaps, wealthier in absolute terms. Poverty can be seen as relative in a second sense, as well. While there are in Marx and Engels's writings clear statements to the effect that workers are paid wages at or about a rate necessary to maintain themselves and their families at subsistence levels, Marx nevertheless argued that:

> the value of labour is in every country determined by a *traditional standard of life*. It is not mere physical life, but it is the satisfaction of certain wants springing from the social conditions in which people are placed and reared up (Marx, 1935:57).

So, while the wages of workers might increase in absolute terms, if this increase is not proportional to the increase in the standard of life of those around them, these workers become "relatively impoverished" in a second, if related, sense of that term.

As capitalism continues to develop, the increasing application of machinery to production boosts productivity and surplus value, while wages decline (relatively, if not absolutely), and the size of the labour force tends to decrease. As a result, "epidemics of overproduction" break out, since the purchasing power of the population fails to keep pace with the production of commodities for sale. These epidemics or peaks in the business cycle are part of the internal contradictions of capitalism and an inherent source of instability in capitalist systems. When they occur, industry must slow down and dispose of its inventories. This depresses wages and creates a floating mass of the unemployed to whom Marx attached the label *industrial reserve army*. When inventories are disposed of, production picks up, wages rise once again, the ranks of the industrial reserve army shrink, and the cycle is set to repeat itself.

While the scenario of recurrent and increasingly severe economic crises culminating in the eventual destruction of capitalism is undeniably present in Marx, it coexists along with other, sometimes very different, scenarios as well. Since it is at once an especially contentious idea and only one of a number of possible projections which might be made into an indefinite future, it will not be entertained further. Our present concern lies with using the principles of Marxism in an attempt to understand the phenomenon of inequality in Canada, and only the deadest of Dead Marxists is likely to read immanent destruction into present events. At the same time, there would seem to be no reason why the notion of business cycles and epidemics of overproduction might not be retained for future use.

Since surplus value is the source of wealth for both bourgoisie and proletariat, and since the bourgeoisie control its distribution, the interests of these two classes must forever be in conflict. If members of a class share common objective interests, this does not mean, however, that they necessarily recognize this fact, much less that they actively band together in opposition to classes whose interests conflict with their own. As long as this recognition is absent, members of a class will remain divided among themselves in competition over their common share of surplus value, and the class will remain a "class in itself." In order for this recognition to develop among the proletariat, and for members of this class to begin to come together and organize in their common interest, that is, for the class-in-itself to become a "class-for-itself," capitalism must develop rather beyond the stage of the initial expropriation of surplus value.

As capitalism matures as a system, the rate of exploitation (and, hence, of relative impoverishment) tends to increase. As the misery this generates rises, and as workers become progressively more alienated from the process and products of work and from themselves as creators, individual discontents intensify and proliferate. At the same time as these factors are at work, capitalism draws larger and larger numbers of people away from "the idiocy of rural life" (Marx and Engels, 1959:11) and brings them together to work in the factories of growing cities. Under these conditions, a subjective recognition among workers that they share a common objective position of exploitation, that is, a "class consciousness," tends to emerge, and the movement from class-in-itself to class-for-itself begins. As machines replace people, an industrial reserve army of the absolutely (not just relatively) impoverished grows, and individual workers see their bargaining power with employers attenuate as their skills are levelled and they become more and more replaceable. The ranks of the industrial reserve army are swelled, not only by castoffs from mechanization, but by new segments of the population — women, children, and others — who find themselves in a position to take on employment once beyond their training and physical skills. Recurrent epidemics of overproduction magnify discontent and stimulate the growth of unions and class-based political organizations. If this is allowed to proceed unchecked — without, for example, the significant intervention of the state into the management of the economy and the administration of large-scale programs of social welfare — the end result is likely to be the overthrow of the bourgeoisie and a revolution in social production.

Transitional Classes and the Internal Differentiation of Bourgeoisie and Proletariat

Marxism has relatively little to say about strictly microstructural and/or distributive matters. The emphasis in Marx and Engels lies in bourgeoisie, proletariat, and the relations between these two social classes. For them, the most important features of capitalist society originate in the dichotomous distinction between bourgeoisie and proletariat. But this simple typology does not exhaust the inventory of classes in capitalist society. And Marx and Engels did comment on the internal differentiation of the various classes.

The bourgeoisie proper are those who own and control the means of production and who employ "free labourers" (i.e., workers with only their labour power to sell) for the purpose of creating and expropriating surplus value. Free labourers who produce surplus value in exchange for a wage constitute, when taken together, the proletariat. In addition to the classical bourgeoisie and proletariat, there are also those who own and control some part of the means of production, but who keep no free labourers in their employ. Members of the *petty bourgeoisie* — mainly free professionals and such independent commodity producers as farmers and fishermen — exist in a state of constant struggle to keep from losing their (typically meagre) holdings and sinking into the proletariat. There are, too, those free labourers who work in the employ of others, but who produce no surplus value, such as servants, valets, private cooks, and the like, but including as well the "new middle class" of white-collar workers. And there are those

> ... vagabonds, discharged soldiers, discharged jailbirds, escaped galley slaves, swindlers, montebanks, *lazzoroni*, pickpockets, tricksters, gamblers, procurers, brothel keepers, porters, *literati*, organ-grinders, rag-pickers, knife grinders, tinkers, beggars (Marx, 1969:442)

and others who are simple parasites, and whom Marx and Engels labelled the *lumpenproletariat.*

The bourgeoisie is not itself an entirely homogeneous class. Its members differ, of course, in the size of their holdings, but they also differ one from another in their function, and this can be cause for cleavage among them. The most important distinction within the bourgeoisie is between those who are actively involved in generating surplus value, that is, the industrial bourgeoisie or "captains of industry," and those who simply siphon off a certain portion of the surplus value available while engaged in circulating and keeping track of money, that is, the financial aristocracy of bankers and others. While the interests of these two categories of capitalist coincide in the long run, they do diverge significantly on occasion. Members of the industrial bourgeoisie, for example, often require infusions of capital in order to maintain or expand their businesses. This is typically accomplished through the borrowing of money from banks and other credit institutions, but only at some rate of interest. Clearly, the industrial bourgeois who borrows money would prefer to minimize the interest rate, while the financial aristocrat who grants the loan would prefer to maximize it. But the fortunes of both ultimately wax and wane together with the overall accumulation of capital.

Just as there are distinctions within the class of the bourgeoisie according to the value of their property, so there are distinctions within the proletariat depending upon the amount of their wage. While the wages of proletarians vary from time to time and place to place along with variations in the size of the industrial reserve army and the traditional standard of life workers expect, wage differentials among proletarians working in the same place at the same time are a regular feature of capitalism. How, then, does this come about?

According to Marx and Engels, unskilled or "simple" labour produces, on the average, commodities with a certain exchange-value in a given period of time. This defines a standard against which to judge the value created by skilled or "compound" labour. "Skilled labor," Marx remarks, "counts only as simple labor intensified, or rather as multiplied simple labor, a given quantity of skilled being considered equal to a greater quantity of simple labor" (1967:44). Skilled labour, therefore, creates value at a faster rate than unskilled labour but, since workers are not paid in proportion to the surplus value they generate, the basis for wage differentials does not derive directly from this fact. It derives, rather, from differences in the relative costs of "producing" skilled, as opposed to unskilled, workers in the first place. In the vocabulary of human capital theory in contemporary economics (see Chapter 6), skilled labour requires greater investment in "human capital" than does unskilled labour. As Marx phrases it:

> In order to modify the human organism so that it may acquire skill and handiness in a given branch of industry, and become labor power of a special kind, a special education or training is requisite, and this, on its part, costs an equivalent of commodities of a greater or lesser amount. This amount varies according to the more or less complicated character of the labor power. The expenses of this education (excessively small in the case of ordinary labor power) enter *pro tanto* into the total value spent in its production (1967:172).

This fact is reflected in corresponding wage differentials, since:

> In a society of private producers, private individuals or their families pay the costs of training the skilled workers hence the higher price paid for the trained labor power comes first of all to private individuals; the clever slave is sold for a higher price, and the clever wage earner is paid higher wages (Engels, 1885:222).

To the extent that capitalism brings with it the rational reorganization of work and the use of sophisticated machinery, however, it should eventually compress this hierarchy and its correlated wage-scale. And wage differentials should diminish, as well, as the costs of education are transferred from individual workers and families to society at large. "In a socialistically organized society, these costs are borne by society, and to it therefore belong also the fruits, the greater values produced by skilled labor. The laborer himself has no claim to extra payment" (Engels, 1885:222).

Neither Marx nor Engels elaborated in any detail a theory which would help account for the internal stratification of the working class. They did appreciate that, in a capitalist system, unskilled labour would command a lower price than skilled labour, since the latter produced more value and cost the worker and/or his family more to produce. But they did not think of this as a special problem, since the real issue for them lay in relations *between* classes, not in differentials *within* them.

> Upon the basis of the wages system the value of labouring power is settled like that of every other commodity; and as different kinds of labouring power have different values, or require different quantities of labour for their production, they *must* fetch different prices in the labour market. To clamour for *equal or even equitable retribution* on the basis of the wages system is the same as to clamour for freedom on the basis of the slavery system (Marx, 1935:39).

Critiques of Marxism

Both Marx and Engels were, of course, greatly influenced by the scholarship of earlier and contemporary thinkers. Most of their major ideas had, in fact, found individual expression in the works of various eighteenth- and nineteenth-century European historians, philosophers, and economists, although never in quite so persuasive a fashion. Hegel's dialectical idealism became, when conjoined with a materialist conception of history drawn from Feuerbach and others, Marxian *dialectical materialism*, although Marx and Engels did not themselves actually use this term. The labour theory of value was well-known and widely accepted as economic doctrine in Marx and Engels's time, most notably in the work of Ricardo, the foremost economist of his day. Marx and Engels borrowed liberally, as well, from analyses of property, class, and conflict by Baboeuf, Sismondi, and, especially, Saint Simon. The idea of recurrent economic crises as endemic to capitalism, finally, was a commonplace of their time, as well as of our own. To be able to show that individual elements in Marxism have historical origins outside the writings of Marx and Engels themselves is only, however, to locate these two men in some context in the history of ideas. Marxism is an elaborate system, remarkably subtle and complex, if also incomplete and internally inconsistent. Should it ultimately prove to be a failure, it may nevertheless have moved us several long steps toward a more adequate social and economic theory.

Weber

The classical critique of Marxism for Western scholars is that of the turn-of-the-century German sociologist Weber (1946; 1964), many of whose major contributions to the discipline were made in explicit response to positions espoused by Marx and Engels in their historical interpretations and in their analyses of the course and direction of capitalism. In particular, Weber provided at least some of the necessary elaboration on the concept of class which Marx had only just begun at the end of the unfinished third volume of *Capital*. He attempted, as well, to amplify and correct the Marxist version of the character of capitalism and capitalist development.

To Weber, the historical materialism of Marx and Engels was not so much incorrect as it was incomplete. While he objected strenuously to the Marxist emphasis on the mode of production as the root cause of structure and change in social and cultural systems, Weber elected to complement it with a parallel analysis of the political realm, rather than to reject it out of hand. As Gerth and Mills observe in their *Introduction* to a collection of his essays:

> Part of Weber's own work may thus be seen as an attempt to "round out" Marx's economic materialism by a political and military materialism. The Weberian approach to political structures closely parallels the Marxian approach to economic structures. Marx constructed economic periods and located major economic classes in them; he related the several social and political factors to the means of production. In political matters, Weber looks for the disposition over weapons and over means of administration (Weber, 1946:47).

Marx and Engels focused their intellectual attention on the phenomena of accumulation and centralization of the means of economic production, and saw the nation-state as essentially the instrument of the bourgeois class. For his part, Weber attributed independent importance to the political process of the consolidation of control over territory on the part of a ruler or group of rulers. "In fact, Weber formulates the very concept of the 'state' in terms of a 'monopoly' of the use of legitimate force over a given territory" (Gerth and Mills in Weber, 1946:48). Weber did not deny that the extension of monopolistic control over territory might often be economically determined or conditioned. He felt strongly, however, that any simple equation of economic with political power did violence to the complexity of the facts.

Central to the Weberian critique and revision of Marxism is the conceptual trio of *class, status,* and *party* (Weber, 1946:180-95). These three terms denote aggregates of people according to their members' market situations (class) and the claims they have on prestige (status) and power (party). Marx and Engels stressed the importance of power and paid scant heed to issues of prestige. For his part, Weber argued that class and status were separate and independently important orders of things — related, to be sure, but conceptually and empirically distinct, and he took the connections among class, status, and party as being more problematic than Marx and Engels often seemed to.

To Weber, a *class* is a plurality of people who share a similar "market position," or set of opportunities for the acquisition of money or material goods. The most crucial determinant of these opportunities is whether or not one owns property, but there are also important distinctions within the propertied and propertyless classes, depending upon the kind of one's property and the nature of one's marketable skills. There are, then, the "positively privileged," or propertied classes, of which there are basically two: the *rentier* (or pure ownership) and the *entrepreneurial* (or acquisitional), with additional divisions of class within each of these. There are, also, the "negatively privileged" classes of those with nothing to sell but their unskilled labour power. And, standing between these, there are a variety of middle classes whose members, while without property, nonetheless possess some marketable skill of one or another kind. While Weber, along with Marx and Engels, stressed the essential significance of property possession as a criterion of class, the Weberian version of class ultimately recognizes as many different classes as there are meaningfully different varieties of property and marketable skill (in contrast to the essentially dichotomous Marxist version elaborated above). Taken at its face, Weber's conception multiplies the number of classes beyond any obvious utility. Moreover, class is a complex and incompletely specified typology, with no clear statement as to just what criteria are used to differentiate the abundance of classes from one another, and no detailed discussion of the importance of these criteria relative to one another.

A *status group* is a collection of individuals who share approximately equal levels of status, and who have in common a certain pattern of consumption or lifestyle. Where class distinctions are grounded in the impersonality and rationality of the economic market, distinctions of status derive from more personal and nonrational sources, such as education, family background, occupation, and ethnicity. While the separate significance of class and status must be acknowledged in any adequate analysis of inequality, the phenomena of class and status are related in all manner of ways, both theoretically and empirically. One's position in the market, especially in respect of property ownership, for example, can and often does provide the basis for a particular style of life, and members of status groups frequently act in concert to monopolize economic opportunities. According to Weber, societies typically exist in some state of tension between an emphasis on class vs. an emphasis on status for, when status groups make incursions into the economic market, they pose a threat to the principle of economic rationality which governs class relations. Social change, in the Weberian view, can often be seen to involve cycles in the shifting importance of class (representing the rational) and status (representing the nonrational) relative to one another in the market.

Weber was at pains to counter a vulgar Marxism which took more or less for granted the transformation of a class-in-itself into a class-for-itself. Class consciousness and collective action organized around class distinctions were, for him, not at all assured. While he did not elaborate in any detail the circumstances under which they might develop, he did point to "cultural conditions," the disparities among the several classes in their wealth, and the perceptions on the part of members of a class that collective action might hold some realistic promise of change and improvement as factors to be incorporated into any theory of class solidarity. In contrast to, and independently of, classes, status groups *are* typically solidary groupings whose members often act together in attempts to monopolize aspects of the economic market and to control access to marriageable women.

Parties, finally, are groups organized for the sole purpose of acquiring and keeping power. As Parkin (1972) points out, however, power is not a distinct "dimension" of inequality on a conceptual par with market position and status in Weber's formulation. These latter two are potential bases for communal action, and this action involves, among other things, efforts aimed at achieving and exercising power. "Now: 'classes,' 'status groups,' and 'parties' are phenomena *of* the distribution of power within a community" (Weber, 1964:181, emphasis mine). While the most consequential single source of power is economic, parties may or may not represent the interests of classes. They can, and often do, represent the interests of status groups or other aggregations.

Weber saw in the transformation of nineteenth-century Europe the master-trends of progressive state monopolistic control and rational, bureaucratic reorganization. He feared these as serious threats to individual freedom, and argued that socialism was fundamentally the extension of state monopolistic control and bureaucracy to the hitherto unregulated sphere of economic activity. Weber recognized class, especially in its property aspect, as perhaps the most crucial element in social inequality, and he acknowledged the historical reality of class and class conflict. He was unwilling, however, to attribute to class conflict the kind of motive force in social change which it exercised in the Marxist model. And he was willing to emphasize — in a way in which Marx and Engels were not — the potentially independent importance of status in relation to party.

To Weber, the advent of capitalistic forms of economic organization could be seen in the larger context of the growth and development of bureaucratic rationality. Where Marx and Engels stressed the internal contradictions in capitalism between the forces and relations of production and, therefore, the ultimate *ir*rationality of capitalist systems, Weber saw capitalism as a preeminently rational phenomenon. The modern corporation brought bureaucratic order and efficiency to the pursuit of economic gain. In it, impersonal rules, task specialization, a division of labour, a hierarchy of impersonal authority, and the rational calculation of gains and losses were all marshalled together and orchestrated for the clearly defined purpose of making profits. The dangers in this lie not in the systematic economic exploitation of one class by another, which is just a special case of the more general process by which individuals are being progressively deprived of their rights in all spheres of activity, not just the economic. They lie rather, in the inevitable loss of freedom it entails.

While Weber's typology identifies an indefinite multiplicity of different classes, there is a tendency in capitalism for class and status to intersect in such a way as to define a relatively small number of major *social classes*. In particular, market position and lifestyle may coalesce to produce an upper class of propertied people, a petty bourgeoisie, a middle class of white-collar people who, while propertyless, possess some skill of marketable value, and a class of manual workers. Of these, the petty bourgeoisie is a kind of transitional class whose position is constantly eroded with the development of capitalism. In some contrast to the Marxist position, however, the petty bourgeoisie is seen as a kind of transitional class who do not become proletarianized as they are dispossessed of their property. They are more likely, rather, to become middle-class, white-collar workers, for this is the class with the greatest potential for growth in capitalist systems. Moreover, the increasing rationalization and bureaucratization which capitalism brings with it creates a class structure which is more, rather than less, differentiated internally as far as the propertyless middle class are concerned. Instead of a deskilled, homogenous proletariat, capitalism generates a highly variegated, propertyless collectivity of middle-class people distinguished one from another in type and degree of trained capacity. And rather than becoming progressively impoverished with the advance of capitalism, members of this propertyless class can be expected generally to prosper economically.

Several of Weber's points are useful contributions to a critique of Marxism. First, although Weber often addressed himself in his writings to issues raised in cruder varieties of Marxism, Marx and Engels did tend to be facile at times in their characterization of the relationship between economy and polity. Weber does caution us to show in detail how economically defined aggregates of people organize to gain and to maintain power and, in particular, to specify the connections between the economy and the nation-state. While he argued that class and party are intimately related, he also showed that party cannot be simply equated with class. Second, Weber's proliferation of class concepts does serve as a useful corrective to the one-sided simplicity of Marx and Engels at their polemical best, and is a valuable supplement to a Marxian definition of class which was never really begun, even if the supplement remains itself incomplete. Indeed, this is a task which Marxists themselves have just recently begun to take up (e.g., Poulantzas, 1975; Wright, 1976, 1978). Third, he did not deny the importance of class and the material conditions of life so much as he attempted to give the study of social inequality analytical balance through the explicit consideration of the phenomenon of status. The concept of status gives expression to the symbolic side of inequality, and the stress Weber placed on it is one aspect of his larger concern with the importance of ideas in social life.

All this being said, however, it is perhaps easy to forget that Weber never attempted to erect anything resembling a full-blown theory of inequality. Much less did he build one to rival any other. And those contributions he undeniably made to a "multi-dimensional" approach to the study of social inequality have sometimes been translated into multi-dimensional models which he would never have recognized as originating in his work. Class, status, and party as he conceived them are not simply three distinct and equally important dimensions of inequality as some (e.g., Kahl, 1957), have treated them. Much less can they be used as part of the rationale for treating such variables as race, income, ethnicity, and education as separate "dimensions" in a "multi-dimensional" model of social stratification, as some, such as House (1978), have interpreted the work of Lenski (1954).

Dahrendorf

One of Marx's better known latter-day critics is Dahrendorf (1959). According to Dahrendorf, Marx was correct in identifying class relations as significant social relations in modern society. Moreover, class relations *are* inherently antagonistic, as Marx and Engels supposed, and class conflict *is* a major source of change in social structure. Class relations are, as well, fundamentally dichotomous, and class conflict can be best understood in terms of two classes doing open or hidden battle with one another. But Marx and Engels's concept of class is only sensible in the context of the historical period in which they lived. Capitalism as they knew it and wrote about it has been since transcended by a post-capitalist, industrial society in which the separation of ownership and control of the means of production has exposed their analysis of class to be but a particular example of a more general case, and now obsolete. Minimally, these developments require that the concept of class be revised, and that the theory of class conflict be reformulated in the knowledge that class relations are only one kind of social relation, and class conflict only one source of structural change.

Dahrendorf's critical "reformulation" of Marxism rests on his analysis of the separation of ownership and control. According to him, Marx and Engels did not fully apprehend the meaning of the separation of ownership and control in the modern corporate enterprise — a phenomenon which they were forced to reckon with only in their later years. In a business firm of this kind, ownership is always for sale in the form of stocks and, thus, accessible to anyone with the money to buy. This opens the door to the separation of ownership and control, in that those who hold stocks in a corporation typically appoint managers to oversee its day-to-day operations, exercising little or no active ownership themselves. Tying the concept of class to ownership as he did, Marx was led by the historical coincidence of ownership and control in nineteenth-century Europe to confuse the particular (i.e., ownership) with the general (i.e., control). "Wherever there is property there is authority, but not every form of authority implies property. Authority is the more general social relation" (Dahrendorf, 1959:137). When there is a separation of ownership and control, therefore, class migrates with control, not with ownership. "Classes," he continues, "are social conflict groups the determinant . . . of which can be found in the participation in or exclusion from the exercise of authority within any imperatively coordinated association" (1959:138). Since an imperatively coordinated association is any organization with an identifiable authority structure, it follows that there is a two-class structure of dominants and subordinates wherever authority can be shown to reside. "Control over the means of production is but a special case of authority" (1959:136). There are "classes," then, in Boy Scout troops and business firms, school classrooms and the state, apartment buildings and religious denominations. But all of these are obviously not equal in importance. In particular, the business firm and the state are of special moment in understanding class and class conflict in modern industrial society.

Although Dahrendorf characterizes the original Marxist treatment of the separation of ownership and control as "brief and somewhat puzzled" (1959:41), it does not seem as brief as he would have it, and it appears generally consistent with Marx's basic theoretical premises. To Marx, the separation of ownership and control appeared as a major and positive development in capitalism, marking the advent of a new era in social production. It brought with it the potential to join managers and workers together as paid employees of the firm, to eliminate owners from the chain of command and confine their role to that of mere expropriators of surplus value, and to socialize ownership through diffusion of stock-holding. The long-term effects of these should be to undermine the very bases of class and class conflict.

In tracing the implications of the separation of ownership and control as he did, Marx seems to have been aware of the phenomenon and of its meaning for his analysis of class and class conflict in capitalism. Rather than having mistaken ownership (the particular) for control (the general), he appears to have understood the distinction between them, consciously located the differentia of class in ownership, and considered just what the consequences of the separation of ownership and control would be under the assumptions of his theory. We are free to judge him wrong in this, but he apparently did not proceed naively.

For his part, Dahrendorf uncovers a nest of nasty issues in redefining class in terms of authority. First, identifying the dominant class in those who participate in the exercise of authority in imperatively coordinated associations casts the net rather widely as far as dominant class membership is concerned. A definition of dominant class which includes shift supervisors in pulp mills, head nurses in hospital wards, and other such minor functionaries can only trivialize the concept. Second, it denotes as many different class structures as there are different imperatively coordinated associations, even if Dahrendorf more or less arbitrarily singles out the economy and the state as being of special significance.

If the Dahrendorfian version of class, class conflict, and the separation of ownership and control is not an acceptable alternative to the Marxist formulation, however, this does not mean that the latter can stand without criticism. First, it rests on the as yet largely undermonstrated assumption that the goals of the new-style managers (or "functionaries without capital") are somehow fundamentally different from those of the old-style capitalists. Just why this should be, however, is not at all clear. In fact, it seems just as reasonable to argue, along with Miliband and others, that they do to some extent share common goals, and that "the differences of purpose and motivation which may exist between them are over-shadowed by a basic community of interests" (1969:34). If there is such a "community of interest," it would stand in clear opposition to the "basic community of interest" of workers in its conception of the appropriate ratio between corporate profits and workers' wages and fringe benefits. The presence of such a conflict of interest provides the basis for latent or manifest class conflict in the long run — something absent in Dahrendorf's model, where the implicit assumption seems to be that dominance and subordination are somehow "naturally" antagonistic conditions.

Second, what happens to the authority positions of owners and managers with the growth and development of the joint-stock corporation in capitalism would seem to depend importantly upon the relative degree of diffusion of stock ownership. Where a small number of people own a majority or a plurality of the stocks in a company, effective control of the firm is likely to reside in the owners. Where stock-holding is widely diffused, however, the control of top management over the activities of the business is probably strengthened. It is difficult for large numbers of geographically dispersed stock-holders to act in concert to influence managerial conduct if the managers form a cohesive group of like-minded people, as often they do.

Moving On

Despite (or, perhaps even, "because of") a hundred years of often profound social change and penetrating intellectual scrutiny, Marxism is a living and growing body of ideas whose popularity in the West has never been greater than it is today, especially in academic circles. but it has neither in the past lived, nor today lives, alone. For this reason, and because the truly important theoretical issues of a period are best revealed in the conflicts among ideas, we move on to consider some further theoretical systems in the next two chapters.

Chapter 3

On The Functional Theory of Stratification and Some of Its Critics

"Who is a functionalist today?" asked a younger sociologist of a group of his academic colleagues. "I am," replied one of the senior members of his own university department who was in the audience (exchange at the Annual Meeting of the Canadian Sociology and Anthropology Association in Montreal, 1980).

Structural-functionalism in social science was first developed in anthropology, partly in reaction to the evolutionary thinking of such nineteenth- and early twentieth-century anthropologists as Tylor and to the culture history approach as represented in the work of Boas and Rivers. Two contemporaries, Radcliffe-Brown (1935; 1948a, b) and Malinowski (1926; 1939), each developed a brand of functionalism which began with the notion that societies can be viewed best as "systems," or organized, integrated wholes whose component parts or "structures" fulfill some social "function." The function of a part is that contribution which it makes to the whole and, for this reason, the significance of individual parts cannot be understood in isolation from the whole. To Radcliffe-Brown, the contribution of a part could be either positive or negative, insofar as it could be seen to contribute to the survival or destruction of the society *as a system*. Malinowski, on the other hand, was ultimately more concerned with the question of the *physical survival* of human beings within a society, and adopted the position that, insofar as a structure exists, it must, by that fact, contribute positively to survival — in the more individual, physical sense of that term.

Building on the work of these two men, Merton (1957) refined their battery of concepts and added a number of influential ideas of his own. One must specify clearly, he argued, just what the system is for which functions are being performed and, he suggested, this need not be at the level of an entire society. It is quite respectable — advantageous, even — in the early phases of theoretical development to work toward "theories of the middle range," in which the unit of analysis is on a scale less grand than that of a total society, and the concepts and variables are something less than the highest of abstractions. Once the system has been specified, its "functional prerequisites," that is, those conditions which must be met if the system is to adapt successfully to its own internal circumstances and to the conditions of its environment, must be identified, although he left it to other writers (e.g., Aberle et al., 1950; Parsons, 1951) to work on this problem. Merton went on, as well, to distinguish between elements of a social system which were "functional" (i.e., contribute to system survival), "dysfunctional" (i.e., contribute to system destruction), and "nonfunctional" (i.e., simply irrelevant to survival). And, where Radcliffe-Brown and Malinowski were vague on how aware individual members of a society necessarily were of the functions performed by social or cultural forms, Merton argued that there were both "manifest" (or generally known) and "latent" (or generally unknown) functions. He also elaborated, finally, the notion of "functional alternatives," or the idea that a function performed by one element in a system can often be performed by another element in that same system, so that no particular element need always be regarded as indispensable to system survival.

The Functional Theory of Stratification

While it is customary in sociology to speak of *the* functional theory of stratification, as if there were but one, there are actually two major versions: one by Parsons (1940; 1953), and the other by Davis and Moore (e.g., Davis and Moore, 1945; Davis, 1948; Davis, 1953). Although sometimes treated as if they were essentially similar or, at least, commensurable (e.g., Kemper, 1976), they were not developed explicitly in relation to one another, and they differ in more than just detail (Lopreato and Lewis, 1963). For these reasons, and since the Parsonian variation has been of relatively little consequence for theory and research in social inequality, attention will be focused on themes elaborated by Davis and Moore.

Davis and Moore begin their argument with the observation "that no society is 'classless,' or unstratified" (1945:242).

> At the same time, although the principle of stratification is universal, its concrete manifestation varies remarkably from one society to another. Consequently, the explanatory task requires two different lines of analysis — one to understand the universal features of stratification, the other to understand the variable features (Davis, 1948:366).

These two aspects of the theory will be dealt with sequentially, beginning with that which has caused the most comment and controversy over the years — the account of "the universal features."

The Universal Necessity of Stratification

Davis and Moore note that all societies however simple or small they might be, are characterized by at least a degree of task specialization and the rudiments of a division of labour, in which different positions necessarily enjoy different rewards, or "rights and perquisites." "The rewards and their distribution become part of the social order, and thus give rise to stratification" (Davis and Moore, 1945:243). And, "if the rights and perquisites of different positions in a society must be unequal, then the society must be stratified, because that is precisely what stratification means" (1945:243). But how is it that societies *must* be stratified? This is so since all societies, if they are to survive, must somehow recruit their members to social positions so as to insure that important positions are conscientiously filled by qualified persons. Recruiting people to positions and motivating them to fulfill the duties attached to them would be no special problem if these duties were equally pleasant to carry out, equally important to social survival (i.e., equal in "functional importance"), and equally demanding in talent and training requirements. But they do vary enormously in each of these respects. In general, less pleasant positions must be better rewarded than more pleasant ones, or they will be less likely to be filled. Too, if positions with high skill demands bring with them enhanced rewards, it is more likely that persons of talent will be stimulated to acquire the necessary training to move into them in the first place and, once in them, adequately moved to carry out their duties (also see Smith, 1937). And, finally, the more functionally important a position, the more important it is for societal survival that its duties be carried out satisfactorily. Better rewards for functionally more important positions are the means by which societies attempt to meet this need.

"Social inequality," Davis and Moore (1945:249) concluded in their original formulation, "is thus an unconsciously evolved device by which societies ensure that the most important positions are conscientiously filled by the most qualified persons." In response to some criticism, however, Davis subsequently qualified his stand. "Actually a society does not need to reward positions in proportion to their functional importance," he later argued. "It merely needs to give sufficient reward to insure that they will be filled competently. In other words, it must see that less essential positions do not compete successfully with more essential ones" (1948:368). And, while the authors of the theory have not specifically commented on this point, presumably the same is true with regard to the unpleasantness of jobs and their skill requirements. That is, positions probably need not be rewarded *in proportion to* their unpleasantness and skill requirements, but only enough that they will be adequately filled.

The rewards societies use as inducements can be conveniently grouped into three broad categories. There are, first, material or economic benefits, such as income, which help the incumbents of positions meet their basic and socially-acquired needs and, depending upon the position, sometimes to do this in a style which goes rather beyond mere necessity. Second, there are numerous advantages of a more recreational or esthetic kind, such as the discretionary and leisure time available to some (e.g., university faculty), but not to others (e.g., farmers). And, third, there are various symbolic (if no less "real") rewards, such as the respect one's position is accorded by others, and the admiration one receives for a job well done.

The Variable Features of Social Stratification

What, then, of the "variable features" of stratification? The rewards which accrue to positions in the division of labour derive largely from two factors:

functional importance and relative scarcity of qualified personnel. Only those positions enjoy high rank which make an important contribution to societal survival *and* which require the most talent or training. Important positions for which there are large pools of qualified persons will not be highly rewarded, while unimportant but difficult-to-fill positions are more likely to disappear than to rise in rank. Important *and* difficult-to-fill positions, however, must carry with them sufficient rewards to attract the qualified. Functional importance and relative scarcity are each, therefore, necessary, but not sufficient, causes of a position having ample rewards. Variations in form and degree among the stratification systems of different societies are, thus, largely determined by conditions which facilitate or place limits on functional importance and/or scarcity of qualified personnel.

While this account may seem plausible, it is necessary briefly to digress and consider Davis's (1948, 1953) response to the criticism of the theory that it rests on assumptions of a competitive order in which individuals vie with one another for positions in the division of labour on the basis of ability and effort. To the extent that this is true, and insofar as, even in the most competitive of societies, the positions which individuals occupy are importantly determined by such factors as their race, ethnicity and family socio-economic background, the theory would strictly apply nowhere, and it would apply only imperfectly to a narrow range of societies, such as Canada and the United States (see Tumin, 1953a,b). Not so, Davis argues, although he concedes the criticism does require an addition to the theory. There are two reasons why this criticism is not fatal to the formulation. First, the functional theory of stratification explains how it is that some *positions* stand high in the hierarchy, while others stand low. It does not address itself to the logically posterior question of how some *people* enjoy high rank, while others do not. Second, even in the most closed of societies, there is always *some* competition for positions. Thus, in the caste system of India, some castes are well rewarded and others poorly so, but this is importantly because of the different functions performed by the different castes, most of which have been historically associated with certain occupations. Moreover, even in this system the hierarchy of castes is not forever fixed but, rather, changes over time as the functions which they perform change. And, beyond this, factions or families within a given caste can rise or fall in the same way, typically by changing their occupations. Thus, functional importance and scarcity are operative everywhere, if not everywhere to the same degree.

People are everywhere to some extent assigned to positions in the economic division of labour in a process of *ascription* on the basis of race, ethnicity, socio-economic background, and other such traits, as well as in a process of *achievement* on the basis of ability and effort (see Chapters 7–10). To be sure, some societies fall toward the ascription end of the continuum, while others fall toward the achievement end. No society could ever rely wholly upon ascription as the means of locating individuals in positions for two major reasons. First, every society has standards of value in terms of which things are evaluated, and this prompts people to strive for upward mobility in even the most rigid of societies. Second, such a society would have to be a totally static one; in which, minimally, each caste or social class would have to reprbduce itself exactly, in both numbers and in social function performed. If this did not occur — as most certainly it never does — then members of one caste or social class would either have to move into the occupations left empty, or these occupations would not be filled. And not filling them would clearly have implications for the future survival of the society. The more important the functions performed by the occupations in question, the more serious the implications for survival.

One of the major determinants of functional importance which Davis and Moore identify is the degree to which particular functions are "emphasized" within a society. Societies vary in the particular functions emphasized, and these functions determine which positions (given relative scarcity of qualified personnel) enjoy high rank. At the same time, certain functions must be performed in every society, and this will mean that there is a broad, overall similarity across societies in the positions which occupy the upper rungs of the stratification ladder. Important among these functions are government, economic activity, and technology.

Government "organizes ... society in terms of law and authority. It also orients ... society to the actual rather than the unseen world" (Davis, 1948:373). Political officials have authority by virtue of office and, thus, their relationships with citizens are necessarily unequal. So obvious is this inequality that political inequality is sometimes regarded as synonymous with inequality generally, although we have already seen that this is not the case. Moreover, the authority of those in office is always circumscribed by the fact that those who govern are only a small proportion of the entire population, that they govern on behalf of the group rather than themselves, and that their authority derives wholly from the offices which they hold, as opposed to any special training or abilities which they might happen to have. "In view of these limiting factors it is not strange that the rulers often have less power and prestige than a literal enumeration of their formal rights would lead one to expect" (Davis, 1948:374).

In capitalist societies, entrepreneurship is functionally important. In any society, some form of active ownership of productive property is necessary, whether public or private. Where there is private ownership, as in capitalism, it is possible for persons to accumulate wealth beyond what they normally spend and, thus, to acquire ownership of captial goods. And, Davis and Moore argue, "presumably such possession is a reward for the proper management of one's finances originally and of the productive enterprise later" (1948: 247).

> But as social differentiation becomes highly advanced and yet the institution of inheritance persists, the phenomenon of pure ownership, and reward for pure ownership, emerges. In such a case it is difficult to prove that the position is functionally important or that the scarcity involved is anything other than extrinsic and accidental (1948:247).

Partly for this reason, they go on, resistance to the institution of private property grows with the growth of industrialism. Possession of capital in varying amounts, as well, "introduces a compulsive element even into the nominally free contractual relationship" (1948:247). Accumulation of capital in the hands of some puts those who must labour in their employ at a disadvantage in striking and maintaining a fair deal for themselves (compare with Marx and Engels on exploitation above).

Positions in the division of labour which involve considerable technical knowledge and skills typically stand relatively high in the stratification hierarchy, given their talent and training requirements. Unlike religious, political, and economic positions, however, technical positions are concerned solely with the means to achieve goals, not with the implementation of goals. Thus, although they will generally be well rewarded, they will not command the very highest of rewards. Still, "the distinction between expert and layman in any social order is fundamental and cannot be entirely reduced to other terms" (Davis, 1948:376), although the position of experts varies widely from society to society and from time to time. Under conditions of extreme specialization in the division of labour, the position of the true expert is usually quite high, although specialization also produces a large number of blue- and white-collar specialists whose talent and training requirements are minimal, and whose rewards are small.

But the idea of a technocratic social order or a government or priesthood of engineers or social scientists neglects the limitations of knowledge and skills as a basis for performing social functions. To the extent that the social structure is truly specialized the prestige of the technical person must also be circumscribed (Davis, 1948:377).

Davis and Moore outline, finally, two processes in the dynamics of the supply and demand for qualified personnel which require mention. First, it follows from the logic of functionalism that, if ample rewards serve to induce people to fill functionally important positions, such rewards also tend to generate oversupplies of qualified personnel, with the result that there occurs a deflation in the status and other rewards which attach to these positions. And, of course, the converse of this can happen as well: a functionally important position inadequately rewarded will generate an undersupply of persons willing and able to fill it, with a subsequent inflation in positional rewards. Second, as opposed to such "natural" scarcities and abundances are those which sometimes develop when particular families or strata come to exercise control over avenues of training to certain important positions, and use this control for their own benefit (also see Durkheim, 1964:374-88; compare with Weber on status groups above).

A Critique of Davis-Moore

As a functional explanation, the Davis-Moore theory asserts that social stratification means differential rewards for those positions which are the most important functionally and the most demanding in talent and training requirements. These rewards are required in order to place individuals in important positions and to motivate them to fulfill the duties of these positions adequately. This is done for the purpose of the survival of societies as systems. The system, then, is "society," and the relevant system state is "survival." The functional prerequisites in this case are the placement and motivation of individuals, and the assumption is that these can *only* be met through differential rewards for positions, or social stratification.

One of the most contentious aspects of the theory has been the assumption that positions systematically differ in their importance for societal survival (Tumin, 1953a,b; Wesolowski, 1962). While they suggest no direct means for assessing the functional importance of positions, Davis and Moore do point in passing to two "clues" to its determination: the uniqueness or irreplaceability of a position, and the degree to which other positions are subordinate to it in a hierarchy of authority. Uniqueness, however, seems essentially to be a matter of specialized training requirements, which are already accorded a role along with functional importance as a *cause* of positional rank. As Wesolowski (1962) points out, uniqueness in this sense cannot be both of *and* apart from functional importance. This suggests, then, that functional importance might be equated with the potentially more tractable notion of location in a hierarchy of authority, which could clarify the concept considerably and point more directly to ways in which it might be measured. At the same time, while Davis and Moore do discuss authority in their analysis of government, it plays only a minor role in the functional theory of stratification as they have set it forth, and they never elaborate in any detail on what their conception of the relationship between authority and functional importance is, choosing instead to stress the role of material, recreational, and symbolic rewards as the *sine qua non* of social stratification.

Is stratification, then, necessary for placement and motivation? It is not logically necessary, of course, or this aspect of the theory would be true by definition, rather than empirically testable and potentially falsifiable. It is possible that people of talent might undertake the training required for functionally important positions and fulfill their duties without differentials in extrinsic rewards, perhaps moved to do so by "alternative motivational schemes" (e.g., Tumin, 1953a, b). Individuals could be socialized to think of it as their self-rewarding duty, for example, to take on important tasks and to do them well, as in the notion of noblesse oblige, a suggestion which Davis (1953) denies but does not refute. Unfortunately, however, we seem to lack convincing contemporary or historical examples of societies with such alternative motivational schemes. But we do not want at all for instances of societies in which individuals are placed in positions largely in a process of ascription, and only incidentally, if at all, in a process of achievement in competition with others (Linton, 1936; Wesolowski, 1962). High caste Indian Brahmins, for example, do not compete with Untouchables for the rewards of being high caste any more than members of the British aristocracy jockey for position with Cockneys for seats in the House of Lords.

It may be, then, that the functional theory of stratification is largely restricted in its application to a narrow range of societies in which positions are achieved in free and open competition with others on the basis of effort and ability. But what of Davis's argument that the theory is designed to account for the location of positions in the hierarchy of social stratification, not of individuals, and that there is always some competition, even in the most rigid of societies? To stand high in this hierarchy, however, a position must be functionally important *and* have a scarcity of qualified personnel. Moreover, the rewards which attach to high-ranking positions are intended to induce people to take them on and to do them well, goals which can scarcely be achieved if large numbers of people are categorically denied access to these positions on the basis of their having certain inherited traits, such as race, ethnicity and family social background.

The question of the necessity of stratification in more or less competitive systems is difficult to assess, due to conceptual problems in the theory and for want of decisive data. It is difficult to think of a good instance of a society which has clearly and obviously "perished" as a consequence of the failure of its system of stratification to place and motivate individuals adequately. Speaking of the Tlingit on the coast of British Columbia, for example, Radcliffe-Brown writes:

> The whole thing is kept going by the potlatch. The social structure itself is what supports the potlatch, and the potlatch vitalizes the social structure. There is a relation of reciprocal action between the two. The maintenance of the structure requires the performance of the potlatch at given intervals (1948a:126).

The potlatch, a periodic display of the conspicious distribution and destruction of property for the apparent purpose of gaining and maintaining status, was a central element in the stratification system of the Tlingit, as well as of many other peoples of the region (Benedict, 1959:156-95). But when it was effectively outlawed and not quickly replaced by some functional alternative, the societies of the Tlingit, the Kwakiutl, the Haida, and others did not simply vanish. They persisted, if in greatly altered form, and at least remnants of at least certain of them persist today. If the society of the Tlingit before was not the same as the society of the Tlingit after, the latter was nevertheless some kind of transformation of the former, rather than something altogether new. In this we have an example of a society whose stratification system underwent sudden and dramatic change, but the functionalist model provides no clean criteria by which we can render the judgment that the society itself failed at some identifiable point to survive.

Summing Up and Moving On

For over thirty years, structural-functional theory (e.g., Parsons, 1951; Merton, 1957) was the most prominent feature in the theoretical topography of North American (especially U.S.) sociology, standing virtually unrivalled, although not without considerable criticism. The philosophers of science Nagel (1956) and Hempel (1959), for example, criticized the logic of functional analysis as a model for social theory. Others, such as Buckley (1958) and Homans (1964), questioned in various ways its explanatory power. Others (e.g., Wrong, 1961) raised doubts about certain of the central assumptions embedded in it. Still others (e.g., Tumin, 1953a,b; Clinard, 1964) criticized in detail the utility of its application to the phenomena of inequality and deviance, respectively. One of its leading practitioners, Davis, was led eventually to abandon it as a "special method" (1959). And Mills summarized a newly emergent radical view of one of the most influential of functionalist treatises, Parsons's *The Social System* (1951), as

> about 50 per cent verbiage; 40 per cent is well-known textbook sociology. The other 10 per cent, as Parsons might say, I am willing to leave open for your own empirical investigations. My own investigations suggest that the remaining 10 per cent is of possible — if vague — ideological use (Mills, 1959:49).

Despite this, structural-functionalism neither collapsed nor withered and died in the 1950s or early 1960s, only to go into unexpected eclipse in the later years of the latter decade. This was true both of functionalism as a general theoretical approach, as well as of applications of functionalism to particular issues and areas. As an attempt to understand the universal and variable features of social stratification, the Davis-Moore application of structural-functionalism seems now generally to be seen as a grand failure — a powerful idea with inherent and, apparently, insurmountable flaws. It sinks or swims according to the flotation generated by such concepts as functional importance, along with assumptions concerning the respective roles of placement-motivation and differential extrinsic rewards, most of which seem inadequate to the task. Still, even if there are apparently terminal problems in a theoretical system, this does not mean that it should be discarded entirely out of hand. It could contain useful ideas around which a more successful theory might be built. We shall have occasion, therefore, to return repeatedly to structural-functionalism in analysing the phenomenon of structured social inequality in Canada.

Chapter 4

Some Contemporary Theories and Outstanding Issues

"But what does all of this mean?" (Talcott Parsons, 1937:359).

If the principal purpose of social theories is to bring together and give meaning to otherwise unrelated and ambiguous observations about social life, theoretical issues in sociology arise at the points of contact between two or more theories, where the interpretations of one are inconsistent with those of another. There are many such points of contact in the regions of inequality, where two theories brush up against one another, and one must eventually yield to the superior explanatory power of the other. Simply identifying these points, however, is not always an easy job, and it is often even more difficult to analyse precisely just what the inconsistencies are when two theories generate conflicting expectations and understandings with regard to the same set of social phenomena. The major aims of the present chapter are: first, to attempt to identify some of the major issues in inequality theory today through a brief overview of some of the central ideas of a number of contemporary theorists and, second, to describe these issues clearly enough so that we will know — at least in principle — how one might begin to go about assessing them empirically. At the same time, it is worth warning that the materials covered in a work such as this are often of a case-study (or "one-shot") kind and not, therefore, well adapted to use in formally testing theories. Consequently, while we will often examine theoretical issues in a Canadian context, we will only seldom be able to say with confidence that one theory applies better than another in helping us understand structured social inequality in this country.

Convergence Theories

Most likely, any successful theory of social inequality developed in the future will be an amalgam of elements drawn from a variety of earlier theories. Moreover, it is likely, as well, to be a reorganization and sythesis of ideas and insights which are presently known, rather than as yet unknown. A decade and more ago, a number of theorists thought they had glimpsed an emergent synthesis between left-wing (or radical) and right-wing (or conservative) theories of inequality, and sought to capture and nurture it in their writings. Among these was Dahrendorf, who attempted to forge a new theory of class and class conflict by welding together revised versions of Marxism and structural-functionalism, arguing that "for sociological analysis, society is Janus-headed, and its two faces are equivalent aspects of the same reality" (1959:159). One of these faces showed society as a set of social relations maintained through coercion and modified through conflict, while the other revealed it to be a functionally integrated system whose coherence and survival rest ultimately upon a consensus on values. And among these, too, was Lenski (1965), who developed an evolutionary typology of societies based on the notion of a hierarchy of technologies of subsistence (from hunting and gathering to simple and advanced horticultural, to agrarian, to industrial). At each level, he argued, social inequalities largely depend upon how the structure and organization of power in society determine the distribution of the available material surplus.

Whether simply premature or necessarily doomed from the start, such attempts as Dahrendorf's and Lenski's to construct so-called "convergence theories" of social inequality failed, and the earlier enthusiasm for a grand theoretical synthesis has since dissipated. At the same time, it would appear both possible and useful to suggest in a general and tentative way how certain theories — in particular, Marxism and structural-functionalism — might be seen to complement one another in several important respects, stopping well short of any effort to meld them into a single, coherent statement of theory. First, while Marx and Engels's writings are not at all confined to issues at this level, Marxism can be viewed as most prominently a macrostructural formulation, while those parts of the Davis-Moore version of functional theory which are least contentious are predominantly microstructural. Second, Marxism primarily represents a relational approach to the study of social inequality, whereas the functional theory of stratification is largely concerned with distributive issues. Thus, while it is true that the macrostructural/relational and the microstructural/distributive phenomena of inequality have important implications for one another, they are analytically distinct orders of things and there is, consequently, some basis for a division of labour between the one theory which concentrates on the former (i.e., Marxism) and the other theory which deals most effectively with the latter (i.e., the functional theory of stratification).

Embourgeoisement Thesis

In the rising affluence of blue-collar workers over the past few decades, some sociologists in Europe, the U.S., and Canada claim to have glimpsed a process of *embourgeoisement*, whereby these workers have increasingly taken on middle-class values, privileges, and lifestyles, and have more and more moved into the middle class in their social relations (e.g., Westley and Westley, 1972). As larger and larger segments of the manual workforce achieve income equality with white-collar workers, it is argued, they migrate to the suburbs and away from their traditional working-class neighbourhoods, abandoning whatever commitments they might have had to labour unions and left-wing politics, and adopting a middle-class, mass-consumption life-style. And this is not simply a consequence of the general decline in blue-collar occupations and the overall rise in white-collar ones. It portends, rather, the demise of the working class as we have known it, and the emergence of a large, new middle class of relatively well-paid, skilled and semi-skilled blue- and white-collar workers (compare, for example, with Weber, above, on the potential for growth of the middle class, as well as with Davis and Moore).

In contrast to the Marxist argument of a progressive proletarianization of white-collar workers, theorists of the embourgeoisement stripe foresee almost the converse — an upward assimilation over time of blue-collar workers into the middle class. Although both envision a kind of melding of the two groups, they differ sharply on the question of which of them is going to move in the direction of the other. And, although both envision a new class of workers differentiated internally by small gradations of income and status, the Marxist version anticipates an eventual coalescence among its members around common issues of class, while the embourgeoisement scenario is a picture of a future new class of more individualistic and competitive workers. The embourgeoisement thesis is less a theory in itself or a critique of Marxism than it is a kind of empirical claim, the reality of which can potentially be determined through research. If, of course, it can be established in this way that there is a trend in the direction of embourgeoisement, and that it is more than just a passing phenomenon, then some fundamental reassessment of certain basic Marxist tenets would seem to be in order. In particular, it is hard to see how the notion of progressive impoverishment (relative or absolute) could be maintained in the face of such findings, much less the Marxist contentions with regard to the emergence of class consciousness, conflict, and organization which flow from it. At the same time, it is not at all difficult to incorporate the idea of embourgeoisement into structural-functionalism or into Weber's analysis of a middle class of propertyless people with some marketable skill to sell.

Post-Industrial Society Theorists

In the past decade or two, theorists from a number of disparate points of view have attempted fundamental reinterpretations of the course and direction of Western society which hinge on the concept of *post-industrialism* — a term which seems to have originated in the writings of Bell (e.g., Bell, 1973). Although their arguments may share little else in common, these theorists typically begin with the assumption that what differentiates the most technically advanced nations of the world (especially the United States) from the rest is, most importantly, that they are moving into a post-industrial phase in their development in which the most important products are services rather than goods — information rather than artifacts. A post-industrial society is one in which a majority of the workforce are employed in the tertiary or service sector of the economy. In the raw-materials producing or primary sector, the jobs people do involve such activities as fishing, farming, mining, and logging. In the industrial or secondary sector, people are engaged in processing or manufacturing. And in the service sector, they are involved in such activities as banking, finance, credit, real estate, insurance, retail trade, providing hotel or motel accomodation, repairing and maintaining automobiles and appliances, dry cleaning, cutting and styling hair, recreation, public transportation and utilities, health care, education, and government at all levels.

Perhaps the most prominent post-industrial society is Bell, who looks ahead to a society dominated by professional and technical workers ("true experts," to use Davis and Moore's term) whose position will derive from their effective monopoly over important theoretical and technological knowledge, rather than possession of productive private property. It will be a society in which class conflict will recede in importance as it becomes more and more contained within such institutions as collective bargaining and compulsory arbitration, and progressively undercut by ethnic, racial, linguistic, religious, and other loyalties. Moreover, it will be a meritocracy (i.e., a society in which rewards are distributed on the basis of ability and effort — see Chapter 6), with the university, rather than business, as the centrepiece, in which effort, training, and ability will be the keys to mobility, and an overarching value consensus will be the cornerstone of a basically harmonious social order. It will not, however, be a society without conflict. Disrupted by periodic disputes between the experts and the public, the politics of post-industrial society are more likely to centre around fine-tuning the system for the greater benefit of the larger number than they are to revolve around issues of class and power. Increasingly we will become concerned with the problems of the environment, making available health care and educational facilities to those who are now denied them, reducing crime, and balancing the costs and benefits of municipal services. And increasingly the "solutions" to these problems will involve greater and greater infusions of both public debate and technical expertise.

Touraine (1971) approaches the analysis of post-industrial society from a neo-Marxist perspective which leads him to differ from Bell in many of his major premises and conclusions, even though he, too, envisions the emergence of a dominant class of the technically learned in a society in which the university is the leading institution. Along with Bell, he sees the rise of this class as a response to the unprecedented possibilities in a computerized age for rational social and economic planning. In Touraine's post-industrial society, however, class conflict does not disappear. Rather, it shifts in emphasis from disputes between capital and labour over the expropriation of surplus value to struggles between technocrats and a public subordinated to their expertise. At the same time, the classical conflicts between bourgeoisie and proletariat persist, and there are conflicts, as well, between the progressive technocratic class and the reactionary class of older capitalistic elements.

Since the post-industrial society theorists are essentially futurists or social forecasters — as witness the titles to Bell's (1973) and Touraine's (1971) major works on the topic — they offer not so much critiques of contemporary theories applied today as they do alternative visions of what is now only darkly seen and remains, in large measure, yet to come. While Bell's view draws importantly upon Weber's work and the Davis-Moore brand of structural-functionalism, Weber seems to have placed much more emphasis on the importance of private property than Bell does, while Davis and Moore argue (if cryptically) that true technical experts (as opposed to mere technicians) can never be expect to rise to a position of dominance as a class.

> . . . The idea of a technocratic social order or a government or priesthood of engineers or social scientists neglects the limitations of knowledge and skills as a basis for performing social functions (Davis and Moore, 1945:247).

Touraine's view is, of course, an elaboration and revision of Marxism designed to take into account anticipated future trends not simply accommodated in the arguments of the original texts. In particular, he argues for possession of important theoretical and technical knowledge as a basis for class formation, to be considered along with ownership of productive private property. This seems to represent a fundamental departure from original Marxist principles, and one which the founding fathers would probably have been hard-pressed to accept — at least from their vantage point a hundred years ago.

While the ultimate utility of the several versions of post-industrial theory remains something for future evaluation, there are certain problems which these versions seem to share at the level of theory. First, the development of technology seems more a cumulative phenomenon within the context of industrialism than it does a break with industrialism. And, if this is so, how does this lead to a wholly new basis for class formation? Second, none of the theories of post-industrial society seems to contain a very convincing account of how it is that the technically learned rise to dominance. They are, after all, only people with expertise to sell, albeit an expertise of a depth and breadth which mark them as a very modern development within industrialism. But this does not explain how it is that they will not largely be taken on in the employ of those — most notably business and government — who can use and purchase their unusual capacities. This is the position which Weber adopted, and which seems more congenial to a Marxist analysis than does Touraine's.

Giddens

Along with Marx and Weber, Giddens begins his analysis of classes in capitalism with the assumption "that, in capitalism, *the market is intrinsically a structure of power,* in which the possession of certain attributes advantages some groupings of individuals relative to others" (1973:101–2). Where the Marxist analysis focuses on differences in bargaining power among groupings which derive from the distinction between those who own productive private property and those who have only their labour power to sell, Giddens sees further class distinctions among people in terms of their relative *market capacities.* In particular, there is in capitalist society a propertyless middle class of persons with educational or technical qualifications to sell and a propertyless working class of persons with only their labour power to sell, as well as the bourgeoisie. Thus, while he rejects Marx's dichotomous model as anchored in what he sees as a misleading distinction between productive and unproductive labour and, consequently, as incapable of apprehending the nature of "middle classes" in capitalism, Giddens follows Weber in also recognizing differences among the latter, although he argues that only a few of the many differentials in market capacity which Weber used to characterize those without property normally give rise to social classes as "historical actors."

In general, the distinctions in market capacity which differentiate those who own productive private property and the propertyless middle and working classes from one another generate identifiable social classes to the extent that inter- and intra-generational mobility across forms of market capacity is limited. This process of the "structuration" of classes, as Giddens terms it, is influenced, as well, by the character of the division of labour among occupations and of the relations of authority within the business firm, as well as by the emergence in society of groupings of people who share common patterns of consumption. In modern industry, "the effect of industrial technique . . . is to create a decisive separation between the conditions of labour of manual and non-manual classes" (Giddens, 1973:108). This effect is heightened by the division between administrative personnel who issue or enforce commands and manual workers who take these commands, while distinctions in authority also divide those at the top into those who have special rights of command as a function of property ownership and those who have no such rights. ". . . the combination of the sources of mediate and proximate structuration distinguished here, creating a threefold class structure," he subsequently goes on to argue in detail, "is generic to capitalist society" (1973:110).

"Moreover, the operation of the 'class principle' may also involve the creation of forms of structuration within the major class divisions" (1973:110). Within the bourgeoisie, for example, it may be necessary to distinguish among individuals in terms of the size of their holdings, if it turns out to be especially difficult for the sons or daughters of small property holders to become big capitalists, or if small property holders themselves find that they are rarely able to increase their holdings by any very great amount. And, within the working class, important distinctions may arise out of differences among members of this class in their training or skill, such that the children of the highly-trained and skilled may find it much easier to move into the middle class than do the off-spring of unskilled or semi-skilled workers.

The existence of class structuration implies a degree of commonality of attitude and belief among members of a class, along with a shared style of life, but it does not suggest that the members of a class recognize that these are tied to membership in a given class, much less that they recognize the existence of other classes whose members share different attitudes, beliefs, and lifestyles. In the former case, we may speak of *class awareness,* but only in the latter of *class consciousness.* Moreover, class consciousness can exist at several levels, sometimes within the same class at the same time. There is, first, the recognition that one is a member of a class which is distinguished from other classes. Second, there is the perception that the interests of the members of one's class are in opposition to those of the members of one or more other classes. And there is, finally, the belief that concerted action on the part of the members of a class can effect a revolutionary reorganization of existing arrangements of power in society. These latter distinctions are important, Giddens argues, since different levels of consciousness arise out of different social conditions. In particular, the second level, *conflict consciousness,* arises out of conflicts of interests between and among classes, such as the conflict of interest between bourgeoisie and proletariat in capitalism, which somehow becomes visible to those involved. On the other hand, the third level, *revolutionary consciousness,* derives from contradictions, or discrepancies "between *an existing and an immanent mode of industrial control*" (1973:114), such as "the clash between a 'backward', agrarian order, and the impact of 'advanced technique'" (1973:117), and is most likely to be found either in groups which are peripheral to an industrial society or in groups most central to it.

"The capitalist state," Giddens argues, "(as both Marx and Weber emphasize) ... necessarily presupposes a dichotomy between the economic order, left open to the play of market forces, and the political order — a dichotomy between 'economic' and 'political man'" (1973:127). Moreover, it is this dichotomy which makes a class society possible, since it makes possible the operation of a market which is at least partially free from political control. As a class society, capitalism necessarily involves exploitation, but it is not an exploitation anchored in notions of productive vs. unproductive labour and the labour theory of value. It is an exploitation which "implies a separation between the social creation of human faculties on the one hand, and the social denial of 'access' to those faculties on the other" (1973:131). But this is not a matter of inequalities in the distribution of material benefits or, as in Marx, of the appropriation of surplus value by the bourgeois class. It is, rather, "*any socially conditioned form of asymmetrical production of life-chances.* 'Life chances' here may be taken to mean the chances an individual has of sharing in the socially created economic or cultural 'goods' which typically exist in any given society" (1973:130-31). In capitalism, class exploitation is effected through differences in market capacity which are revealed most obviously in material inequalities, but also in inequalities in access to education and in opportunities for jobs which are satisfying, creative, and conducive to a full life.

In contemporary capitalist societies, the extension of civil, political, and socio-economic rights to the masses, the accumulation and centralization of capital, and the separation of ownership and control are all signal outcomes in the evolution of capitalism as a system, but they do not require that we abandon the concept of capitalist society. In the case of civil, political, and socio-economic rights, their extension represents "more of a 'completion' or consolidation of capitalist development rather than an undermining of it" (1973:158). As regards the accumulation and centralization of capital, the Marxist category of "monopoly capitalism" is an accurate description of no current society. And, finally, the separation of ownership and control seems to have led not to conflict between shareholders and managers, but to "an overall homogeneity of value and belief, and a high degree of social solidarity, as manifest in interpersonal contracts, friendship and marriage ties ..." (1973:171).

The new middle class of workers in capitalist society is differentiated from the working class in market capacity and hence in income as well. Moreover, since occupational mobility in this kind of society is largely short-range, most of it takes place within the boundaries of class, rather than across them. This source of class structuration is reinforced, in the case of the middle and working classes, by differences between them in their opportunities for advancement, in the kinds of work they perform, and in their isolation from one another at work and at home. It is not difficult to understand how it is that the middle class are relatively reluctant to join unions, especially militant ones, given their location in the authority structure and their opportunities for upward mobility, along with their "class awareness stressing 'individualism,' cognitively and evaluatively" (1973:191). The growth of the new middle class and the increasing mechanization and automation of clerical work have not proletarianized white-collar workers and fused them with the working class in a "historic bloc" with revolutionary potential. Instead, it is closer to the truth to see in this the emergence of an upgraded white-collar workforce, highly trained and specialized, and freed from routine, repetitive work.

Where Marx looked ahead to increasing class conflict as a consequence of the development of capitalism, industrial and political conflict in modern capitalism have become separated as a result of the separation of the economy and the polity, and the intensity of class conflict has been more and more contained within the boundaries of institutionalized forms of arbitration. "Conflict of interest has been recognized and formalized, and thereby held in check" (1973:201). This is not to say, however, that the working class does not have a degree of class consciousness resulting from their aggregation in large plants and the routinized character of their work, just as Marx expected. Contrary to Marx, however, these are sources of *conflict* consciousness, not of revolutionary consciousness, and even this conflict consciousness is tempered by the persistent division of workers into different categories of skill. "As Dahrendorf and many others have pointed out, Marx was wrong in supposing that the trend of capitalist development was towards the elimination of the skilled worker ..." (1973:204) This conflict consciousness manifests itself in trade union organizations which focus on issues of economic gains for their members, but which do not bring seriously into question the relations of authority in industry, since the former is in the economic realm in capitalism, while the latter is in the political. As a consequence of this, coupled with the increasing affluence of the capitalist nations in the twentieth century, the working class has become progressively more affluent over time, although its structural separation from the middle class and its distinct lifestyle have prevented any overall movement in the direction of embourgeoisement.

Some Outstanding Issues

While our concern with matters theoretical is far from ended, it is time to isolate and identify what some of the more important theoretical issues seem to be, and then to put these theories to work for us. In observing how well and why they do not work in helping us interpret the phenomena of social inequality, we will come to know them and their strengths and weaknesses much better than we do now. At the same time, we cannot properly regard many of the uses we put these theories to as "tests" of them, since much of the material in this book is really part of a case study of a single society. In order to test a theory — even weakly — one must have measurements on multiple units at the same point in time and/or multiple measurements on one or more units at several different points in time. Case study data can be used as a source of theoretically relevant examples and illustrations, and theories can be employed to order and arrange such data in particular patterns. But only rarely will we be in a position to state with some confidence that the data do or do not support one theory over another. Moreover, applying Marxism as an interpretive tool in the analysis of single societies is made doubly problematic by the fact that the "system" to which it refers is ultimately the world-as-system, not an individual society or nation-state. Capitalism knows no such boundaries as those which separate societies or nations. "The need of a constantly expanding market for its products chases the bourgoisie over the whole surface of the globe. It must nestle everywhere" (Marx and Engels, 1959:10). In the higher stages of capitalism, the bourgeoisie will be truly an international class, as will the proletariat. Class and class conflict will eventually take on global dimensions, and the revolution against capitalism, should it come to that, will be ultimately a world-wide revolution, and not events locked within the confines of national borders. It is in this sense that, in elaborating the theme of revolutionary social reorganization, Marx and Engels would often describe the conflict between bourgeoisie and proletariat as "the last class conflict," and the proletariat as "the last class."

The Sources of Social Order

One of the major sets of issues separating Marxism and structural-functionalism has to do with the nature of the mechanism by which societies cohere or fail to cohere (Mann, 1971; 1973). The Marxist canon is laced with the rhetoric of force and coercion, and it is clear that capitalist societies, in the end, hang together in this version through the strength of the exploitative grip the bourgeoisie have on the proletariat. But there are several fingers to this grip, not all of which necessarily exercise it in any crude or direct way. Through their control over the means of production, the bourgeoisie are able to manipulate the various super-structures of society to their own advantage. In particular, they are to a degree able to impose their own attitudes, values, and beliefs (i.e., their own ideology) on society in general through their control over what is and what is not learned through educational institutions, organized religion, and the content of the mass media of television, radio, and newspapers. As Marx and Engels express it: "the ideas of the ruling class are in every epoch the ruling ideas, i.e., the class which is the ruling *material* force of society is at the same time its ruling *intellectual force*" (1965:64). To the extent that the ideology of the dominant class is also the ideology of the people generally, then the members of the several subordinate classes can be described as existing in a state of "false consciousness." That is, their attitudes, values, and beliefs serve the interests of the dominant class, not their own. When there is ideological hegemony imposed from above, members of subordinate classes will be unaware of the fact that they share a common exploited position or, if aware of it, they will remain divided among themselves along ethnic, religious, or other lines. Basic to the structural-functional model, on the other hand, is the assumption that social order is fundamentally anchored in an overarching consensus of attitudes, values, and beliefs in the population (Parsons, 1951). This consensus is not imposed from above but, rather, reflects a kind of natural harmony of interdependent, individual interests. It makes social order possible and is the major reason why the classic, Hobbesian condition of "the war of all against all" does not everywhere prevail.

The Marxist position holds that consensus may or may not obtain in a society but that, in either case, social order is based on coercion. Where there is consensus in capitalist societies, this is the result of an ideological hegemony imposed from above in which the members of subordinate classes are falsely conscious. The notion of "false" consciousness, however, has proved to be especially provocative and contentious, for it rests on an independent judgment that some attitudes, values, and beliefs are "true," while others are "false." It can be divested of some ot its more problematic aspects if we can equate "true" with "awareness of common exploited position" (in the case of subordinate classes), and "false" with an absence of such awareness. As well, there are always certain elements in any ideology which are amenable to empirical test as "true" or "false," such as the belief that everyone begins life with a roughly equal opportunity to acquire material wealth and fame. In structural-functionalism, it is essential that there be consensus in any society on such central issues as these. If instances could be found of societies which continued to cohere, despite the absence of any such consensus, this could be comprehended more readily from a Marxist than from a structural-functionalist perspective.

Changing Class Structure

From a Marxist standpoint, the continued development of capitalism should be accompanied by an overall simplification of the class structure, in which the various "transitional" classes, such as the petty bourgeoisie, disappear and are absorbed into a swelling proletariat. Marx was vague, however, on the future fate of a growing "new middle class" of clerical, administrative, and scientific workers, who generate no surplus value directly on their own. It is difficult to see them as members of the bourgeoisie, but they do not quite qualify as classic proletarians either. The problem here seems to stem from Marx's reliance on the labour theory of value in his interpretation of capitalism — a reliance he maintained long after many other of the economists of his day, including Ricardo himself, had abandoned it. If it is assumed that the sole source of value lies in labour, then the idea of surplus value and a system founded upon its appropriation lead logically to a distinction between "productive" and "unproductive" labour, corresponding to the distinction between those who produce surplus value and those who live off the surplus value produced by others. Many white-collar workers do not create surplus value directly through their labour, but they can be seen to perform tasks whose effect is to increase the total amount of surplus value generated within a business firm. To the extent that they possess no share in productive private property, exchange their labour for a wage, and create surplus value indirectly, they are more proletarian than they are anything else. In addition to these white-collar workers, however, are others to whom Marx occasionally refers as the "surplus middle class" of propertyless persons engaged in such "clearly" nonproductive white-collar activities as banking, real estate, and insurance, which are capitalistic functions *par excellence*. Unfortunately, Marx never developed his analysis of this class very far, but it is important to keep in mind the distinctions among proletariat proper, new middle class, and surplus middle class in comparisons and contrasts between a Marxist analysis of the class structure and a structural-functional one.

In some contrast to the Marxist model, the structural-functional theory of social stratification generally envisions an *in*creasing differentiation of social positions and the positional reward structure with increases in specialization and the division of labour. With regard to the almost-proletarian new middle class, it should follow from the premises of a more or less traditional Marxism that the increasing introduction of machinery and advances in the rational reorganization of the work process will lead to decreasing skill requirements and an ever-larger pool of replaceable white-collar workers performing standardized, repetitive tasks. From a structural-functional point of view, this should be to some extent true of the lower layer of white-collar workers, perhaps, but it should be accompanied at the same time by a counter-balancing trend in which an upper layer of "true technical experts" emerges. The two models seem to part company most in their respective analyses of what is likely to happen to the stratum of engineers, scientists, and lower-level administrators who exchange their labour power for a salary or a wage. While it is anything but completely clear on this point, the Marxist perspective would seem to have this group becoming progressively proletarianized over time (see, for example, Anderson, 1974:52-56; Braverman, 1974:Chapter 18). Consistent with Weber's general argument, the structural-functionalist analysis would have it increasingly differentiated internally in skill requirements and rewards, and increasingly affluent as well.

Class, Stratum, and Consciousness

With the increasing internal differentiation of society which comes with societal size, urbanization, and industrialization, rates of upward mobility, according to the orthodox structural-functional view, tend to rise and stratum solidarity falls. People become progressively more concerned with inching their individual ways up the many-runged ladder of material and symbolic success, and less and less moved by any notion that they share common fate with others like them. While Marx and Engels have relatively little to say about individual mobility as such, their vision of the future development of capitalism is, again, quite different. The course they chart for capitalist systems leads in the long run to a polarized, two-class system of class-conscious people, and to a politicized and organized proletariat whose members find the old avenues to mobility no longer open to them.

Government and the Economy

In structural-functionalism, the political and the economic tend to be seen as relatively discrete realms of activity organized around separate social functions which need bear no close relation to one another. And, by implication, this should be increasingly the case as societies grow in size and level of internal differentiation. Government is a more or less autonomous institution which acts on behalf of all its constituencies, of which big business is but one. Although they do not explicitly elaborate the theme, Davis and Moore do state that ownership of capital goods is a source of power, and it is only a small theoretical leap from this observation to the inference that this power might be used on occasion to give capitalists an advantage over lesser creatures. Their discussion of the limits to political power makes it clear, however, that this would be a real exception rather than a regular practice. The Marxist position stands in some contrast to this. With the maturation of capitalism, the bourgeoisie consolidate their hold over the superstructure of politics until government becomes, more than anything else, the organized expression of bourgeois political interests. The political becomes, in the end, importantly (although not altogether simply) subordinate to the economic.

Momentum of Meritocracy

Another issue on which there is real division at the level of theory is the extent to which societies such as Canada can be seen to move in the direction of reward according to merit (or "meritocracy" — see Chapter 6). That people should be increasingly rewarded in some proportion to their contributions is an easy inference from the premises of the functional theory of stratification, from Weber's emphasis on increasing rationality in the market, and from Bell's version of the trend to a technocratic order. In each case, the clear expectation is that rewards on the basis of gender, ethnicity, and other ascriptive criteria will eventually disappear, to be replaced by rewards in terms of achievement. While Marx thought he could see a tendency toward the reduction of workers' levels of skills and a general levelling of skill differentials within the working class and, as part of this, a diminution of wage disparities among different social categories, he did not see in this any movement in the direction of meritocracy. Rather, he looked ahead to a relatively homogeneous and (absolutely or relatively) impoverished working class in capitalism, along with an increasingly affluent bourgeoisie. Among neo-Marxists, though, a variety of different positions on this matter can be found. Touraine, for example, appears to envision a future, post-industrial society in which merit largely determines rewards, while others, such as Anderson (1974), see continuing ethnic, gender, and other inequalities which serve the interests of the bourgeoisie by keeping wages and other work benefits down.

Summing Up

The current chaos that is social theory makes it tempting to adopt an eclectic stance, using bits and pieces of theory here and there as they seem useful. But selecting and rejecting issues and information on such unsystematic grounds ignores the fact that issues are made important and information made relevant *by* theories or, perhaps more precisely, by their being located on the lines of combat where two or more theories clash. A free-wheeling eclecticism would, at best, leave the otherwise uninitiated reader with a disorganized mélange of ideas and facts without any real sense of how they might be organized, what their larger meaning might be, or why these ideas and facts, as opposed to others, were chosen.

Since structural-functionalism and Marxism, however flawed and incomplete, remain the major contenders doing battle in the regions of social inequality even yet, more attention has necessarily been paid to them than to any others. Still, it is impossible here to do much more than to outline the central features of even these two theories, to identify a number of the more important points at which they seem to converge and diverge, and to point to certain ways in which they can be seen as more complementary than as either redundant or opposed to one another. And it was impossible, as well, to avoid discussion of a least certain of the contributions to theory of Weber, Dahrendorf, Bell, Touraine, Giddens, and others. The reader concerned with acquiring more than just an introduction to concepts, theories, and issues in the analysis of social inequality would do well to consult some of the original sources mentioned here.

A critical exposition of the main features of a version of contemporary Marxism and of the structural-functional theory of social stratification according to Davis and Moore hardly boxes the theoretical compass of our time. And to add to it something of the contributions of Weber, Dahrendorf, Bell, Touraine, Giddens, and others is to do little more than to allude to what is now a vast and still growing literature on social inequality. Still, contained within Marxism, structural-functionalism, and the juxtaposition of the two are most of the major issues of the field today. They are usually there in substance, if not always in name. And, while there have been undeniable, recent theoretical advances, it is an easy judgment to make that there are currently no theoretical systems in social inequality which match Marxism or structural-functionalism as systems, or which conclusively resolve the issues raised but not resolved in these two great bodies of thought. This is not to say, however, that we can effectively ignore the remaining corpus of inequality theory. We shall meet some more of it soon enough, but more in the context of using theories than in just talking about them.

Part II

On the Distributions
of Rewards and Merit

Chapter 5

Some Changing Distributions of Rewards

"What's a million?" (remark frequently, if erroneously, attributed to C.D. Howe, Canada's World War II Minister of Munitions and Supply.)

"I've been rich and I've been poor," the saloon singer Sophie Tucker once reflected, "and, believe me, rich is best." And most Canadians doubtless agree — even if they have to rely upon the opinions of Miss Tucker and others to know that it is so. for few of us are (or ever will be) very rich; and most of us are not (or ever will be) very poor. Still, some of us are rich; some of us are poor; and there are real differences in affluence among the remainder of us who fall somewhere between these two extremes. That is, income and wealth are unequally distributed in our society, and it is the basic purpose of this chapter to describe how unequal these distributions are, how these inequalities have changed over time, and how Canada stands relative to some other nations in this regard.

Income

Changing Distribution

Comparatively, Canada is a wealthy nation, and it has been so throughout the period following World War II. It has consistently ranked among the top few nations of the world in per capita Gross National Product (i.e., the combined value of all the goods and services produced in a country in a given year, usually abbreviated as GNP, divided by the population size) — a common measure of the wealth of nations. The per capita GNP increased from $1,503 to $9,812 in the years 1951–78, and there was an accompanying increase in the average income of individuals from $2,086 in 1951 to $10,244 in 1978. In this same period, however, the cost of living rose substantially and, therefore, some better gauge of the affluence of Canada and Canadians can be gained by expressing these figures in *constant*, rather than in *current*, dollars. One way of doing this is to use the Consumer Price Index as an indicator of the cost of living, setting it equal to 100 for the base year 1961, and then expressing all dollar values as if they were in 1961 dollars. If the index were 100 in 1961, it was approximately 88 in 1951, 133 in 1971, and 257 in 1978. By this yardstick, then, a dollar was worth about three times as much in 1951 as it was in 1978 (i.e., 257 divided by 88). Expressed in terms of 1961 dollars, the per capita GNP increased from $1,707 in 1951 to $3,818 in 1978, with an accompanying increase in the average individual income from $2,370 in the former year to $3,986 in the latter. Even allowing for inflation, then, there was a 124 per cent increase in the per capita GNP and a 68 per cent increase in the average individual income in the period 1951–78. At the same time, the upward trend in real incomes stopped in the latter half of the 1970s, and (as of this writing) has not yet begun again.

Both Canada as a country and individual Canadians on the average, then, have continued to fare better and better economically, in all but very recent times. Changes in per capita GNP, however, do not translate themselves in any simple or direct way into changes in individuals' incomes, and changes in individuals' incomes tell us only part of the story of the purchasing power of individuals. One reason for this is that most people belong to family units, and a majority of families currently have more than one income earner. While single individuals who live alone may typically have only their own economic resources to draw upon, people who are members of families can often draw upon the income of more than one person. At the same time, it is normally individuals, and not families, who receive income, although it was once fairly common for employees to be paid according to their marital status and number of children. For some purposes, then, it is appropriate to analyse family incomes (e.g., to study economic resources) while, for other purposes, it is appropriate to analyse individual incomes (e.g., to study wage and salary determination). Table 5–1 shows the changing distribution of families by the number of income recipients, 1951–71. As these data show, the modal pattern of an earlier time, whereby the economic fortunes of the family were tied to the income of one person, has been

Table 5-1

Percentage of Families by Number of Income Recipients, 1951-71.

Number of Income Recipients in Family	1951 [a]	1961 [a]	1971	Change: 1951-71
None	0.4%	0.5%	0.3%	– 0.1%
One	57.0	53.2	34.7	–22.3
Two	29.7	34.7	47.6	+17.9
Three	8.7	8.6	11.6	+ 2.9
Four	3.0	2.4	4.3	+ 1.3
Five or more	1.1	0.6	1.4	+ 0.3

[a] Excludes families with one or more farmers.

Sources: Dominion Bureau of Statistics. *Income Distribution* (Cat. 13-529, Table 14).
              Statistics Canada. *Income Distribution by Size in Canada* (1971: Cat. 13-207, Table 25).

replaced by a pattern in which the Canadian family is likely to have two or more income recipients.

In 1951, the average income among families and unattached individuals in Canada was $3,185. This increased to $4,815 in 1961, $8,845 in 1971, and $17,710 in 1978. This twenty-seven-year period, then, saw family and unattached individuals' incomes register a more than five-fold increase in current dollars. If we express these figures in constant (1961) dollars, however, the increase has been less spectacular. In 1961 dollars, the average income among families and unattached individuals in Canada was $3,619 in 1951, $4,815 in 1961, $6,650 in 1971, and $6,891 in 1978 — a less than two-fold increase (see Table 5-2). Moreover, real incomes for these units began to fall in the latter half of the 1970s, and (as of this writing) have not yet begun to rise again. Between 1977 and 1978, for example, the average income for families and unattached individuals rose from $16,764 to $17,710. This was a *gain* of 6 per cent in current dollar income, but a *drop* of 3 per cent in real income, and the second consecutive year in which such a drop was recorded.

While an analysis of increases and decreases in real income is informative in its own right, it, too, tells us only part of what we might wish to know about the changing economic resources of Canadians. In particular, it does not tell us anything in itself about income inequalities, since some families and unattached individuals make much less than the average, while others make much more. Table 5-2 contains information on the changing distribution of the incomes of families and unattached individuals in Canada, 1951-78. These data show that,

Table 5-2

Percentage of Total Before-Tax Income Going to Families and Unattached Individuals by Quintile, 1951-78.

Income Quintile	1951 [a]	1961 [a]	1971	1978
Lowest	4.4%	4.2%	3.6%	3.9%
Second	11.2	11.9	10.6	10.4
Middle	18.3	18.3	17.6	17.7
Fourth	23.3	24.5	24.9	25.5
Highest	42.8	41.4	43.3	42.5
Average in constant (1961)	3,619	4,815	6,650	6,891

[a] Excludes families with one or more farmers.
Source: Derived from Canada (1974a: Table 7.4; 1978a: 18).

although real incomes rose by about 90 per cent in the period surveyed, there are large and persistent inequalities in the distribution of incomes. The bottom quintile (i.e., 20 per cent) of families and unattached individuals never received more than 4.4 per cent of the total income going to these units in the years represented in the table, while the top quintile never received less than 41.4 per cent of the total family income (also see Henderson and Rowley, 1977, 1978a, b). As well, there has been a small, but measurable, tendency for the top two quintiles to increase their hold upon the available income at the expense of the bottom three quintiles (also see Hamilton and Pinard, 1977 and Johnson, 1977). In 1951, the top two quintiles received 66.1 per cent of income going to families and unattached individuals. This decreased slightly in 1961 to 65.9 per cent, rose in 1971 to 68.2 per cent, and then dropped slightly to 68 per cent in 1978.

The levels of family income inequality in Canada over the past thirty years appear to be broadly similar to those in the United Kingdom (Atkinson, 1975) and the United States (Thurow, 1975) in the same period — slightly higher than in the former, perhaps, and slightly lower than in the latter. They are, however, clearly higher than those in at least certain of the Eastern bloc countries, such as the Soviet Union, Poland, Czechoslovakia, and Hungary (Lane, 1971), although the available data are inadequate to provide any very precise comparisons between nations and the East and West.

Taxes and Transfers

The data on income distributions presented to this point have concerned before-tax income only. Many of us take at least some comfort, however, in the notion that Canada has a system of progressive taxation, whereby those with high incomes pay proportionally more in taxes than do those with low incomes, with the result that the tax structure has an equalizing effect on the overall income distribution. In fact, the system of taxation in Canada seems not to be progressive at all, and actually appears to be regressive at the low end of the income range. That is, when direct and indirect taxes from all sources — federal, provincial, and municipal — are taken into account, there is a general tendency for the well-to-do to pay proportionally *less* of their incomes in taxes than the less well-to-do. As Maslove puts it in his detailed analysis of taxation in Canada, "by far the most striking conclusion to be draws from an examination of total tax payments is the extreme regressivity of the system at the lower end of the income scale and the lack of any significant progressivity over the remainder of the income range." "Indeed," he continues, "over the lower portion of the income scale, the system tends to contradict the ability-to-pay principle by taxing the poor at a higher rate than those who are better off" (1972:64). Some more concrete idea of the magnitude of this pattern can be gleaned from the data in Table 5–3, which show that the regressivity and lack of progressivity observed by Maslove reveal themselves in all taxes taken together, as well as in federal, provincial, and municipal taxes considered separately. Those at the very bottom of the income scale paid, on the average, 120.3 per cent of their incomes in taxes, while those in the next-to-bottom category paid 60.6 per cent, and all those with incomes of $6,000 and above paid about 40 per cent. Instead of the well-to-do and the rich subsidizing the poor, the poor to some extent subsidize everyone else. The overall effect of the taxation system in Canada, then, is to increase rather than to decrease income inequality.

Table 5–3

Average Tax Rates before Transfer Payments, Families and Unattached Individuals, Canada, 1969 [a]

Income	Federal	Provincial	Municipal	All Taxes
Under $2,000	48.7%	40.7%	30.8%	120.3%
$ 2,000–$ 2,999	25.7	20.7	14.3	60.6
$ 5,000–$ 5,999	20.9	15.1	6.1	41.9
$ 6,000–$ 6,999	21.0	14.3	5.4	40.8
$ 9,000–$ 9,999	21.5	13.7	4.9	40.1
$10,000–$10,999	21.8	13.6	4.6	39.9
$15,000 and Over	23.7	13.6	3.8	40.9

[a] Percentages based on "broad income," which includes certain non-money income components, such as the imputed value of food and fuel produced on farms.
Source: Maslove (1972: Table 5.15).

As Table 5–3 shows, there are certain segments of the population (i.e., those with very low incomes) who pay out more in federal, provincial, and municipal taxes than they receive in income exclusive of government *transfer payments* (e.g., the family allowance, unemployment insurance, the Canada Pension Plan, welfare, and the like). And this is true even when income is broadly construed to include such components as the imputed value of food and fuel produced and consumed within the household — an important component of farmers' incomes, for example. Thus, people whose monetary plus imputed incomes were on the order of $1,000 in 1969 paid, on the average, about $1,203 (i.e., 120.3 per cent of $1,000) in taxes. This is only possible because of the existence of government transfer payments, but it means that a significant proportion of the transfer payments which people receive is spent to pay the taxes levied on them.

The express purpose of government transfer payments is to maintain some minimum standard of living for those who would otherwise have little or no income. Although they amount to many millions of dollars every year, they make up but a small part of the total income Canadians receive. In 1951, they made up 5.2 per cent of the total income of families and unattached individuals in this country, increasing to 7.0 per cent in 1961, and decreasing to 6.6 per cent in 1971 (Canada, 1974a: Table 7.19). At the same time, they do form a significant component of the incomes of at least some Canadians — most notably those who receive no salary or wage. Transfer payments are of little benefit to those who are employed, regardless of their wage or salary level (Johnson, 1974).

Since transfer payments represent a significant proportion of the incomes only of persons who receive no wage or salary, they have litle effect on the overall distribution of incomes of individuals, of income earners, or of families (Love and Wolfson, 1976) — despite the expansion of social security programs in the postwar years whose apparent purpose has been to redistribute income. The inclusion of transfer payments in income does eliminate the phenomenon of people paying out more in taxes than they receive in income, but the basic pattern of regressive taxation for the lowest income categories remains, if in somewhat weakened form (Maslove, 1972:72). The pattern of taxation for the remainder of the income scale is unaltered through the inclusion of transfer payments, as one might expect.

The systems of taxation and social security in Canada, then, seem to effect no significant redistribution of incomes, despite their stated purpose of doing so. In fact, the taxation system is actually regressive at the lower end of the income scale, and neither particularly regressive nor progressive through the remainder of it. With regard to the taxation system, the poorest 22 to 39 per cent of all families, depending upon the province, fall into the regressive range when broad income (i.e., income before taxes, including the imputed value of nonmonetary components, and minus transfer payments) is used. When full income (i.e., income before taxes — including, again, nonmonetary components — plus transfer payments) is used, the poorest 17–28 per cent of families, depending upon the province, fall into the regressive range. Moreover, the more local the unit of government, the more regressive the taxes it levies tends to be. In fact, the personal income tax — the one we tend to think first about when we think of taxes — is the only one which is progressive for all income levels. Most other federal taxes are regressive for at least certain income levels, including the federal general sales tax, which is regressive for all income levels. This is, of course, a feature of all taxes based on consumption. At the provincial level, the progressivity of the personal income tax (a proportion of which is either returned to the provinces or, as in the case of Quebec, collected by the province itself) is offset by the regressivity of sales and excise taxes. Municipal taxes, finally, are the most regressive of all including, most importantly, municipal property taxes, which are regressive at almost all income levels.

Perhaps most surprising is the apparent failure of the massive and increasingly expensive social security system in Canada to redistribute incomes in any real way. A major reason for this would seem to be that, despite the seemingly large amounts of money involved, they have been small and relatively constant as a proportion of total income earned over the years, and they benefit, by and large, only those who do not work for a wage or a salary. And another major reason could be that increases in transfer payments over the past thirty years have come in a period when the poorer income earners have been losing in *relative* purchasing power and, most recently, in *absolute* purchasing power as well. If this is true, "then it should not be surprising that 'redistributive' programs are failing to 'redistribute.' Like Alice, in *Through the Looking Glass,* they are running as hard as they can to stay in the same place" (Johnson, 1977:342).

In general, then, taxes and transfer payments in Canada seem at most to have only a small redistributive effect with regard to incomes. Just how Canada fares in this regard relative to other nations cannot be determined very precisely, although Hewitt (1977) presents some data for a number of Western countries which suggest that direct and indirect taxes, coupled with government social service expenditures, in Canada have only a modest redistributive effect relative to elsewhere (also see Atkinson, 1975:71). At the top of the list of seventeen countries (in order) were Sweden, Austria, the Netherlands, Germany, Norway, and New Zealand. In the middle were Belgium, Denmark, the United Kingdom, Finland, and Switzerland. And at the bottom were the United States, Australia, France, Canada, Ireland, and Japan. The relative positions of the U.S. and Canada on this list are consistent with Pipes and Walker's (1979) analysis, which suggests that the overall tax rate is higher for all income categories in Canada than in the U.S., with the largest differences occurring in the lowest income categories and the smallest differences in the highest categories.

Poverty

One major reason why income is important is that it is a means to acquire "things that contribute to sustenance and comfort." It may be useful, therefore, to get some sense of the levels of sustenance and comfort which are achieved by persons at different income levels in Canada. As one approach to this, we might attempt to assess the extent to which the incomes of Canadians are sufficient to permit them to live above a line which represents "poverty." From the very beginning (e.g., Rowntree, 1901), however, studies of poverty have been plagued with difficulties in definition — in particular, is the concept best defined by reference to some absolute or some relative standard?

Although the current consensus is that poverty is most usefully defined in relative terms, it is worth pointing out some of the problems involved when an attempt is made to give it absolute definition. First, there is no such thing as a subsistence diet. Instead, there are all manner of different diets which permit different levels of physical vitality for people whose requirements vary as a function of their physical activity (e.g., office workers vs. manual labourers). Second, people are widely ignorant as to how to obtain the best nutritional value for their money. Third, even if it were generally known how to obtain the best nutritional value, social conventions would prevent many people from eating these foods (which might include such items as soybeans, beef liver, and skim milk, for example). Consequently, attempts to give the concept of poverty absolute definition necessarily involve a certain amount of arbitrariness, even in what is probably the most clear-cut case, food. What level of physical vitality is implied by the term subsistence, for example, and must we specify different diets for people depending upon their physical activity? If people do not make the best possible use of their food dollars, do we exclude them from the category of the poor if they have enough money for an adequate diet but do not know how to obtain it? And, likewise, do we exclude those people from the category of the poor if they have enough money for an adequate diet but refuse to eat what they can afford? Not surprisingly, such problems of arbitrariness multiply when we move to consider issues of what is minimally adequate housing, clothing, recreation, and the like.

In adopting a relative definition of poverty, we recognize that what is considered to be poor is so by reference to the standard of living and customs of the time and place in which it is found. Thus, for example, Rainwater (1972) found that people's definitions of what constitutes poverty are hinged directly to whatever the average income is at the time, and that they estimate their families' needs at just slightly above half of the average level of family consumption — whatever that happens to be. This means, of course, that most poor Canadians would not be poor when judged against the corresponding criterion used to define poverty among the inhabitants of the subcontinent of India. But it does not necessarily mean that there will always be poverty, since it is quite possible that someday no families will consume less than half of what the average family consumes.

One widely-accepted approach to the definition of poverty lines was first developed by Poduluk, working at Statistics Canada, and later adopted by the Economic Council of Canada (Podoluk, 1968; Economic Council of Canada, 1968). Taking as its initial point of departure the results of a survey of about 2,000 families selected at random in Canada, which showed that the average family spent approximately 50 per cent of its income on food, clothing, and shelter, it was (admittedly arbitrarily) assumed that those families were poor which spent 70 per cent of their incomes on these basic necessities. When this criterion was applied to the population of Canada for 1961, it classified some 25 per cent of the population as poor. Since this result was generally regarded as a "reasonable" estimate at the time, the 70 per cent figure was retained for use in subsequent revised poverty lines. At the same time, the procedure has been criticized on several grounds (e.g., Special Senate Committee, 1971:7). First, it makes no provision for families larger than five, and there is a good reason to believe that a significant part of poverty in Canada is to be found in precisely such families. Second, the 70 per cent figure may have been appropriate enough at an earlier time, but it is likely that the average family today spends rather less than the 50 per cent of its income on basic necessities than the average family spent some fifteen years ago. And third, the formula adopted by the Council for future revisions of its poverty lines allowed for increases in the cost of living, but not for increases in the average standard of living. To the extent, then, that the average living standards of Canadians rise over time, the difference between the poverty lines and this average standard will progressively increase.

A Special Senate Committee struck in 1968 to study the problem of poverty in Canada elected to pursue a somewhat different course from that of the Economic Council. First, it began with an estimate of the annual costs of basic necessities for a family of four. Second, it generated a procedure in which the basic principles of Podoluk's method for adjustments according to family size were applied to the initial cost estimate for a family of four, and then extrapolated to families up to size ten. This yielded a set of basic need lines which, when treated as if they made up 70 per cent of a poverty line income, generated a series of poverty lines for families of different sizes. In the Committee's words:

> As the total number of individuals covered by Statistics Canada's *Survey of Incomes* (1969) was just under 20.5 million, the overall poverty rate for that year was approximately 25.1 per cent; that is, one Canadian in four was a member of a family unit whose income was below the poverty line. ...the incidence of poverty (the poverty rate) was highest among unattached individuals, two-person families, and families with five or more members. The lowest incidence was among families with three and four members (Special Senate Committee, 1971:11).

> Furthermore, it should be borne in mind that 6.2 persons represent only the *average* size of these five-or-more person families. While the general poverty rate for these families is about 28.5 per cent..., research by the Committee indicates that in the very large families of seven, eight, and more persons, where there are likely to be many small children, the poverty rate approaches 40–50 per cent. These facts are even more significant when it is realized that the data...include transfer payments — family allowances, old age security pensions, welfare allowance, etc. (Special Senate Committee, 1971:13).

These estimates of rates of poverty, however, treat the poor as a homogeneous category, whereas some are much poorer than others. Among unattached individuals who fell below their poverty line in 1969, approximately 440,000 (or 70 per cent) had incomes which were less than 70 per cent of their poverty line. In other words, 70 per cent of all poor unattached individuals had incomes insufficient to meet (according to the Committee's criteria) their basic requirements for food, clothing, and shelter. And over 1,240,000 (or almost 50 percent) of those in poor families of five or more were similarly impoverished. In all, something on the order of 2,636,000 (or about 51 per cent) of poor unattached individuals and members of families falling below their poverty line in 1969 had incomes inadequate to feed, clothe, and shelter themselves at what the Committee took to be a level of subsistence only (Special Senate Committee, 1971:14).

Since the Special Senate Committee completed its work, the real incomes of Canadians have risen somewhat. Thus, if we were simply to apply the Committee's criteria as we have described them, adjusted for the cost of living, this would probably lead to the conclusion that the rate of poverty has declined slightly since that time (see Harp and Hofley, 1980:Chapter 1). That is, if the Committee's original poverty lines define some level of minimal adequacy in standard of living, then increasing real incomes would necessarily mean that a smaller and smaller proportion of Canadians would be unable to live at that level. The Committee, however, opted for a definition of poverty indexed to the "average living standards" of Canadians. They generated a procedure whereby subsequent adjustments to poverty lines could be made according to changes in the total disposable income (i.e., the total amount of personal income, including transfer payments, less the total amount of personal income taxes paid) of Canadians.

Convinced "that the Senate committee was not going to live up to its mandate" (Adam et al., 1971:v), which was "to discuss the actual production of poverty in Canada — the roles played by the tax system, corporate autonomy, collective bargaining and the rest," four members of its research staff defected to write their own report. Entitled *The Real Poverty Report*, it characterized the Statistics Canada-Economic Council of Canada and Senate Committee poverty lines as "misleading measurements" (Adams et al., 1971:11) and proposed, instead, "a poverty line drawn at one-half of the average living standard of Canadians" (also see Rainwater, 1972), with adjustments for family size based on the same principles used in the earlier poverty lines. Unlike these earlier poverty lines, however, which are simply indexed to the Consumer Price Index (in the case of Statistics Canada-Economic Council of Canada) or to average disposable income (in the case of the Senate Committee), the Relative Poverty Line (as its authors called it) begins by defining poverty in terms of average living standards (1971:12-15).

If poverty is such an elusive phenomenon, how is it that it has received so much attention? One reason might be that poverty is preeminently a political concept, and that defining it and enumerating the poor become important activities when governments decide that certain inequalities in income require official attention (see, for example, Special Senate Committee, 1971:207-13). In a political environment where a degree of inequality is considered both natural and just, but where some people are seen as poor through no real fault of their own (i.e., "poor but honest," in Dickens's phrase), a working definition of poverty is a necessary administrative device, permitting official agencies to identify "the poor" and to minister to them.

Since any distinction between poor and non-poor is necessarily at least somewhat arbitrary, and since the principal concern of the present work lies with an analysis of inequalities, it would not seem particularly useful to add the notion of poverty as such to our already cluttered conceptual armamentarium. Affluence is more or less continuously distributed among the population, all the way from enormous wealth down to grinding poverty, even as it is unequally distributed. Deciding who is poor and who is not requires that we find some point along this continuum below which the economic resources of people are unacceptably low. But it is, after all, a continuum, and there is, therefore, no natural poverty line. Moreover, the issue of poverty would not arise at all if affluence were not unequally distributed in the first place. Economic inequality can be seen from this point of view as the general problem, of which poverty is a special case.

To argue that there is no clearly and qualitatively defined state separate from other states which we might usefully define as poverty is to suggest that it probably makes little sense to have specific theories of poverty apart from our theories of material inequality generally. Thus, the poor might be seen from a structural-functional point of view as simply those with the least economic resources, although one version of structural-functionalism exists in the *culture of poverty* thesis (e.g., Lewis, 1961). Briefly, this thesis argues that the poor form a socially, culturally, and psychologically distinct group whose social arrangements (e.g., family structures), beliefs, values, and attitudes keep them and their children poor. Certainly it is true that social, cultural, and psycho- logical factors vary with the locations of individuals in society, but what is not clearly true is that these factors are *causes* of poverty. From a Marxist stand- point, they are most readily seen as *consequences* of one's location in society. Thus, the poor comprise some fraction of the working class, along with members of the industrial reserve army of the unemployed and the flotsam and jetsam of the lumpenproletariat. Their poverty derives from their location in a system of class relations, and their social arrangements and their consciousness derive ultimately from this source. Thus, if we are studying a family headed by an unemployed mother, whose members do not believe firmly that hard work and ability lead to success, and who are oriented very much to the present, with little tendency to defer gratification, are these factors causes of their poverty, or are they consequences of their class?

Wealth

Assets, Debts, and Economic Worth

Issues in the distribution of economic resources in a society are often dealt with in terms of income, especially those readily measurable components which derive from wages and salaries. A substantial amount of what Canadians receive in income, however, typically evades our scrutiny, since no comprehensive and systematic accounting of overall income is made on any regular basis. Income in kind, for example, generally falls into this category, as do inheritances and bequests, capital gains (or losses), refunds from pension plans, settlements from insurance policies, and all manner of gifts. But, even if we had detailed information on total incomes of Canadians, this would still not give us an entirely satisfactory measure of the economic resources to which they have access. It would tell us much of what we might like to know about the rate at which new wealth was flowing in, but it would not tell us anything in itself about wealth already in hand (Henretta and Campbell, 1978). And the value of the new depends importantly upon the store of the old. An income of $15,000 per year for a husband, a wife, and two children, for example, would mean one thing to a family with a 95 per cent mortgage on a newly acquired, $55,000 home, with furniture and automobile time payments to make and no investments, and quite another to such a family with no mortgage or time payments to make and a substantial portfolio of blue-chip stocks.

If the available data are inadequate for any definitive study of income, they are woefully inadequate for any very penetrating study of wealth. Table 5-4 shows the cumulative shares of totals assets held by all families and unattached individuals in Canada in 1970. According to these data, fully 93.3 per cent of all assets were held by the "most wealthy" 50 per cent of families and unattached individuals, leaving 6.7 per cent to be distributed among the remaining 50 per cent. Or, to put it another way, the average assets held by the top 50 per cent are on the order of fourteen times the average assets held by the bottom 50 per cent. And the most wealthy 1 per cent of Canadian families and unattached individuals held a total of 12 per cent of all assets — twelve times what one would expect if assets were equally distributed among the population. This inequality in wealth is much higher than the corresponding inequality in income observed earlier in the chapter.

Table 5-4

Cumulative Shares of Total Assets Held by All Families and Unattached Individuals, 1970.

Percentage of Total Assets held by:

Most wealthy 1 per cent	12.0%
Most wealthy 2 per cent	17.4
Most wealthy 5 per cent	28.6
Most wealthy 10 per cent	41.8
Most wealthy 20 per cent	60.8
Most wealthy 50 per cent	93.3

Source: Canada (1974a: Table 7.18).

For all income groups, the largest single asset is the estimated market value of home and vacation home, although only those toward the top end of the income scale, of course, are likely to have both (Canada, 1974a:Table 7.12). These two items taken together constitute well over half the total assets for all income groups, except the very highest (i.e., those with annual incomes in excess of $25,000), where they constitute about a third. The second largest component of total assets for all but the very highest income group (where it is non-liquid financial assets, such as publicly-traded stocks) is liquid assets, including cash on hand, bank and savings deposits, and various types of bonds. Non-liquid financial assets form an important component of the assets of only the top income group, as does investment in other real estate. And the estimated market value of automobiles is a significant asset for no income group. Almost all families and unattached individuals in Canada, then, have almost all of their assets tied to the market value of their homes and vacation properties, in cash, or in something readily convertible to cash. Only the very highest group has much in the way of investment in other real estate or non-liquid financial assets.

Assets, though, show only the credit side of the ledger of wealth. Rich or poor, most people have various liabilities which must also be taken into account in any determination of their financial worth (Canada, 1974a:Table 7.12). If the largest asset for most people is the market value of their home and vacation home, the largest debt for all income groups is the mortgage(s) on these. In general, and with the significant exception of the very highest income group, the higher the income group, the greater the percentage of total debt involved in home and vacation home mortgages. The second largest debt for all but the very highest income group (where it is "other" personal debt) is consumer debt — charge accounts and instalment debt, loans from consumer loan companies, loans from Credit Unions and Caisses Populaires, and the like. As a percentage of total debt, consumer debt is considerably larger for low- and middle-income groups than it is for high-income groups. And, finally, other personal debt, including bank loans against collateral or securities, loans from insurance companies, home improvement loans, and various unsecured debts, is a significant percentage of the total debt for low and high income groups both, although much more so for the latter than for the former.

Table 5–5 shows total assets, total debts, and net worth in (1977) dollars for families and unattached individuals by income group in 1977. The average assets for these units were $54,482 in that year which, when reduced by the average debts of $8,209, left an average net worth of $46,273.

Although comparisons among nations in the matter of the concentration of wealth are extremely hazardous as a consequence of the generally poor quality of the data and of different definitions used in determining what is to be regarded as wealth, it would appear as if wealth is less concentrated in the U.S. than in Great Britain (Atkinson, 1975:Chapter 7), and less concentrated in Canada than in the U.S. Thus, Atkinson has estimated that the top 1 per cent of families in Britain held between 28.4 and 33.4 per cent of the wealth in that country in 1968, while the corresponding figure for the United States was in the range of 20 per cent. The Canadian figure (Table 5–4) for 1970 was close to half that for the U.S.

The Family Home

Canada is a nation of people who own their own homes or who would like to. In recent decades, however, the percentage of families living in owner-occupied dwellings has decreased, while the percentage living in rental accomodation has increased. In 1971, 63.6 per cent of all dwellings in the country were owner-occupied — down from 66.2 per cent in 1966 and 67.6 per cent in 1956 (Canada,

Table 5–5

Average Total Assets, Total Debts, and Net Worth of Families and Unattached
Individuals by Income Group in Current (1977) Dollars, 1977.

Income Group	Total Assets	Total Debts	Net Worth
Under $3,000	$ 18,121	$ 1,464	$ 16,657
$ 3,000–$6,999	25,455	1,763	23,692
7,000– 10,999	34,950	3,715	31,235
11,000– 14,999	40,794	6,897	33,897
15,000– 19,999	50,974	10,362	40,612
20,000– 24,999	60,701	14,134	46,567
25,000– 34,999	82,224	14,285	67,939
35,000 and over	228,129	22,269	205,860
Totals	54,482	8,209	46,273

Source: Derived from Canada (1979: Tables 17 and 22).

1974a:214). Along with this has come a drop in the percentage of housing which
is of the single detached variety — the type which most Canadians seem to prefer
— and a rise in the percentage of other kinds of dwelling units: single attached
(e.g., townhouses, maisonettes), apartments and mobile homes. In 1951, 66.7 per
cent of all dwelling units in Canada were single detached (Canada, 1974a:212).
This decreased slightly to 65.4 per cent in 1961, and decreased further to 59.4 per
cent in 1971. Single attached units rose from 7 per cent to 11.3 per cent in this
same period, while apartments and flats rose from 26 per cent to 28.2 per cent.
While the percentage which are mobile homes has risen as well, they currently
make up an inconsequential 1 or 2 per cent of all dwellings in Canada. What
seems likely in the future is a convergence of the two major trends — a decreasing
percentage of families living in owner-occupied, single detached housing and an
increasing percentage living in rented, single attached units and apartments.

For most Canadian families, the home is a uniquely important family
possession. It is the major component of both assets and debts, and it makes up
well over half the net worth of all families taken together. Table 5–6 shows the
estimated equity families and unattached individuals had in homes by income
group in 1977. In general, the higher the income group, the higher the estimated
equity, although this equity represents a much larger percentage of net worth for
lower- and middle-income families (over 50 per cent for those with incomes less
than $35,000, and about 28 per cent for those in the $35,000 or over category).
For those middle- and lower-income families who own homes, then, the equity

they have in the home represents the bulk of the wealth they have been able to accumulate over the years.

Table 5–6

Equity in Home of Families and Unattached Individuals by Income Group in Current (1977) Dollars, 1977.

Income Group	Equity in Home
Under $3,000	$26,911
$ 3,000–$ 6,999	28,513
7,000– 10,999	31,684
11,000– 14,999	28,988
15,000– 19,999	29,850
20,000– 24,999	31,914
25,000– 34,999	39,267
35,000 and over	59,250
Total	33,968

Source: Derived from Canada (1979: Table 20).

For a variety of reasons, housing prices increased at a much faster rate than did incomes in the first half of the 1970s, and the dream of owning a single de-tached home rapidly became just a dream for many middle- and (especially) lower-income Canadians. In the future, it seems likely that more and more Canadian families will have to content themselves with what they regard as less and less. As housing prices, and, in the latter half of the 1970s, interest rates, have risen, fewer and fewer families have been able to raise the necessary down payment for a single detached home, or to meet the monthly instalments on the "high-ratio" mortgages (i.e., mortgages which are 75 per cent or more of the purchase price of a dwelling) which these rising prices have made necessary. This underscores the fact that many people who "own" their own homes do not own them outright and, indeed, may have little or no actual equity in them. For many, ownership is little more than a thinly-veiled legal fiction which is per-haps better described as an elaborate (and maybe even costly) form of rent entered into with the "cooperation" of a bank, trust company, or other credit institution. At the same time, many people do have some equity in their homes, and this implies a more equal distribution of wealth than would otherwise be the case. To the extent that home ownership is decreasing, therefore, this suggests an increase in inequalities in wealth.

Home ownership represents a form of private property, but it is not the *productive* private property which provides the basis for class formation in Marxist theory, although there are people who own property and who derive some or all of their incomes from renting it to others. These landlords represent a form of rentier capitalist, and they can properly be regarded as members of the capitalist class. Those who "own" the dwellings in which they live and those who simply rent them do not, however, by this fact alone belong to different classes in the Marxist sense. In fact, those homeowners who own nothing other than their homes and certain other personal effects belong in the same (nonpropertied) class as do those renters who own nothing other than their personal effects. At the same time, homeowners and renters are probably often usefully regarded as different fractions within the same class, since they are distinguished from one another in important ways. First, their economic interests are not always the same, as in the case of certain tax and mortgage issues (e.g., mortgage interest deductibility, whereby some or all of the interest paid on a mortgage can be deducted from personal income tax, which is the practice in the U.S. and which was an item in the ill-fated 1979 federal budget). Second, and partly as a consequence of this, where owners and renters live in the same neighbourhood, the former often regard the latter as less committed to the local area and, sometimes even, as a threat to property values. Third, although home ownership is often regarded as an investment by homeowners, it may be better regarded as an investment of consequence to the owners' children than to themselves, since the owners can derive real economic benefit from ownership only if they subsequently move into a less expensive house or into rental accomodation, while inheriting the value of their parents' homes is an important (if poorly researched) source of wealth and of inequality in wealth in the children's generation.

Dividend Income

In an economic system such as Canada's, which is dominated by family-owned firms and joint-stock corporations, participation in the ownership of private enterprise is an important source of income and form of wealth. One aspect of this participation is stock ownership and, in Canada, about one income recipient in fifteen received at least some of his or her income from the ownership of stocks in 1976 — down from abut one in ten in 1970. And there are large differences among these one in fifteen in the amount of income which they receive from their holdings. Table 5-7 shows the percentage of dividend income which went to individuals for each quintile of income recipients in Canada since 1950. As these data show, dividend income is very unequally distributed — much more so than income generally, and more so even than total wealth. In the four widely-separated years surveyed, the top quintile of income recipients never shared less than about 78 per cent of the total dividend income received by individuals, while the bottom quintile never shared more than about 5 per cent. Or, to illustrate this in a slightly different way, the top 1,698 income recipients in Canada in 1976 shared among them $116,031,000 in dividend income — about as much as the bottom three quintiles of income recipients taken together.

Table 5-7

Percentage of Individual Dividend Income by Income Quintile, Canada, 1950-76.

Income Quintile [a]	1950	1960	1970	1976
Lowest	5.1%	3.5%	2.1%	1.3%
Second	5.8	4.7	5.5	3.1
Middle	5.4	5.1	4.5	6.2
Fourth	5.6	6.9	8.8	8.9
Highest	78.1	79.8	79.1	80.5

[a] Quintiles are not exact, due to grouping in the original data.
Source: Canada, *Taxation Statistics* (annual).

Over time, the trend seems to have been in the direction of increasing inequality in the distribution of dividend income. For one thing, the percentage of income recipients who have dividend income has declined quite sharply, at least in recent years. And, for another, the percentage of dividend income going to the top two income quintiles has progressively increased, from 83.7 per cent in 1950 to 89.4 per cent in 1976, while the percentage going to the bottom two quintiles decreased from 10.9 to 4.4 per cent in this same period. While it would be tempting to infer from this that inequalities in wealth have increased in the past two or three decades, these are far from the ideal data to base such an inference on, partly since they refer to individual income recipients, not to families, and families are more properly regarded as the repositories of wealth. Thus, the trends observed in Table 5-7 could be the result of an increase in overall concentration of wealth in Canada, but they could also be the result of other factors, such as the increasing labour force participation of women, who are over-represented in the bottom quintiles of income recipients and who probably hold fewer stocks on the average than men do.

Conclusions

As we have seen, Canadian society has been long characterized by substantial and persistent inequalities in income and wealth. In the case of income, the purchasing power of families and individuals has on the average increased in the post-World War II period, except for very recent years while, at the same time, the trend has been in the direction of increasing income inequalities. As for wealth, the data permit no such firm generalizations, although it is doubtless true that the average net worth of families and individuals has increased over time and, whether increasing (as they appear to be) or decreasing, inequalities in wealth are much greater than inequalities in income. And we have also seen that Canada is not at all unique in these respects.

To discuss inequality is invariably to raise issues of equity (i.e., fairness), for social scientific questions always turn out to involve questions of what is fair or unfair. Any analysis of inequalities in the distributions of income or wealth must, therefore, also deal with the justice of these distributions, even though problems involved in developing "a theory of justice" (Rawls, 1971) may ultimately prevent us from judging any one distribution as either just or unjust in some degree. For, as Thurow puts it, "there are intelligent and unintelligent statements to be made about...equity" (1975:23). Thus, to establish that income and wealth are unequally distributed in a society is not necessarily to show that these distributions are inequitous, since there is no such simple connection between equality and equity. In fact, it could be true in any given instance that equality is unfair, that small inequalities are more unfair than large ones, and that increasing inequality implies increasing fairness. And, to establish that income and wealth are inequitably distributed (by some criterion) at any particular time is not necessarily to show that the system by which income and wealth are distributed at that time is itself inequitous, since these inequities could have been inherited from a previous period when the system was unfair, and were simply preserved after it became fair.

There are a number of useful insights to be gained into issues of inequality and inequity from a comparison between Marxist and structural-functional theories. Marxism and functionalism resemble one another quite closely in what they identify as sources of inequality, while differing in the relative importance which they attribute to each. Thus, from a Marxist perspective, the major inequalities in capitalism are seen to be material class inequalities deriving from the appropriation of surplus value by capitalists from workers. But Marx and Engels were also alert to the fact that workers tend to be paid in some relation to the standard of living of the time and place, as well as that, in capitalism, differences in pay originate in individual differences in talent and training. And, from a functionalist view, the principal inequalities are identified in the differences in the rewards which individuals receive as a consequence of the functional importance, scarcity of qualified personnel, and pleasantness of the positions which they occupy. But Davis and Moore also locate sources of inequality in the inheritance of wealth, the purchase of opportunities to learn or otherwise get ahead, the capacity of advantaged classes to control avenues of training, and ownership of capital.

Whether the principal sources of inequality are as Marx and Engels identified them or as Davis and Moore did is an empirical question to be discussed below. What is more to the present point, however, is that, although they may proceed from different premises, Marxism and functionalism come very close to a common analysis of the nature, causes, and consequences of inequity. In Marxism, inequalities in material rewards anchored in differences in talent or training — like them or not — make sense in terms of the logic of capitalism. Talented people produce more and, since they sell their capacity to work in exchange for a wage or a salary, they must be paid more. And trained people have invested something in themselves in order to become more productive, so that they must also be paid more. In functionalism, inequalities in rewards are necessary in order to place people in functionally important positions and, once placed, to motivate them to carry out their duties as diligently as the importance of their positions requires. In neither case, then, are such inequalities seen as unjust and, in fact, the functionalist argument is that there are understandings shared among the population that they are just.

In the Marxist view, the fundamental inequity in capitalism is the exploitation of workers by capitalists, whereby the former receive less than full value for what they produce and the latter receive something for nothing. And this process, if unchecked, carries with it the strong likelihood of organized attempts at redress on the part of the working class. From the functionalist side, factors such as class control of access to training or jobs and the ownership of capital permit some people to be rewarded out of proportion to what is generally believed to be appropriate to their position. And these factors, if permitted to persist or develop, are not only harmful from the point of view of the effective utilization of talent and, therefore, of the survival of the society, but they can also bring about organized opposition and, perhaps even, class conflict. As they relate to issues of equity, therefore, Marxism and functionalism alike identify differences in rewards which derive from differences in (especially class) power as unjust, and both point to such injustice as a source of social cleavage, conflict, and change.

By these criteria, then, is it possible to make some judgments about the distributions of income and wealth which have been described and discussed in the present chapter as either just or unjust in some degree, and either increasingly or decreasingly so? This is a tall order for, to be able to fill it completely, we must know what people regard as just, how unjust they see departures of a given magnitude from justice to be, and the extent to which the differences between what people actually receive and what people think their positions entitle them to originate in differences in power. Unfortunately, our knowledge of these matters is far from complete, although Jasso and Rossi (1977) have recently provided some of the hitherto missing information. Specifically, these investigators undertook to determine if there was some consensus on the levels of pay which people thought appropriate for men and women with different levels of education, types of occupation, marital statuses, and family circumstances to receive. Their conclusions were that there was consensus of this kind, and that people with some combinations of these attributes (i.e., married males with sixteen years of formal education and the very highest prestige jobs) were thought to deserve as much as two and one-half times as people with other combinations (i.e., single females with seven years of formal education and the very lowest prestige jobs). As we have seen, however, the actual differences among people in their incomes are often many times this size, and this suggests that they may be regarded as considerably larger than they ought to be. Moreover, we have also seen that these differences have increased over time, and this implies that they could be viewed as increasingly unjust.

Chapter 6

On Merit: Education, Occupation, and Rewards

"Intelligence and Effort together make up Merit (I + E = M)"
(Young, 1961:94).

*"'Go West, young man!' advised Horace Greeley in 1851. A
century later, he might have said:'Go to college!'" (Bowles and
Gintis, 1973:3).*

When asked why he persisted in the practice of robbing banks, the legendary
Willie ("The Actor") Sutton replied: "Because that's where the money is." In a
more conventional approach, "a man [*sic*] qualifies himself for occupational life
by obtaining an education; as a consequence of pursuing his occupation he
obtains income" (Duncan, 1961:116). This is certainly true. But it may raise
more questions than it answers. First, how does a person's education "qualify"
him or her for a particular occupation? Second, how are a person's life-chances
determined in a market where his or her capacities are exchanged for material
and other benefits? Third, how important is occupation for rewards, and what
are the attributes of different occupations which allow those who have them to
"obtain" different amounts of them?

Outside the social sciences, at least, and perhaps inside them as well, the
most widely held view of how material and symbolic rewards are distributed is
that an individual's share of the available rewards is determined most
importantly by his or her combination of intelligence and effort (which Young
refers to satirically in the above quotation as "merit"), which come together in a
formal education and are put to use in the pursuit of an occupation. According
to this version of merit, which is a central set of ideas in structural-functionalism
in sociology and forms the core assumptions in its counterpart in economics,
human capital theory (Becker, 1964), people largely acquire the knowledge and
skills necessary to carry out the tasks of their occupations through the
mechanism of schooling, and they are generally rewarded in rough proportion to
the value of their contributions to the goods and services which they help to
produce in their work. In general, the more knowledge and skill (and, hence,
formal education) which an occupation requires, the more valuable are its
contributions to production and, therefore, the better rewarded are its
incumbents. The principal purpose of the present chapter is to import this
structural-functional/human capital theory analysis of the distributive process
in an attempt to see how useful the conventional, meritocratic interpretation

seems to be, relative to certain other (mainly Marxist) interpretations, in giving meaning to the changing relations among education, occupations, and rewards in Canada in the period of the twentieth century. But, before this can be done, we must first consider some of the facts which these theories are given charge to explain.

Education, Occupations, and Social Change

Levels of Educational Attainment and Inequality

Over time, and in a process which quickened in the 1950s and 1960s and still shows little real sign of slowing, more and more Canadians have been staying in school longer and longer (Martin and Macdonell, 1978). About four people in five in the age group 5–24 are currently enrolled full-time in some kind of educational institution, be it primary or secondary school, community college, university, or some other. This is the highest rate ever in Canada, and currently among the highest rates in the world. Enrolments rose rapidly throughout the 1950s and 1960s, as the post-war "baby boom" intersected with increasing rates of educational participation. And rates of educational participation seem likely to remain high for some time, although there was a shift from universities to community colleges in the 1970s, and only the echoes of the baby boom remain.

All of the provinces have had compulsory school-leaving laws since at least 1943, when Quebec and Newfoundland adopted theirs, and most have had them for much longer. Consequently, almost all children between six and fourteen years of age are enrolled full-time in school across Canada, and this has been true for many years. Increases in school retention rates at the level of public school, therefore, have occurred largely for those persons fifteen years of age and over. For fifteen year-olds, the percentage remaining in school increased from 88.9 per cent in 1961 to 96.6 per cent in 1971, while the corresponding increase for sixteen year-olds was from 69.9 to 87.8 per cent, and that for seventeen year-olds was from 50.8 to 65.8 per cent (Canada, 1974a:Table 4-4; the 1971 figures omit data from Quebec). As a consequence of more Canadians staying in school longer, the percentage remaining through to completion of secondary school has increased to the point that, by 1971, approximately 56.1 per cent of those leaving school had at least completed secondary school. And, if this trend continues, the percentage will rise to about 65.0 per cent by 1980 and 68.8 per cent by 1985.

At the post-secondary level, too, enrolments have continued to rise. In 1962/63, post-secondary enrolment as a percentage of the age group 18–24 stood at 11.1 per cent. By 1975/76, it had reached its (to that point) peak of 19.6 per cent (Canada, 1977:97). Of those leaving school in 1971, some 36.0 per cent had completed at least some post-secondary training, and it is expected that this percentage will rise to about 45.0 by 1980 and 53.3 by 1985 (Canada, 1977:94). There is apparently a large pool of people in Canada who have not in the past stayed in school as long as they will in the future.

These trends have meant a general upgrading in the educational qualifications of the Canadian population, and they have been paralleled by similar trends in most other countries — First, Second, and Third World alike. And they have led to a progressive reduction in the level of educational inequality in this country — a reduction which does not seem easy to reconcile with at least certain of the increases in material inequalities observed in Chapter 5.[1] For, if the differences among people in their educational qualifications lie importantly behind the differences among them in their material rewards, then one might expect a decrease in educational inequality to lead to a decrease in material inequality. But apparently it has not.

So, how is it that more people are staying in school longer and longer? A number of explanations for this have been proposed (see Squires, 1977). In general, functionalists and human capital theorists point first to what they see as increasing needs in industrial society for the skills and knowledge of educated labour (e.g., Becker, 1964; Bell, 1973; Clark, 1962; Davis and Moore, 1945), while Marxists generally argue that the principal factor behind rising levels of educational attainment is the increasing requirement in capitalist (some would say industrial or industrializing) society for a reliable and compliant workforce respectful of the dominant ideology (e.g., Bowles and Gintis, 1976; Crompton and Gubbay, 1977; Schecter, 1977). These various explanations then, tend to join in the assumption that rising occupational "requirements" lie behind the trend of rising educational attainment, whereas they seem to separate in the interpretation of what these requirements are.

Consistent with both functionalist (and human capital theory) and Marxist explanations for rising levels of educational attainment, there have been real increases in the educational requirements for occupations in the period of the past hundred years, although this correlation between the two does not in itself permit us to identify which, if either, is the cause and which the effect. For it is just as possible that increases in the availability of educated labour have prompted employers to raise their educational requirements as it is that increasing educational requirements have stimulated people to obtain increasing amounts of education.

Prior to World War II, the requirement of high school graduation was quite rare, as was the requirement of a university degree for any occupation. Prior to World War I, they were rarer still. Today, they are common. Employers in search of unskilled and semi-skilled workers now sometimes require that successful applicants have a high school diploma, where they would seldom even have demanded evidence of literacy fifty or more years ago (Bradwin, 1928, 1972). Companies hiring clerical workers may restrict their choices to persons with some post-secondary training, where literacy would once have sufficed. Relatively recently, a university degree has become mandatory for a person to sit for bar examinations, to qualify as a professional engineer, or to be licensed as a

---

[1]   For example, the coefficient of variation (a measure of inequality in quantitative distributions, defined as the standard deviation divided by the mean) for educational attainment among persons 14 years of age and over in Canada decreased from 1.75 in 1960 to 1.59 in 1965 to 1.48 in 1969 (author's own calculations from Canada, 1974a: Table 4.1, with estimated category mid-points). The higher the coefficient, the greater the amount of inequality it signifies.

psychologist. Universities rarely hire new faculty members in the social sciences, natural sciences, or humanities who do not have their doctorates, and many companies only take on aspiring executives who have degrees in engineering or business. And it may not be long before university graduation will be required for people to tutor the young in the schools, provide counselling for a fee to the maritally troubled, or perform many tasks which can currently be done without benefit of sheepskin.

Whether functionalist, Marxist, or of some other theoretical stripe, sociologists tend typically to assume that education and occupation are simply and closely connected, and it is true that occupations differ considerably in the levels of educational attainment of those in them, as Tables 6-1 and 6-2 show. Still, it is easy to exaggerate the bond between the two, since it is also true that the levels of educational attainment of persons *within* particular occupations vary quite widely, as indicated in the example of Table 6-3.

Table 6-1

Percentage of Labour Force 15 Years and Over with Nine Years or More Formal Education, by Occupation Division, for Canada: 1941, 1951 and 1961.

Occupation Division	Percentage			Change
	1941	1951	1961	1941–61
White Collar	75.8	79.8	83.8	+ 8.0
Proprietary, managerial	56.9	66.5	73.6	+16.7
Professional	92.7	96.6	95.5	+ 2.8
Clerical	82.4	84.3	87.1	+ 4.7
Commercial, financial	65.8	69.0	73.6	+ 7.8
Blue Collar	36.7	39.3	45.6	+ 8.9
Manufacturing, mechanical	41.7	41.9	47.2	+ 5.5
Construction	33.5	38.0	43.8	+10.3
Labourers [a]	24.3	26.3	33.8	+ 9.5
Primary	19.0	23.2	31.1	+12.1
Agricultural	19.4	24.0	31.9	+12.5
Fishing, hunting, trapping	12.1	15.8	22.0	+ 9.9
Logging	11.9	15.9	22.7	+10.8
Mining, quarrying	26.3	30.0	38.5	+12.2
Transportation, communication	36.3	41.6	48.4	+12.1
Service	37.3	40.4	47.2	+ 9.9

Source: Derived from Meltz (1969).
[a] Except those in Primary

Table 6-2

Percentages of Males and Females, 15 Years and Over, in the Labour Force, with Nine Years or More Schooling, by Occupation Division, for Canada, 1971.

Occupation Division	Percentage Males	Females
Managerial, administrative and related	93.7	94.3
Natural sciences, engineering and mathematics	95.9	96.0
Social Sciences and related	97.3	96.1
Religion	93.4	79.9
Teaching and related	98.8	98.7
Medicine and health	92.0	92.0
Artistic, literary, recreational and related	89.2	93.4
Clerical and related	85.4	94.1
Sales	82.4	80.1
Service	65.2	61.7
Farming, horticultural and animal husbandry	51.7	55.2
Fishing, hunting, trapping and related	32.2	46.7
Forestry and logging	43.3	57.4
Mining and quarrying	55.4	61.8
Processing	56.8	46.7
Machining and related	62.4	57.3
Product fabricating, assembling and repairing	63.7	44.7
Construction trades	55.0	61.6
Transport equipment operating	56.0	70.6
Materials handling, not elsewhere classified	60.1	56.6
Other crafts and equipment operating	75.1	71.8
Not elsewhere classified	59.3	58.6
Not stated	64.4	67.2
Total	69.2	79.3

Source: Derived from *1971 Census of Canada*, Cat. 94–729.

Acknowledging the less than one-to-one relationship between education and occupation, it could nevertheless still be the case that the key to rising levels of educational attainment lies in rising knowledge and skill requirements for occupations brought about by changes in the occupational distribution and technological advances in production. If low skill/knowledge occupations have decreased or high skill/knowledge occupations have increased in their representation over time, or if the skill and knowledge requirements of existing occupations have been upgraded over the years, then rising levels of educational attainment might be seen to make sense from a functionalist or human capital theory point of view. But perhaps these processes have either not taken place at all or not developed very far *and* it can be shown that educational institutions

Table 6-3

Levels of Educational Attainment, Elementary and Secondary School Teaching
and Related Occupations, Males, Canada, 1971.

Level of Educational Attainment	Percentage
Less than Grade 9	0.5%
Grades 9 and 10	1.0
Grade 11	2.1
Grades 12 and 13	9.5
Some University	24.2
University Degree	62.7
Total	100.0

Source: Calculated from *1971 Census of Canada.*

serve to satisfy an emergent need for workers whose attitudes and values adapt
them well for work in industrial (or capitalist) society. If so, then rising levels of
education might be amenable to a more Marxist interpretation. And there may
be other possibilities as well.

Changing Occupational Distribution

In the past century or so, Canada has been transformed from a rural,
agrarian country of farmers and self-employed artisans, small business
proprietors and professionals to an urban, industrial country of (in the early
phases) blue-collar factory and (more recently) white-collar clerical, managerial,
professional, and other workers. Table 6-4, although it relies upon a set of
occupational categories which is far from ideal from a sociological point of view,
shows something of the changes which have occurred in the occupational
composition of the labour force in the period 1901-61. These changes are
brought more up to date in Table 6-5, which shows the changing occupational
composition of the labour force, 1961-71, using a slightly different set of
occupational categories to permit comparisons with the 1971 *Census of Canada.*[2]

While the overall size of the labour force has grown enormously since the
tun of the century, this growth has not touched all occupational categories
equally. Some, in fact, have actually experienced large, numerical declines.
During this period, there was a substantial increase in the proportion of white-
collar workers, while, by contrast, the proportion of primary workers decreased
sharply. The representation of blue-collar workers has remained quite stable
over time, while that of transportation and communication workers, as well as of
service workers, has increased.

---

[2]   Note the large figure for "Unknown" in 1971. This suggests caution in comparisons.

Table 6–4

Percentage Distribution of Labour Force 15 Years and Over by Occupation Division, for Canada: 1901, 1921, 1941, and 1961.

Occupation Division	Percentage				Change
	1901 [a]	1921	1941	1961	1901–1961
White Collar	15.3	25.3	25.3	37.9	+22.6
Proprietary, managerial	4.3	7.3	5.4	7.8	+ 3.5
Professional	4.6	5.4	6.7	9.8	+ 5.2
Clerical	3.2	6.9	7.2	12.7	+ 9.5
Commercial, financial	3.1	5.7	6.0	7.6	+ 4.5
Blue Collar	27.8	25.8	27.1	26.6	– 1.2
Manufacturing, mechanical	15.9	11.4	16.1	16.1	+ 0.2
Construction	4.7	4.7	4.7	5.2	+ 0.5
Labourers [b]	7.2	9.7	6.3	5.3	– 1.9
Primary	44.3	36.2	30.5	12.8	–31.5
Agricultural	40.3	32.6	25.7	10.0	–30.3
Fishing, hunting, trapping	1.5	0.9	1.2	0.6	– 0.9
Logging	0.9	1.2	1.9	1.2	+ 0.3
Mining, quarrying	1.6	1.5	1.7	1.0	– 0.6
Transportation, communication	4.4.	5.5	6.4	7.7	+ 3.3
Service	8.2	7.0	10.5	12.4	+ 4.2
Unknown	–	0.2	0.2	2.6	+ 2.4

Source: Derived from Ostry (1967:50–51).
[a] 10 years and over in 1901.
[b] Except those in Primary.

Among white-collar occupations, all four categories listed in Table 6–4 have experienced some growth, especially clerical occupations in the 1941–61 period. The proprietary and managerial category as a whole has grown least rapidly, but growth patterns for occupations within this category have been far from uniform. In general, independent proprietors have decreased as a proportion of the labour force, while managers have increased (Ostry, 1967:11). The professional category increased fairly steadily in the period 1901–41, and rather more rapidly since that time. And commercial-financial occupations have continued to grow.

Among blue-collar occupations, the construction category has varied little

Table 6-5

Percentage Distribution of Labour Force, 15 Years and Over by Occupation Division, for Canada: 1961–71.

Occupation Division	Percentage		Change
	1961	1971	1961–1971
White Collar	*37.3*	*41.5*	*+4.2*
Managerial	8.3	7.9	–0.4
Professional and technical	9.7	12.6	+2.9
Clerical	12.9	14.8	+1.9
Sales	6.4	6.2	–0.2
Blue Collar	*28.9*	*24.9*	*–4.0*
Craftsmen, production	23.6	20.1	–3.5
Labourers	5.3	4.8	–0.5
Primary	*12.7*	*7.4*	*–5.3*
Farmers and farm workers	10.0	5.8	–4.2
Fishing, hunting, trapping	0.5	0.3	–0.2
Logging	1.2	0.6	–0.6
Mining, quarrying	1.0	0.7	–0.3
Transportation, communication	*6.1*	*5.0*	*–1.1*
Service	*12.3*	*11.7*	*–0.6*
Unknown	*2.6*	*9.5*	*+6.9*

Source: Calculated from *1971 Census of Canada* Cat. 94–716.

since the turn of the century in its representation, while the other two categories have been rather more volatile. The proportion of labourers increased quite markedly in the early years of the century, only to begin a decrease which has continued to the present. The greatest change which has occurred in the occupational distribution since the turn of the century has been the decline in the agricultural sector. In 1901, fully 40.3 per cent of the labour force were engaged in agriculture. By 1961, this had dropped to 10.0 per cent, and it is currently about half that figure. In fact, the actual number of persons engaged in agricultural occupations increased in the period 1901–31. Since 1941, the representation of the agricultural sector had decreased, both proportionally and in absolute numbers, to the point that, as of 1951, the manufacturing-mechanical category replaced the agricultural as the largest one. The remaining occupational categories — transportation-communication and service — have grown fairly slowly and steadily since 1901.

This changing labour force composition can be interpreted against a backdrop of changes in economic production in post-Confederation Canada. At the time of Confederation, Canada was about 80 per cent rural, with over 50 per cent of the labour force engaged in agriculture, fishing, and lumbering, and about 13 per cent involved in manufacturing and handicrafts. "In 1870, there were 38,898 establishments engaged in manufacturing, employing 181,679 people, or an average of less than five persons per establishment, with an average capital investment of only $1,900" (Clement, 1975:69). Not only were these productive units typically small, but their markets were generally local, and their outputs were mostly geared to the needs of a rural economy. Over the past twenty years, the number of manufacturing establishments in Canada nearly doubled, and they grew in size and capitalization, stimulated by the protective tariff of Sir John A. Macdonald's National Policy, an influx of direct investment from the United States, large-scale immigration, and the opening up and settlement of the West through the completion of the first transcontinental railway (McDougall, 1968; Chodos, 1973).

"If the 1880s witnessed the rise of the factory system, the period 1890 to 1920 was one of concentration of production. The 70,000 manufacturing units of 1890 dwindled to 22,000 by 1920, a reduction which indicated more rather than less industrial activity" (Rinehart, 1975:39), and each employed an average of 25.8 workers (Urquhart and Buckley, 1965:463). Between 1909 and 1913 alone, 56 mergers absorbed 248 separate business firms (Myers, 1972:xxxii). And the joint-stock corporation emerged as a prominent organizational form. Not only were manufacturing units considerably fewer and larger, but they were also better capitalized, more often national and international in their markets, and increasingly organized according to the principles of modern business practice.

Between 1867 and 1920, the factory replaced the independent craftsman as the characteristic productive unit in Canadian manufacturing (Kealey, 1973). Hand tools gave way to power-driven equipment. And a self-paced journeyman working alone or in tandem with a couple of others and some apprentices in a small shop yielded to a relatively large number of workers engaged in more specialized tasks, whose efforts were scheduled and paced by machine and coordinated in some overall division of labour under the active supervision of management. As markets expanded beyond the confines of a local trading area, business establishments were forced to grow in size, to rationalize the work process, and to mechanize, in order to maintain their share of an increasingly competitive market.

If these events did not increase the proportion of the labour force working in manufacturing occupations by any dramatic amount, they did increase the proportion of white-collar workers. Increases in productivity could apparently be effected through increases in the scale of manufacturing operations, the rational reorganization of work, and mechanization, without corresponding growth in the relative size of the industrial work force. They did, however, require a newly-created cadre of white-collar managers, professionals, clerks, and others to perform the administrative, supervisory, record-keeping, marketing, and other tasks of modern business. Between 1901 and 1921, the proportion of the labour force in manufacturing-mechanical occupations actually decreased, while the proportion in white-collar jobs increased from 15.3 to 25.3 per cent.

Agriculture, too, was affected by the same kinds of forces (MacDougall, 1973). As Johnson observes: "in the long-settled areas, a decline in number of farm units was already under way as early as 1901-11 in the Atlantic region" (1972:148), and the period 1901-21 saw a decline in the percentage of the labour force engaged in agriculture from 40.3 to 32.6. As in manufacturing, this was accompanied, not by a decrease in farm productivity, but by an increase in agricultural output, as farms grew larger in size and became more mechanized.

These trends continued through the 1920s, only to be stopped by the economic collapse of 1929 and the subsequent depression of the 1930s. The relative size of the white-collar sector following the revival of the economy in the late 1930s and the advent of World War II was about the same as it had been in 1921, while the proportion of workers in manufacturing-mechanical occupations increased and that in the labouring category decreased in this period. At the same time, the proportion engaged in agriculture continued to decline, even as the total number of farm units in Canada increased somewhat as agriculture expanded further into the West. "It was," finally, "the Second World War, and C. D. Howe's program of industrialization and rapid expansion of the capitalist sector through guaranteed wartime profits, which . . . completed the transformation of the Canadian economy to industrial capitalism and . . . incorporated most of Canadian labour into advanced modes of industrial capitalist production" (Johnson, 1972:171; also see Newman, 1975, 1979). Companies expanded through growth and merger, and the processes of rationalization of the labour process and automation accelerated. In response, the proportion of white-collar workers increased by about 50 per cent between 1941 and 1961, while the proportion of blue-collar workers remained about the same. And the proportion engaged in farming decreased dramatically, as farms grew larger and more productive with greater infusions of capital, increasing rationalization of work, more mechanization, and (most recently) the introduction of automated equipment.

Standing at some distance from this detail, we can see that the development of industrial capitalism in Canada has been associated with major changes in the occupational distribution and the nature of work. Among the more visible of these changes have been the decrease in agricultural work, the displacement of independent crafts workers by blue-collar factory workers, and the growth in the complement of white-collar (especially clerical) workers, coupled with tendencies in the direction of the greater rationalization, mechanization, and automation of work. What, then, has this meant for changes in the knowledge and skill requirements of occupations? Have they generally increased or decreased, or have they increased for some occupations and decreased for others?

And how have these changes been related to changes in the educational requirements of occupations?

Changing Knowledge and Skill Requirements

The shift from the older, primary occupations to the newer blue- and (especially) white-collar ones is often interpreted as involving an overall increase in knowledge and skill requirements (e.g., Kerr et al., 1960). The most recent and comprehensive data on this issue, however, do not seem to bear this out. In his analysis of the changing occupational distribution in the U.S. between 1900 and 1970, for example, Dubnoff (1978) found evidence of an overall decrease in the complexity of work involving data, little overall change in the complexity of work involving people, and an overall decrease in the complexity of work involving things — most of which changes could be attributed to the movement out of agriculture and the growth of the clerical sector. In addition, women's occupations appeared to decrease in complexity of work with people, while those of nonmanual workers increased and those of manual workers decreased in complexity of work with things.

In his analysis of the shift away from primary occupations, Braverman concludes that "it is . . . not in terms of direct assessment . . . that an assembly line worker is presumed to have greater skill than a fisherman or oysterman, the forklift operator greater skill than the longshoreman, the parking lot attendant greater skill than the lumberman or raftsman" (1974:430). And, speaking of the turn-of-the-century farm labourer, he continues:

> . . . a great many — perhaps most — were fully qualified farmers who had themselves owned and operated farms and lost them, or who had grown up in farm families and learned the entire broad craft. The farm hired hand was able to be of assistance to the farmer because he was the product of years of farm life and had a mastery of a great many skills involving a knowledge of land, fertilizer, animals, tools, farm machinery, construction skills, etc., and the traditional abilities and dexterities in the handling of farm tasks (1974:433–34).

Compare this with what is required of the modern urban labourer or of the semi-skilled machine operative since, ". . . with the routinization of machine operation, there is less and less reason to rate the operative above many other classifications of laborers" (Braverman, 1974:430). Or compare it with what is demanded of the contemporary clerical worker. It is not obvious in such comparisons that most primary occupations are lower in knowledge and skill requirements than the bulk of blue- and white-collar occupations.

If the knowledge and skill requirements of primary occupations cannot be judged to be measurably lower on the whole than those of most blue- and white-collar occupations, the movement away from the former and toward the latter probably did stimulate some educational upgrading. The knowledge and skills involved in farming, fishing, trapping, and logging are the kinds of things which, at the turn of the century, could often be acquired as a matter of course in growing up in a society where most people worked at these for a living. This was not true to the same extent of the newer, blue- and white-collar occupations which the sons and daughters of primary workers increasingly had to enter. The requirements of office or factory work — most notably the ability to read, write, perform simple arithmetic calculations, and operate certain kinds of mechanical equipment — were often new, and a ready place to acquire some facility in many of them was the formal setting of the school.

Too, the increasing rationalization, mechanization, and automation of work have helped add to the payroll scientists, engineers, and other technical specialists responsible for producing new knowledge, improving technology, and increasing worker efficiency, along with many other experts in marketing, personnel, public relations, accounting, finance, corporate law, and the like. And, as in the case of the newer, blue- and white-collar occupations, the verbal, quantitative and other knowledge and skills involved in this "expert" category are scarce in a rural, agrarian society, and are probably best acquired through at least some formal education.

So, if the shift away from the older, primary occupations to the newer, blue- and white-collar ones and the growth in the expert category may not have meant an overall increase in the knowledge and skill requirements of occupations, it may well have generated some educational upgrading of the labour force through the introduction of requirements which were new, and which were most readily satisfied by people with some formal education. At the same time, evidence from an analysis of educational upgrading in the U.S. suggests that only a small part (perhaps 15–25 per cent) of it can be attributed to the changing occupational mix, and that the bulk has been educational upgrading *within* existing occupations (Folger and Nam, 1964; Rodriguez, 1976). If this is true, then it implies that the answers we seek — assuming that formal education and occupations are tied together by way of job-related knowledge and skills — are to be found in the changing requirements within occupations.

In general, the productive work of the modern factory seems, if anything, more and more to be done by workers who can fairly be described as essentially unskilled, or whose skills are required in a process of on-the-job training lasting (typically) a few weeks or (more rarely) months (Walker and Guest, 1952; Aronowitz, 1973). Moreover, this work often makes sense only in the context of the particular firm and factory in which it is done, so that the knowledge and skills acquired on the job may have little general market value. In the evolution of the modern factory, the process of mechanization may lead in its early stages to a general increase in knowledge and skill requirements (Braverman, 1974:184–235). In the stages which lie beyond, however, the skills of the worker seem to be progressively replaced by the capacities of the machinery, especially as the workers' equipment is made more and more automated.

The skilled trades have also been transformed under modern conditions of production, but not in ways which would necessarily suggest any overall increases in knowledge and skill requirements (Braverman, 1974:184–235). Often, the tasks involved in them seem to have become more routinized and circumscribed over time, and important elements of the mental labour which they once entailed have frequently been taken over by others. In the building trades, for example, carpenters increasingly make use of prefabricated, modular units (e.g., doors, doorframes, and cupboards), where once they would have been involved in phases of building construction, including planning, selecting the materials, and actually building almost everything. Those who do the metal cutting in a machine shop may be little more than operatives who make adjustments to semi-automated devices, rather than highly-trained machinists who, after lengthy apprenticeships, could run a variety of different and complicated kinds of equipment.

A century or two ago, clerical workers constituted a small stratum of relatively favoured employees (Lockwood, 1958; Crozier, 1965, 1973; Braverman, 1974; Lowe, 1977). "...by and large, in terms of function, authority, pay, tenure of employment (a clerical position was usually a lifetime post), prospects, not to mention status and even dress, the clerks stood much closer to the employer than to factory labor" (Braverman, 1974:295). Largely a male preserve, clerical work displayed many craft-like components, and a clerk typically learned his job from others in something resembling a master–apprentice relationship. Frequently, there was the prospect of a future partnership in the business in reward for service, for the clerk's skills in maintaining the accounts and otherwise handling the paperwork of the firm were special ones in real demand. With the remarkable growth in clerical occupations which began in the latter part of the nineteenth century, however, came important changes in the character of clerical work. As offices grew in size, clerks began to be differentiated in skills and organized in a division of labour. With the influx of women into the occupations, a sexual division of labour emerged among clerks, with males dominating upper-echelon and females largely confined to lower-echelon positions. The progressive introduction of office equipment, beginning with the typewriter and including, as time went on, a variety of increasingly more sophisticated machines, seems to have had the long-term effect of undercutting the privileged position of bookkeeping, stenography, and other highly-skilled specialties, and of rendering the class of clerical workers increasingly homogeneous. The advent of the business school and the incorporation of commercial training into the curricula of the schools, where the typing, shorthand, bookkeeping, and certain other basic clerical skills could be acquired in a short time, further diminished the craft-like aspects of clerical work and helped make available the mobile legion of more or less interchangeable and low-paid clerical workers which we have today. On those days when Bob Cratchit was ill, Scrooge probably had to make do as best he could. Were he alive today, he might just call Office Overload.

Although the increasing rationalization, mechanization, and automation of work may have had some overall, long-term effect in diluting the requirements of many factory, skilled trade, and clerical occupations, this has not been true of all occupations. Shepard (1971), for example, studied a number of insurance companies in the U.S., and found that the introduction of key-punch machines for recording data and electro-mechanical devices (e.g., counter-sorters) for processing them destroyed the craft-like components of clerical work, and divided the labour up among a larger number of more specialized jobs. With the introduction of automated systems of electronic data processing, however, the low-level, routine clerical work was reduced, and many of the separate functions of the specialized jobs in the immediately preceding phase were once again brought together, but this time in the fairly high-level jobs of account control clerk and computer operator. These latter, however, were still essentially clerical, rather than managerial, in character, despite their relatively high salaries. And, although computer jobs in an earlier period typically involved a wide range of skills and a good deal of autonomy, these, too, have apparently become more and more specialized and routinized (e.g., Greenbaum, 1976).

Although most of the educational upgrading which has taken place has been within existing occupations, these case study materials do not suggest that the knowledge and skill requirements of occupations generally have increased or decreased very much in the past forty or fifty years, and this is consistent with what has been found in more comprehensive and large-scale studies (Horowitz and Herrenstadt, 1966; Spenner, 1979). In fact, the educational requirements for occupations generally have risen, even as the knowledge and skill requirements of many occupations have fallen with the increasing rationalization, mechanization, and automation of work. These long-term trends in work have resulted in a complex division of labour in which a large number of highly specialized, standardized and repetitive jobs have been linked together and articulated with one another. At the same time as the technology involved in many kinds of work has become increasingly sophisticated, then, the tasks involved have often become more and more circumscribed and simplified. As a result, it is not clear that the progressively more scientific character of work has not been more than counterbalanced by the increasingly narrow simplicity of many occupations. It is clear, though, that increasing task requirements of occupations do not lie importantly behind the rising levels of educational attainment.

For most occupations, job-related knowledge and skills do not seem to provide the major connection between the formal education requirements of occupations and the work which people do. Among manual workers, for example, there is evidence that graduates of high school vocational programmes are no more likely to secure employment than are high school dropouts (Duncan, 1964). Formal retraining is not extensively used in industry as a means of upgrading the skills of manual workers whose jobs are affected by technological change. And the majority of skilled manual workers develop their skills in the course of learning on the job (Clark and Sloan, 1966:73). The common denominator of most modern clerical jobs is some minimum of verbal and quantitative skills, plus the ability to type. These do not require lengthy formal training, and the special skills of even the more highly-paid clerical occupations, such as legal secretary, are largely acquired on the job. In the case of professional occupations, there are some, such as medicine, which probably require special formal education beyond the basic verbal and quantitative skills normally acquired in school (see Doctor X, 1965, on the importance of on-the-job training for physicians), although there are others, such as law and engineering, which have only recently required a university degree, suggesting that on-the-job training may be sufficient to give practioners of these arts the skills they need to work at them successfully. And there are others, as well, in which there are relatively little in the way of special bodies of knowledge and technique which can be imparted in the context of a classroom, such as school teaching and social work, although, of course, these do demand the basic cognitive skills. Despite the tenuous connection between formal educational requirements and occupational tasks, however, the level of educational attainment of workers and the formal educational requirements for occupations have both continued to increase.

Education and "Style/Ability"

How is it, then, that some occupations require more schooling than others, and that, within occupations, employers seem generally to prefer better-educated workers? If extended experience in educational institutions is not of major moment for the learning of job-related knowledge or skills — at least for most occupations — this does not necessarily mean that educational requirements for occupations are purely arbitrary, or that most people merely mark time in school, emerging unchanged at graduation. If education does mean something important for occupations, though, we will have to explore this meaning further to understand what it might be.

In his study of "what is learned in school," Dreeben argues that schools are, before anything else, places where "pupils learn to accept principles of conduct, or social norms, and to act according to them" (1968:44).

> Specifically, they accept the obligations to (1) act by themselves (unless collaborative effort is called for), and accept personal responsibility for their conduct and accountability for its consequences; (2) perform tasks actively and master the environment according to certain standards of excellence; and (3) acknowledge the rights of others to treat them as members of categories (4) on the basis of a few discrete characteristics rather than on the full constellation of them that represent the whole person (Dreeben, 1968:63–64).

Similarly, Bowles and Gintis (1976) point to acceptance of hierarchical authority, a willingness to self-discipline under a set of rules, and an ability to suppress personal feelings in relations with others as the crucial outcomes of schooling, along with the capacity to be motivated in what one does, not by any intrinsic satisfactions which may come with the activity, but by the external rewards which follow successful performance. While this learning undoubtedly takes place through direct teaching, it also occurs simply through the long-term, day-to-day experience of participating in the bureaucracy of the modern school, with its hierarchy of authority, impersonal rules, regular routines, and the like. And Collins (1971) stresses the role of the school as a mechanism for the transmission of "status cultures" (also see Prentice, 1977, Chapter 3). From his perspective, "schools primarily teach vocabulary and inflection, styles of dress, aesthetic tastes, values and manners" (Collins, 1971:1010). The public schools, he continues, have as their task to transmit respect for middle-class culture, while the private schools of the upper class have as their special task the preservation of elite culture (see Porter, 1965; Clement, 1975; Newman 1975, 1979).

Although they proceed from different sets of assumptions, these analyses of schooling outcomes arrive at broadly similar conclusions. To Dreeben, what employers value in their employees is primarily the *normative content* of what is learned in school, and which matches the criterion for adequate job performance in modern, industrial society. To Bowles and Gintis, what is learned in school and important for work are ways of feeling, thinking, and behaving which adapt people to conditions of labour in industrial capitalism. And Collins argues that "educational requirements for employment can serve both to select new members for elite positions who share the elite culture and, at a lower level of education, to hire lower and middle employees who have acquired a general respect for these elite values and styles" (1971:1010-11). Experience in a particular kind of educational institution, then, can be taken as a sign that one has been exposed to and has taken over elements of a particular status culture.

In apparent contrast to the common view of the principal goal of schools as to provide "intellectual training" (Ausubel, 1968:29) or "to give or impart knowledge" (Geer, 1977:5), then, we have an analysis of the first purpose of education as to transmit knowledge of and respect for middle- and upper-class culture. But how different are these? One conclusion which emerges from the study of human intelligence is that it may not even make sense to distinguish between intellectual abilities, on the one hand, and learning (i.e., knowledge of some culture), on the other. And, when we actually attempt to measure intelligence, it turns out that I.Q. tests are designed "to measure verbal ability and to predict school performance" (Ausubel, 1968:228), both of which are culturally-defined and acquired through learning. Moreover, those things which one must learn in order to succeed in school or to do well on I.Q. tests — even the so-called "basic skills" — are class-related, being integral to middle- and upper-class, but not to lower-class, culture (see, for example, Bernstein, 1971). Consequently, at least a major part of what we *mean* by the term "intelligence" in Western society *is* those verbal, quantitative, and other capacities which distinguish middle- and upper-class from lower-class culture (Davis, 1948; Kagan, 1974).

If the significance of some combination of diplomas and degrees (or lack of them) lies most importantly in an amalgam of cognitive abilities and cultural styles which we might call "style/ability," it is still not clear why people seem to be hired in terms of it and occupations apparently require more or less of it. First, style/ability does not imply the capacity to carry out the tasks involved in an occupation, since job-related knowledge and skills are largely learned on the job, and the connection between education and occupation is, as we have seen, fairly loose. Second, style/ability does not appear to be related to productivity, since the available evidence does not suggest that, among individual workers, the better-educated are on the average more productive in their work (Berg, 1970:85–104, 143–47; Braverman, 1974:441–42). In fact, at least for certain blue-collar and lower echelon white-collar occupations, better-educated workers may even be less productive and more given to absenteeism and turnover than their less well-educated counterparts, although these workers' supervisors apparently do not perceive this to be the case (Berg, 1970:16–17). And, at the level of nations, it is true that high levels of educational attainment are associated with high levels of economic development. But longitudinal studies suggest that "the main contribution to economic productivity. . .appears to occur at the level of the transition to mass literacy, and not significantly beyond this level" (Collins, 1971:1006; also see Thurow, 1975:65–66). Apparently, then, most people can be trained to the requirements of most jobs and, once trained, can carry out the duties associated with them about as competently as the next person.

This analysis suggests that style/ability implies a number of general capacities or qualities which, while not specifically job-related, do help people learn certain technical and social requirements of jobs, and that, more generally, the labour market does not consist so much of fully-formed workers competing for jobs in terms of their occupational qualifications as it does of people jostling for openings on the basis of the apparent ease with which they will learn to adapt. And the importance of formal education lies in its role as a kind of indicator of, or *market signal* (Spence, 1974) for, an individual's style/ability, since labour markets are typically too large for employers to know prospective employees beforehand, and it would be too expensive for them to attempt an independent assessment of all such employees or to try just anybody out to see how quickly they became socialized to the job. Worker style/ability, in this version, then, signifies the relative ease with which an individual is likely to move into a particular job and work group and play his or her part. The closer the match between the style/ability attributes of the worker and the technical and social requirements of the job, the easier this move will be; and, the higher the style/ability attributes of the worker relative to those of his or her competitors, the more likely he or she will be hired.

Of course, *level* of formal education as such (i.e., the *number* of years of schooling alone) will not serve as a market signal for the ease with which a person is likely to be socialized to occupational requirements of *any* kind. Thus, McLaughlin (1978) analysed occupational requirements and found that occupations could be described in terms of their cognitive, manipulative and social skill, along with their physical strength, requirements. Hunter (1980a) found a fairly strong relationship between the level of formal education of workers and the *cognitive* (but not the other) requirements of their jobs. No doubt a more fine-grained study would show that certain kinds of formal education (e.g., in the humanities) are more closely related to some kinds of occupational requirements (e.g., verbal ability) than to others (e.g., quantitative skills. And there is probably a whole range of market signals other than those involving formal education which represent individuals' capacities to be socialized to occupational requirements other than just cognitive ones.

Finally, we might ask how it is that, if level of formal education operates as a market signal for the relative ease with which an individual is likely to learn certain technical and social requirements of occupations, the relationship between education and occupation is so weak. While the reasons for this can only be mentioned in passing here, there would appear to be at least three. First, as pointed out above, level of formal education as such refers to a general set of capacities or qualities which are likely to be related only to a general set of occupational requirements. Thus, all sorts of otherwise different occupations will probably resemble one another in these requirements, precisely because they are so general. Second, as suggested above, as well, formal educational market signals are probably only a subset of a larger set of such signals. And it seems likely that it is the relative weighting of various market signals considered together which is important for access to an occupation, not just those market signals involving formal education. And third, whether or not a particular type of person gains access to a certain kind of occupation is probably best viewed as a probabilistic (as opposed to deterministic) process which must simultaneously take into account both the attributes of the queue of available people *and* the list of job openings at different times and places (Thurow, 1975). Since most people can be trained to fill most jobs, employers will choose the "best" workers they can get. But the best at one time and place may be much better or worse than the best at other times and places.

Over-Education of the Labour Force

Although the several interpretations of the meaning of formal education for occupation converge closely, we are still left with divergent views as to the reasons behind increasing levels of educational attainment. The functionalist/ human capital argument is that industrialization requires workers with constantly upgraded job-related knowledge and skills, but we now see that these latter are largely learned on the job. Dreeben interprets educational upgrading as a response to increasing requirements for a workforce inured to the regimens of industrial labour. And Bowles and Gintis view it as tied specifically to the development of capitalist labour markets. Neither Dreeben nor Bowles and Gintis, though, presents any very convincing body of supportive evidence on their own behalf, and Bowles and Gintis's formulation seems flawed by their failure to address the issue of how rising levels of educational attainment can be an inherently capitalist phenomenon, when they have occurred both within and without the capitalist world (but see Crompton and Gubbay, 1977, for a Marxist interpretation which makes no qualitative distinction between western-style capitalism and eastern-bloc socialism, focusing, instead, on the functions of capital and labour with and without the institution of private property).

Unlike the others, Collins's argument does not depend upon any assumptions about increases in the demand for workers with certain kinds of qualities.

Instead, he suggests that rising levels of educational attainment can have a dynamic of their own, and may originate largely in the competition among people for jobs under conditions where the better-educated are preferred. That is, since people compete with one another for jobs at least partly on the basis of their educational qualifications, there is a tendency over time for them to get more and more education, simply to keep ahead of the competition. But, since their competitors are doing the same thing, an "educational arms race" results, and the general level of educational attainment rises. This is a simpler explanation than the others and, hence, otherwise to be preferred, since it shares a common set of assumptions with them, but depends upon a smaller number of assumptions overall.

Where competition for jobs has the effect of continuously raising the general level of educational attainment, many people who prepare for the competition by aiming at certain kinds of occupations will find that their educational qualifications are inadequate by the time they are ready to go to work — unless, of course, there has been some compensatory growth in the job market at the same time. That is, where the general level of educational attainment rises as a consequence of competition for jobs where the better-educated are chosen first, the educational requirements for these jobs will tend also to rise. As a result, there is likely to be some fairly widespread feeling on the part of workers that their occupational aspirations have not been realized, and that they are over-educated for what they do (Harvey, 1974). Perhaps this lies behind the apparent fact that, within particular occupations, the better-educated may actually be less productive and reliable employees on the whole than the less well-educated. It may be that the better-educated tend disproportionately to be working at jobs which they regard as beneath them.

To the extent that the better-educated within particular ocupations come to be seen as less desirable employees than those with the "right" amount of education, the connection between formal education and occupation will become realigned over time (Harvey, 1974). And, along with this, the rate of increase in the general level of educational attainment should slow. In fact, this could help explain the phenomena which can be observed in both Canada and the U.S. of a convergence in the (rising) rates of unemployment for persons with different levels of education (Braverman, 1974:442–43; Canada, 1977:119), and a slowing in the rate of increase in university enrolments. Over time and in both countries, the rates of unemployment for the well-educated and the less-well-educated, while rising for both, have risen faster for the former than for the latter. And, while university enrolments have grown in recent years, this growth has been gradual overall and quite uneven across different programmes of study. Still, it is doubtful that there will be any decrease in the level of educational participation of Canadians in the near future. A "good" education is still a necessary condition for a "good" job, even if it is not a sufficient condition. If an accumulation of diplomas and degrees is not an airline ticket to success, it is still a lottery ticket. And there seems to be no real dampening in the desire of Canadians to take the chance.

Income

Most of the income which Canadians receive comes from working, either for one's self or for somebody else. In any one year, just over four-fifths of all income reported in tax returns comes from employment earnings (i.e., wages, salaries, and commissions), just over one-twentieth from self-employment earnings (i.e., business and professional income), and just over one-twentieth from investments. To understand how people obtain earnings from working, then, is to know the processes which largely determine income distributions.

Occupation and Income

An important determinant of a person's income is the kind of occupation which he or she has. Table 6–6 gives the average incomes of men in different occupa-

Table 6–6

Average Incomes for Males 15 Years and Over Who Worked in 1970,
by Occupational Division, for Canada, 1971.

Occupational Division

Managerial, administrative and related	$13,407
Natural sciences, engineering and mathematics	8,905
Social sciences and related	10,971
Religion	4,738
Teaching and related	9,014
Medicine and health	14,175
Artistic, literary, recreational and related	6,545
Clerical and related	5,823
Sales	7,120
Service	5,276
Farming, horticultural and animal husbandry	3,321
Fishing, hunting, trapping and related	3,340
Forestry and logging	4,544
Mining and quarrying	6,966
Processing	5,957
Machining and related	6,695
Product fabricating, assembling and repairing	6,402
Construction trades	6,175
Transport equipment operating	6,190
Materials handling, not elsewhere classified	5,141
Other crafts and equipment operating	7,528
Not elsewhere classified	4,496
Not stated	5,418
Total	6,574

Source: *1971 Census of Canada*, Cat. 94–768.

tions for 1970. As these data reveal, the direct economic benefits which attach to different occupations vary considerably, even when very broad categories of occupations are considered. On the average, men in medical and health occupations, for example, received over four times the income in that year that men in farming, horticultural, and animal husbandry occupations earned, and about twice the income that men in sales occupations received.

When particular occupations are considered, the contrasts in income from occupation to occupation can be even greater than those reported above. Table 6–7 shows the average incomes of men in a selected set of specific occupations for 1970. On the average, male physicians and surgeons, for example, received about thirty times the income of newsvendors, and some eight and one-half times that of fishermen.

Table 6-7

Average Incomes for Males 15 Years and Over Who Worked in 1970, Twelve Selected Occupations, for Canada, 1971.

Occupation	Males
Physicians and surgeons	$26,990
Veterinarians	14,912
Architects	14,405
University professors	13,667
Civil engineers	11,417
Commercial travellers	8,935
Insurance agents	8,680
Funeral directors	8,155
Bartenders	4,213
Cooks	4,000
Fishermen	3,141
Newsvendors	901

Source: *1971 Census of Canada*, Cat. 94-768.

Not only is there a rather pronounced pattern of differences in occupational incomes, but this pattern has been quite stable over time, although there was a general narrowing trend during World War II and, more recently, a widening trend (Meltz and Stager, 1977). These trends broadly parallel those in the income distribution documented in Chapter 5, and probably lie at least partly behind them. At the same time, (the author's own) calculations from Meltz and

Stager's data suggest that it may not be the case that income inequalities in Canada have increased as a consequence of the changing occupational mix (i.e., of people moving out of middle-income occupations into lower- and higher-income ones). But as the data in Table 6–8 illustrate, the changes which have occurred from decade to decade in relative occupational incomes have sometimes been very large (e.g., lawyers and notaries, 1941–51, and physicians and surgeons, 1961–1971), sometimes negligible (e.g., firemen, 1951–61), but typically modest (e.g., policemen, 1961–71, and electrical engineers, 1951–61). Thus, those occupations which have been well above average at some point in time (e.g., physicians and surgeons) tend to have been well above average throughout the entire thirty years covered in Table 6–8; and those occupations which have been around or below average at one point in time (e.g., bus drivers

Table 6–8

Incomes of Selected Occupations as Percentage of Average Income, Males, Canada, 1941–71.

Occupation	1941	1951	1961	1971
Lawyers and Notaries	541	187	201	221
Professors	285	169	194	183
Physicians and Surgeons	238	200	188	300
Dentists	233	207	200	276
Electrical Engineers	226	179	200	169
Teachers	221	125	151	148
Locomotive Engineers, Firemen	195	156	152	134
Firemen	160	122	121	135
Telegraph Operators	156	127	112	108
Power Station Operators	153	124	135	139
Tool and Die Machinery	149	131	123	123
Movie Projectionists	149	122	103	98
Architects	143	174	183	189
Policemen	139	117	118	134
Subway and Streetcar Operators	136	120	126	125
Bus Drivers	119	111	98	90
Mail Carriers	109	99	91	87
Flour and Grain Milling	94	91	81	84
Secretaries and Typists	92	103	100	97
Brick and Stone Masons	79	99	82	90
Barbers and Hairdressers	77	85	72	68
Taxi Drivers and Chauffeurs	74	79	67	62
Plasterers and Related	69	101	85	90

Source: Calculated from Meltz and Stager (1977: Tables C1–C4).

and barbers and hairdressers) have likewise tended to maintain something re-sembling their relative income positions. This suggests that there is some system-atic connection between the attributes of occupations and the incomes associated with them which endures over fairly long periods of time, and that we should seek to discover what it is.

One clue to occupational income differentials seems to lie in formal education, or in factors related to it. The average levels of educational attainment of persons in different occupations, for example, are directly related to the average incomes of these occupations, and changes in the incomes of occupations over time are directly related to changes in the educational levels of their incumbents (Meltz and Stager, 1977). That is, the better educated the people in an occupation are, the higher the income of that occupation tends to be, and increases in the level of educational attainment of persons in an occupa-tion are associated with increases in the income of that occupation. How might this happen? Earlier, it was argued that formal education can be seen as a market signal for style/ability, including cognitive skills and, consistent with this inter-pretation, McLaughlin (1978) has found that a fairly large proportion (c. 40 per cent) of the differences among occupations in their incomes can be accounted for by differences among them in their cognitive requirements. This suggests that, the more important style/ability is for ease of training to the social and technical requirements of an occupation, the more employers will pay in order to hire people with high style/ability. Although most people can be trained to the requirements of most jobs, training in some jobs no doubt comes more quickly to those with high style/ability, and this may often be enough reason for employ-ers to pay more for them. One factor behind occupational income differentials, then, may be differences among occupations in style/ability requirements, coupled with the fact that, since people who can meet such requirements are rarer the higher these requirements are, they command better pay on the average. And, since the style/ability requirements of occupations relative to one another change only slowly over time, the relative incomes of occupations are generally quite stable from decade to decade.

Central to both structural-functional and human capital theories is the idea that people in different occupations will earn different incomes because they somehow differ in the value of their contributions. In the functionalist formula-tion, this notion takes the form of the argument that occupations are rewarded according to their functional importance, that is, in the value of their contribu-tion to the maintenance or survival of society, and that — other things being equal — their rewards are commensurate with their functional importance. And human capital theory involves assumptions that people in different occupations are paid in some proportion to their contributions to the price of that which they help produce, that is, according to the value of their marginal products, in the technical vocabulary of marginal productivity theory in contemporary micro-economics. If either of these views can be sustained, then we will have a further clue to occupational income differentials and some version of a meritocratic interpretation of them can be seen to make sense. Unfortunately, however, neither of these arguments has been put to a successful test. As we saw in Chapter 3, the concept of functional importance has thus far defied attempts at clear explication and has consequently been largely abandoned. And direct tests of marginal productivity theory have shown no strong or consistent relationships between the values of the marginal products of occupations and occupational incomes (Thurow, 1975). Some occupations (including sales, managerial, supervisory, and professional) have much higher incomes on the average than marginal productivity theory would predict, while others (including the skilled trades, clerical and service workers, and labourers) have much lower ones. If occupations differ in their incomes according to some meritocratic principle, then, it remains to be discovered what this principle is.

Income Differences within Occupations

Although occupation and income are tied together, this connection is actually quite loose. Jencks et al. (1972), for example, estimate that perhaps as little as one-quarter of the differences in earnings among U.S. men are attributable to differences among them in their occupations, and that as much as three-quarters may be earnings differences *within* occupations. And similar results were found for women. This phenomenon is illustrated in the data in Table 6-9, which shows the income distribution for teachers and professors in Canada for 1976. Thus, while about one teacher or professor in eight earned less than $10,000 in that year, another one in eight earned $25,000 or more.

What, then, might account for these income differences within occupations? One possibility is that the better-educated within occupations are paid more, and we have seen that there are real differences within occupations in the

Table 6-9

Distribution of Annual Incomes for Teachers and Professors, Canada, 1976.

Income Category	Per Cent
Less than $5,000	1.4%
$ 5,000–$10,000	11.6
$10,000–$15,000	27.8
$15,000–$20,000	28.7
$20,000–$25,000	17.6
$25,000 and over	12.9
Total	100.0

Source: Calculated from Canada, *Taxation Statistics* (1978).

levels of educational attainment of those in them. Thus, Gunderson (1976:138) found that Canadian men who worked full-time in 1970 and had 1–3 years of high school earned, on the average, $861 more in that year than did their counterparts with only an elementary school education or less. Those with 4–5 years of high school earned $739 more again; those with one university degree earned an additional $2,478; and those with an M.A. or Ph. D. degree made $1,195 more again. This was true after the effects of age, marital status, and rural–urban residence had been taken into account. And similar results were found for women. When the relationship between education and income is examined within particular occupations, however, it almost entirely vanishes. That is, the better-educated within occupations do not tend on the average to be paid measurably more than the less well-educated. Education is relevant to gaining access to an occupation; and those occupations with higher educational requirements do tend to pay more; but, once individuals are trained to the requirements of an occupation, differences in their levels of educational attainment are largely irrelevant to their pay.

It was at about this point (in a more detailed argument) that Jencks et al. (1972) were led to conclude that income differences among individuals are mostly determined in a process of "luck." That is, whether a person's income is high or low or somewhere in between depends largely upon him or her being at just the right place at just the right time with just the right market capacity or talent. Moreover, although many have disagreed with this conclusion, none has successfully refuted it. And there is almost certainly at least an element of truth in it. Being in the U.S. in the 1980s with the ability to throw a football well, for example, being in the Yukon in the 1890s with a claim to some land, or being in England in the 1600s with some navigational skills and a grant from the Crown — all these, and a variety of other equally improbable combinations of circumstances — gave some individuals the opportunity for material success beyond conventional explanation. Still, it would probably be a mistake to accept the principle that luck is the rule and not the exception, since we will never discover what the "real" rules might be if we do not continue the search.

One of the criticisms which can always be made of analyses such as that by Jencks and his associates is that, somehow, all of the "right" variables were not included, although this is an empty criticism in the absence of any good suggestions as to what these variables might be. But there do seem to be a number of possibilities which are not often considered, even though they hold promise to explain an additional proportion of intra-occupational income differences.

If we can assume that people tend to be paid in some relation to their productivity (or, perhaps, labour power), then this should be revealed in income differentials which can be at least partly explained by differences among workers within occupations in their *expertise* and their *labour time*. If different levels and kinds of formal education act as market signals for the capacity to learn different kinds of knowledge and skills which are subsequently largely acquired on the job, then expertise is likely to be found in some (perhaps fairly complex) combination of both formal education and on-the-job experience (see, for example, Stolzenberg, 1975). And labour time simply means the number of hours in a given period in which people actually work at their jobs.

What seems likely is that, for some occupations, it is primarily the accumulated knowledge and skill (as opposed to hours of work) which bring economic returns and, although working harder or longer than the next person may prove advantageous in the end (e.g., in helping a person keep his or her job), it has little short-run payoff. Since this expertise is largely acquired on the job, differences in pay among persons in the same occupation can be expected as a consequence of differences among them in their experience. Thus, for example, although merit pay is often used in reward of apparently superior academic performance, most of the earnings differences among academics (within the same department and university) are explained by differences among them in their teaching experience. For other occupations, it is primarily how many hours in a given period that one works (as opposed to expertise) that determines income, although pay may in fact be pegged directly to hours worked, indirectly by way of some version of piece-work pay, or to some combination of these two. So, for instance, differences in pay among construction labourers working on the same construction site are probably almost completely determined by differences among them in the number of hours which they work. At the same time, although expertise may be the major factor in some occupations and labour time in others, both probably operate together in most occupations. There are part-time academics, those on sick-leave at reduced salary, and those who work at institutions which allow or encourage extra teaching for extra pay, for example, and there are often advantages to experienced construction labourers in being hired on a job in the first place, offered the chance to work overtime once hired, and the like.

Finally, although there is much to be said for attempts to explain occupational earnings, and these efforts can undoubtedly be made more successful through consideration of additional individual variables (such as expertise and labour time) and certain extra-individual factors (see Chapters 7–10), what is at issue here may be better described as the *total benefit packages* which people receive, rather than just earnings as such. Narrowly conceived, this would constitute pay, plus fringe benefits of an economic kind, including employer pension contributions, health insurance, life insurance, and so on. Somewhat more broadly viewed, it might encompass job security and such employee advantages as access to athletic or other recreational facilities, free parking, and even annual picnics and Christmas parties and such. And most generally construed, it might also include the status and various perquisites which a job carries with it, since it could be that increased benefits of a material kind sometimes help compensate for an absence of benefits of a nonmaterial kind, or vice versa, although we know that, in general, occupations which are blessed with one kind of reward tend also to be blessed with other kinds of rewards as well. Perhaps, then, these models would be more successful if they attempted to take more than just pay into account.

Wealth

As we saw in Chapter 5, the distribution of wealth in Canada is much more unequal than the distribution of income. At least part of this is not difficult to understand, since, not only can those who earn more save more, but the *rate* at which people save and invest what they earn is higher for those who earn a lot than for those who do not. Consequently, initial equalities in wealth turn into inequalities over time in a process of income accumulation, and small initial differences grow into large ones later on. For example, two people who have equal wealth but different incomes at one point in time will differ in their wealth later on, since one will be able to save more (both absolutely and relatively) than the other. Thus, while the data presented in Chapter 5 may have suggested that people's wealth is roughly proportional to their incomes, this was probably because of the way the data were collapsed into crude categories. Although it is based on U.S. sources, a more accurate version of the relationship between income and wealth is probably that people earning about $25,000 per year have average wealth of about *half again* that amount; those who make on the order of $50,000 per year have about *twice* that much wealth; and people who earn about $100,000 per year have wealth of about *ten times* that amount (Projector, 1964).

While most people probably gain what they own through some combination of a patient process of saving from income and receiving modest inheritances in mid-life, great wealth cannot be accumulated in this way. For, if it were, it would take even those who earn stratospheric incomes several lifetimes to make their way into the rarefied regions of the very rich. And yet there are a few people in this country who do have — even by international standards — enormous wealth, and it would be useful to know something of how they gained it. We shall continue this discussion in Chapter 9 when we analyse the process of inheritance.

Status

If mid-twentieth-century European sociology tended on balance to pay more heed to Marx than to Weber, the converse may have been more characteristic of North American (particularly U.S.) sociology, where the study of inequality concentrated largely on issues of social stratification (rather than of class) and among these, especially on matters relating to *social status* (see, for example, the work of Warner et al., 1960; 1963). Considerable research in the U.S. between the 1930s and 1960s was concerned to analyse the phenomenon of social status — the evaluative judgments people make of one another as worthy human beings — often against the theoretical background of Weber's discussion of social honour and status groups.

Among the major conclusions to emerge from U.S. community stratification research were that, at least in communities below a certain size, people form overall judgments of one another's social status, and that they generally agree with one another in these judgments. Moreover, the status judgments which people make can be predicted quite accurately from knowledge of a few of the status characteristics of the persons being judged, including educational attainment, occupation, and income. This fact often enabled investigators to dispense with the time-consuming task of having to ask members of a community actually to judge one another's status directly. Instead, they could simply determine how individuals measured up on certain status characteristics, and then combine this information into a summary measure of overall social status. More important than just the ease this afforded in research, however, were the insights it may have provided into the apparent processes by which overall status judgments are formed, that is, as the consequence of people's evaluations of a limited set of status characteristics (also see Hamblin, 1971, 1974).

Educational Status

Among the several things that different levels of educational attainment signify (e.g., style/ability) is status. The higher the level of education, the greater the status it brings with it. At the same time, each additional year of education adds a larger increment of status than the one before it, so that when appropriate measurement procedures are used, the amount of status is approximately equal to the *square* of the number of years of education (Hamblin, 1971, 1974; but see Baker, 1977). Thus, for example, a person with half the number of years of formal education of another receives considerably less than half the status.

Occupational Status

There is also a symbolic significance to occupation, such that some occupations are perceived as standing higher in status than others (e.g., National Opinion Research Center, 1947; Hodge et al., 1966; Pineo and Porter, 1967). In the only national study to date of occupational status conducted in Canada, Pineo and Porter had a sample of 793 people rate the "social standing" of about 200 separate occupational titles. On a 100-point scale, the aggregated judgments of these people produced ratings ranging from a high of 89.9 for Provincial Premier to a low of 14.3 for garbage collector. Table 6–10 shows the status scores for a selected set of occupations included in this study.

Economic Status

Economic resources may be important to people, not only in terms of the purchasing power which they represent, but also in terms of the status which they carry with them. Warner and his associates (1960), for example, found that both source and amount of income were related to an individual's reputation in the community. Those with inherited wealth tended to receive the highest status followed, in turn, by persons whose income was derived from earned wealth, profits and fees, a salary, wages, private relief and, finally, public relief and "nonrespectable" income (also see Pineo and Porter, 1967, Appendix I). And, within each of these categories, the higher the amount of one's income, the higher his or her status tended to be. Subsequent research has added refinement to this latter finding, such that, the greater the income, the greater the status it brings with it, except that each additional dollar seems to add a smaller increment of status than the one before it (Hamblin, 1971, 1974). Or, more

Table 6–10

Status Scores, Twelve Selected Occupations

Occupation	Status Score
Physician	87.2
University professor	84.6
Architect	78.1
Civil engineer	73.1
Veterinarian	66.7
Funeral director	54.9
Insurance agent	47.3
Travelling salesman	40.2
Cook	29.7
Cod fisherman	23.4
Bartender	20.2
News peddler	14.8

Source: Pineo and Porter, "Occupational Prestige in Canada." *Canadian Review of Sociology and Anthropology*, 4 (1967).

precisely, when appropriate measurement procedures are used, the amount of status is approximately equal to the *square root* of income. For example, a person who has twice as much income as somebody else receives less than twice as much status.

The Meaning of Status

Up to this point, the term status (or prestige) has been used in two apparently different ways. First, it has been used in a distributive sense to refer to evaluative judgments which people make of one another and of one another's attributes, such as education, occupation, and income. Second, it has been employed in a relational sense to indicate deference in social interaction. While these are two distinct orders of phenomena and ought not to be confused, they can be seen to be related in a way which provides a rationale for using the same term to describe them, as long as the context of the discussion indicates clearly which of the two meanings is intended. Briefly, it seems useful to think of distributive status as the subjective experience of relational status or, to use Kahl's words (paraphrasing Weber), "prestige is a sentiment in the minds of men [*sic*] that is expressed in interpersonal interaction: deference behavior is demanded by one party and granted by another" (1957:19).

The Status-Attainment Process

In the period since the publication of Blau and Duncan's 1967 epic, *The*

American Occupational Structure, a considerable amount of research has been conducted on the "status-attainment process," using "status-attainment models," although there is very little published research on this topic as it relates to Canada (Turrittin, 1974; Cuneo and Curtis, 1975; McRoberts et al., 1976). Basically, there are two related status-attainment models which are often identified in the literature, the Blau–Duncan and Wisconsin models (Alexander et al., 1975), of which only the former has begun to be examined in any detail in the Canadian context.

As it relates to issues of the present chapter, the Blau–Duncan model focuses especially on the relationship between education and occupation — specifically, the causal connection between an individual's level of educational attainment and the status of his or her occupation — using quantitative, causal models as a means of representing this relationship. Such causal models are often given pictorial representation in the form of *path diagrams,* as in Figure 6-1, where the variables of educational attainment and occupational status are depicted as standing in causal relation to one another, and the concern is to estimate very precisely, using (linear, additive) statistical procedures, how many units of change in the dependent variable (or effect) are produced by a unit (say a year of education) of change in the independent variable (or cause).

Figure 6-1 THE CAUSAL CONNECTION BETWEEN LEVEL OF EDUCATIONAL ATTAINMENT AND OCCUPATIONAL STATUS

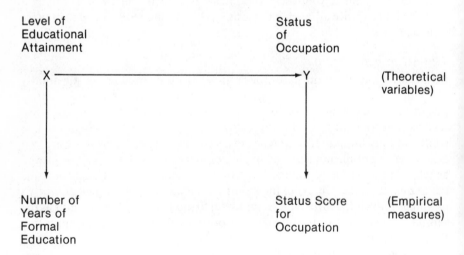

In one of its more recent incarnations, the Blau–Duncan model has been extended by a number of investigators (e.g., Duncan et al., 1972) to include income as the dependent variable, with occupational status causally prior to it, and educational attainment causally prior to both of these two variables. And, even more recently, wealth (or net worth) has been treated as dependent upon income, occupation, education, and a number of other variables (Henretta and Campbell, 1978). In models of this kind, however, the causal ordering of the variables relative to one another must be unambiguously clear, since these methods can only cast insight into the extent to which *known* causes have effects, not whether one variable *is* causally prior to another. If the investigator puts his or her variables in the wrong order, then, numerical results will still be obtained, although they will not be meaningful. In the case of occupational status and income, it is not obvious which, if either, is the cause and which the effect, so that the results obtained with income as the dependent variable should probably not be accepted uncritically. And, at any rate, these models have been much less successful in accounting for income than for occupational status — as one might have expected from the analysis of occupation and income above. As for wealth, finally, much the same cautions apply (e.g., some people accumulate wealth from income, and some derive income from wealth, so that it is not clear that income can easily be treated as the cause of wealth, rather than the other way around, or as the two variables causing one another). And, even if wealth could be dealt with as if it were dependent upon income, we have already seen that great wealth, at least, comes to people in other ways than through saving from income.

Especially as we will see later, there have been real payoffs from this research tradition, particularly in its success in documenting and explicating the phenomena of social ascription. As an approach to the understanding of the matrix of relationships among education, occupation, and rewards, however, it has some limitations which ought to be identified. First, despite the title which has been given it, it is worth mentioning that it does not deal with "status attainment" as such but, rather, with *occupational* status attainment. Second, it isolates only two specific aspects of education and occupation for analysis, namely *level* of educational attainment and *status* of occupation. Third, although the results obtained in empirical tests of this part of the Blau–Duncan model are often given interpretation in terms of the functional theory of stratification or human capital theory (Horan, 1978), these tests cast no light on *how* it is that education and occupation are connected the way they are — a major concern of the present chapter. Fourth, the use of causal models assumes that the variables in question are related to one another deterministically, whereas education and occupation are probably best seen as related probabilistically. Fifth, most attempts to use Blau–Duncan models have not taken into account the possibility that the relationship between education and occupation might vary importantly as a consequence of changes in the supply and demand for educated labour (but see Hauser et al., 1975; Sorenson, 1979). And sixth, these models focus on issues of individual attainment, while paying relatively little heed to the changing structure and organization of the larger society generally (and not just of the changing supply and demand for educated labour).

On Merit

In an analysis of inequalities in the distribution of life-chances, an attempt was made in this chapter to assess the extent to which a structural-functionalist/human capital interpretation (that people are generally rewarded according to their abilities and efforts, i.e., their merit) could be sustained against certain other (mainly Marxist) interpretations. According to this version of merit, ability and effort directed at obtaining a formal education result in the acquisition of knowledge and skills which qualify people for jobs whose rewards are at least roughly commensurate with their merit. Early on, however, it appeared as if, in order to maintain such a meritocratic interpretation, a number of the assumptions underlying it had to be expanded at some length and sometimes significantly reformulated in light of recent information and interpretations. An essentially technical analysis of the importance of formal education for occupations, as contained in both functionalist and human capital theories, for one thing, seems inadequate when it is appreciated that, for most jobs, job-related knowledge and skills are acquired at work, and not in the classroom. And, for another thing, the better-educated within particular jobs do not seem generally to be more productive than their less well-educated colleagues. Following an examination of the outcomes of schooling and the task requirements of jobs, it was suggested that formal educational qualifications may operate as market signals for the relative ease with which persons are likely to be socialized to the technical and social requirements of different occupations. Also, there is probably no simple equation connecting formal educational qualifications and notions of individuals' market capacities, as is often thought, precisely because of the importance of on-the-job experience for job-related learning. Rather, the concept of market capacity may be best conceived of as implying a range of different combinations of types and amounts of both formal education and on-the-job experience. At the same time, it was possible only to hint at just how the particular capacities which are signalled by different kinds of educational certification adapt people to learn the technical and social requirements of different jobs, much less to develop a full-blown typology of market capacities generally, and then to link this to the job market in detail, although a number of suggestions were made.

First, *level* of formal education as such seems to signal a general amalgam of cognitive abilities and cultural styles (labelled "style/ability") which appears to have a counterpart in the requirements of occupations. But, partly because style/ability is a very general collection of qualities, and partly because it is only one of an unknown number of relevant market signals and job requirements, it does not in itself provide any clear clues to the ties between people and occupations. Second, it may be that occupations tend to fall along a continuum defined at one end by those in which *expertise* is the principal basis for remuneration and, at the other end, by those in which the major determinant of pay and other occupational rewards is *labour time*. Perhaps, then, as Weber (and, following him, Giddens) suggested, one can simplify the complex set of market capacities which are taken to define individual's memberships in different classes in terms of a broad class of persons who exchange technical knowledge and skills for rewards in the market, and a class of those with only their capacity to work to sell, although the line of demarcation which separates them is neither clear nor obvious.

Other links in the chain of the functionalist/ human capital, meritocratic argument were strained when it could not be determined that occupational incomes are related in some close and systematic way to the value of the contributions of different occupations or that inequalities in the distribution of wealth derived essentially from a patient process of saving from earned income. Whatever the processes are by which members of some occupations earn more on the average than others or by which some people become fabulously wealthy while others are desperately poor, these do not appear to be wholly, or even largely, connected to merit.

The fact of the very loose connections between education and occupation, and between these two and income and the accumulation of great wealth, has led researchers off in a number of different directions, with some arguing for the importance of "luck" or chance, others suggesting various refinements of and additions to the basic approach, and still others adocating other things. As for chance, its importance may have been over-stressed by some and, rather than thinking in terms of "dumb luck," it might be more useful to entertain the possibility of genuinely probabilistic (as opposed to deterministic) explanations for many of the phenomena considered here. As for refining and adding to the basic approach, some of the more promising possibilities may lie not on the side of the *supply* of labour (e.g., strengthening the conceptualization and measurement of market capacities), but with elaborations on the side of the *demand* for labour (e.g., considering aspects of *both* the jobs which are open *and* the people who are available to fill them). Although it is not inherent in the basic approach, investigators working in this general tradition have concentrated on issues of supply and largely ignored matters of demand. Too, when one considers both the supply of and the demand for labour with different market capacities, one must also take into account that scarcities and surpluses occur, so that the connection between the market capacities of people and the requirements of jobs will necessarily have some element of probability attached to it and thus will necessarily vary somewhat from time to time and place to place.

While functionalists and human capital theorists do make assumptions about the market, it tends to be seen as the open market of neoclassical economics, that is, perfectly competitive, in which all actors have full information, move freely to maximize their gains, and receive returns in line with their contributions, and where the principal dynamics are those of supply and demand. Davis and Moore did point to the inequalities of opportunity and inequalities of reward apparent in the inheritance of great wealth, for example, and recognized such "imperfections" in the market as those which arise when different social classes or groups control avenues of access to certain privileged positions. But they tended to see such phenomena as these as detrimental to the survival of society in the long run and, hence, as likely to disappear in time. Yet, as we have glimpsed and will see even more clearly, even in a society as advanced in industrial development as Canada, inheritance persists as a major source of great wealth and other social advantage and, although the data do not permit any definite determination of trends in this regard, there is no evidence of any clear and consistent decrease in such inheritance.

Weber, too, made assumptions about the market, and he was also alert to such phenomena as the inheritance of great wealth and the control of avenues for mobility by certain social groups, although he never carried his analysis very far. For his part, these features of the market were seen as evidence of a cyclical rotation in the mechanisms of distributive systems, whereby there are periods when class (or economic rationality) is the major determinant of life-chances, followed by periods in which status (a nonrational principle) is the major determinant, and so on. In his emphasis on the master-trends of increasing rationalization and bureaucratization in social life, however, he can be seen to argue along lines which resemble those of the functionalists or human capital theorists, at least in terms of the conclusions which they arrive at. Or, as Bell forecasts into the post-industrial future: "a post-industrial society, being primarily a technical society, awards place less on the basis of inheritance or property (though these can command wealth or cultural advantage) than on education and skill" (1973:xviii).

Whether or not some version of the meritocratic, post-industrial society lies ahead of us, it is clearly not with us yet. But, if not merit, then what? In the following section, an attempt will be made to identify the extent to which rewards can be seen to be distributed according to such criteria as gender, ethnicity, and social background, and to describe the principles of distribution which these appear to involve.

Part III
Beyond Merit

Chapter 7

Gender Inequalities

"Women belong horizontal on their backs and should only be allowed to stand up once in a while" (Harold Ballard, Canadian sports entrepreneur, to Barbara Frum, host of the CBC radio program, As It Happens).

"Mr. Speaker, as a woman vertical in this House, I must say God in Her wisdom says 'nuts' to Harold Ballard" (Iona Campagnola, one-time Liberal Minister of Fitness and Amateur Sport and former Miss Prince Rupert).

In the previous chapter, almost all of the data presented were for men only and, consequently, the interpretations offered of them may best apply or, perhaps even, *only* apply to the male experience. Because we must find this out, and because the male and female circumstances only make sense in relation to and as part of one another, the present chapter is devoted to a description of gender inequalities.

Education

Throughout the present century, the percentages of males and females 14 years of age and under enrolled full-time in school in Canada have been approximately the same (Robb and Spencer, 1976:55; Synge, 1977). Prior to 1951, though, the percentage of females in the age group 15–19 enrolled full-time consistently exceeded the percentage of males in that age group enrolled, while this pattern has since been reversed. In the 20–24 age group, proportionately more males than females have been enrolled full-time in school in every census year since 1911, and the differences between them have shown a tendency to increase over time, especially since 1951. As the data in Table 7–1 show, the higher the age group, the greater the *difference* in enrolment rates in favour of males tends to be, and the greater the difference has tended to become in the past few decades. To put these trends in better perspective, however, enrolment rates for both males and females at all ages beyond 5 years have either continued to increase or, as in the case of those 14 years of age and under, reached their saturation level.

In 1951/52, females enjoyed a slight edge over males in the percentage in the age group 15–17 enrolled full-time in high school, and a considerable edge over males in the percentage in the age group 18–21 enrolled full-time in

Table 7-1

Enrolment Rates in Full-Time Education by Sex, Canada, Selected Years

		1951/52	1961/62	1966/67	1971/72
Elementary-Secondary					
Age 5	Male	27.7%	57.7%	70.3%	n.a.
	Female	28.9	58.4	70.6	n.a.
Age 6	Male	79.9	96.4	96.7	96.6
	Female	80.3	97.2	96.8	98.2
Age 15	Male	69.7	88.9	94.7	94.7
	Female	70.8	87.1	94.0	94.5
Age 16	Male	50.6	70.0	83.4	84.9
	Female	53.1	65.1	80.7	83.5
Age 17	Male	31.5	50.8	63.2	64.8
	Female	31.9	41.5	55.4	58.7
Non-University, Post-Secondary (relative to 18–21 age group)					
	Male	1.4	3.2	5.3	12.0
	Female	5.0	7.3	6.6	10.3
University Transfer [a] (relative to 18–21 age group)					
	Male	n.a.	n.a.	0.3	4.2
	Female	n.a.	n.a.	0.1	2.8
University Undergraduate (relative to 18–21 age group)					
	Male	11.0	17.5	20.6	22.9
	Female	3.1	6.3	10.5	14.0
University Graduate (relative to 22–24 age group)					
Male		1.0	1.8	3.9	4.9
Female		0.2	0.3	0.8	1.4

n.a. — not available.
[a] University transfer students are registered in non-university, post-secondary institutions and, as such, are part of the above category.
Source: Robb and Spencer (1976:56).

nonuniversity, post-secondary institutions, as shown in Table 7-1. By 1971/72, the advantage had turned to males by a large margin at the high school level, and by a small margin at the nonuniversity, post-secondary level. In the universities, males have always outnumbered females and, although rates of increase in full-time enrolment have been higher for females than for males in the past few decades, the university population is still close to 60 per cent male.

Some small part of the educational disadvantage of females revealed in the data for full-time enrolment may be made up, however, in part-time university and nonuniversity study, which has become increasingly common over the past twenty years, and much more so for women than for men (Robb and Spencer, 1976:61–62). At the university undergraduate level, women actually outnumber men as part-time students, although this has only happened within the last few years, and men still outnumber women as part-time students by a margin of 3:1 at the university graduate level. As well, there may also have been an increasing tendency for women in older age groups to resume their education after marriage or a period in the labour market (Synge, 1977:303) — a fact not reflected in the data in Table 7-1.

Despite the conclusions which one might leap to on the basis of certain popular beliefs about "women's lib," then, women may have "come a long way," but men may actually have come even farther, at least in education. Still, men and women in Canada do not differ much overall in their average levels of educational attainment. One reason for this is that many men and women are still alive from that earlier period in which women were more likely to complete high school, while another is that the differences between them in educational participation have occurred at a level which relatively few Canadians ever reach. About 82 per cent of the total population 14 years of age and over in 1972 had no more than a secondary school education — down from 90 per cent in 1961/62 vs. 92.9 per cent in 1951/52 (Canada, 1977:93). Those male-female differences in educational participation which are both long-standing and of some magnitude, however, have occurred at the level of university, and only a small proportion of the population has either attended university or received one or more degrees. In 1971, some 4.7 per cent of Canadians 15 years of age or above and not attending school had a university degree, and an additional 5.1 per cent had some university education (Kubat and Thornton, 1974:130). So, even if men are far more likely to attend university and to receive university degrees than women, this is only a big difference for a small (if increasing) number of people. At the same time, men now hold the advantage over women in educational participation at all levels beyond the compulsory school attendance age and, taken together, the trends over time in male-female enrolments point to a continuing (and not obviously decreasing) advantage in education for males over females.

If males and females differ in their levels of educational attainment and in their rates of educational participation, they differ, as well, in the kinds of education they receive. These differences begin in the very earliest grades in school and become more pronounced at every higher level within the system, especially in the final years in high school and at the level of post-secondary education (Stacey et al., 1974). Table 7-2 shows the percentage distributions of full-time male and female undergraduates in Canadian universitites in 1962/63 and 1972/73 by field of specialization. As these data show, there are significant and persistent differences between men and women in the university programmes they pursue, although the overall differences between them have diminished slightly in the period covered. For the male-female differences to have disappeared in 1962/63, approximately 40 per cent of the men (or 40 per cent of the women) would have had to have moved from their actual programmes of study into some other programme, while the corresponding figure for 1972/73 was about 36 per cent.

Table 7-2

Full-Time Undergraduate Enrolment by Sex and Field of Study, Canada, 1962/63 and 1972/73.

	1962/63			1972/73		
	Males	Females	Difference [a]	Males	Females	Difference [a]
Arts	38.5%	50.3%	-11.8%	31.0%	44.5%	-13.5%
Science	12.7	6.2	+ 6.5	19.3	11.3	+ 8.0
Commerce and Business Administration	7.7	0.8	+ 6.9	10.1	2.8	+ 7.3
Education	7.4	19.8	-12.4	8.5	18.4	- 9.9
Fine and Applied Arts	0.0	0.2	- 0.2	0.8	1.7	- 0.9
Household Science	0.0	4.7	- 4.7	0.0	3.2	- 3.2
Law	2.9	0.4	+ 2.5	3.8	1.3	+ 2.5
Music	0.2	1.1	- 0.9	0.7	1.3	- 0.6
Medicine	4.0	1.2	+ 2.8	3.1	1.4	+ 1.7
Nursing	0.0	5.7	- 5.7	0.0	4.3	- 4.3
Other Health	1.4	3.2	- 1.8	1.0	3.1	- 2.1
Social Work	0.2	0.9	- 0.7	0.4	1.5	- 1.1
Other	28.6	5.5	+23.1	21.3	5.2	+16.1
Total	100.0	100.0		100.0	100.0	
Number, All Fields	95,827	36,854		175,377	109,781	

[a] A "–" signs means that females are over-represented relative to males;
    a "+" sign means that males are over-represented relative to females.
Source: Adapted from Robb and Spencer (1976:60).

As Table 7-2 shows, women were over-represented relative to men in both time periods in education, arts, nursing, household science, and health programmes other than medicine or nursing, while men were over-represented relative to women in commerce and business administration, science, medicine, and law. Moreover, while the differences between them have decreased somewhat over time in education, household science, nursing and medicine, they have either remained about the same or increased (as in arts, science and commerce and business administration) in all other fields. Even though there seems to have been a small overall decrease in the differences between men and women in their areas of university study, then, this decrease summarizes a pattern of both decreases *and* increases across a number of different fields of specialization.

There is, then, a changing pattern of sometimes substantial differences between men and women in enrolment, attainment, and field of specialization in education. And, though there is probably a long-term trend in the direction of sexual equality in education, it is neither consistent nor pronounced.

Employment and Occupations

Women are much less likely to be employed or seeking employment than are men, and this has been true throughout the period of the present century, as Table 7-3 shows. However, labour force participation rates for men have slowly declined as men have spent more and more of their lives in school and retired at younger and younger ages, while the rates for women have risen more or less continuously, despite these dual processes of educational upgrading and earlier

Table 7-3

Labour Force Participation Rates by Sex, Canada, 1901-76.

	Participation Rates	
Year	Male	Female
1901	87.8	16.1
1911	90.6	18.6
1921	89.8	19.9
1931	87.2	21.8
1941	85.6	22.9
1951	83.9	23.5
1961	79.8	28.7
1971	76.1	36.5
1976	75.5	45.0

Source: Canada (1977: Table 6.1) and *1976 Census of Canada.*

retirement. Overall, this has meant that there has not been much change in the total percentage of adult Canadians in the job market in the twentieth century.

The increasing labour force participation of women has come about partly as a consequence of the movement of women into occupations whose representation in the occupational structure has grown over the years. For this reason, it would be useful to analyse the changing sex composition of occupations to see the extent to which certain jobs have become increasingly or decreasingly dominated by members of one sex or the other. Having done this, and knowing from our earlier analysis the changing representation of different kinds of jobs in the occupational structure, we will get some notion as to where the demand for female labour within certain occupations has combined with the changing occupational structure to stimulate rising rates of female labour force participation. Table 7–4 shows the sex composition of broad occupational categories for every other census year, 1901–61, while Table 7–5 brings this information up to date using the broad occupational categories of the *1971 Census of Canada*.

As these data show, women have moved into clerical and commercial-financial (mainly retail sales) jobs much more rapidly than men in the past seventy years, and this has also been true, although to a much lesser extent, of agricultural, proprietary-managerial, transportation-communication, and labouring jobs as well, while men have moved more quickly than women into service and manufacturing-mechanical jobs. And the remaining broad occupational categories have shown little change in sex composition in this period. Since all of the white-collar occupational categories have experienced relative growth in the twentieth century — especially the clerical — the massive influx of women into the labour force has basically taken the form of movement into white-collar (except professional) jobs, just as these jobs were experiencing a period of rapid growth. And added to this was their movement into another occupational sector which has grown steadily over the years — transportation-communication. Since both agricultural and, to a lesser extent, labouring jobs have declined in relative (and, in the case of agricultural, in absolute) representation, the movement of women into these two categories has not been a major factor in their increasing labour force participation, although it is notable that women now occupy one in five of all agricultural jobs. As for men, their movement into manufacturing-mechanical jobs has occurred at a time when this category has been declining in relative representation, and the only category into which men have moved more rapidly than women, which is also on the incline, is service jobs.

Since the increasing demand for female labour has, for the most part, involved the recruitment of hitherto unemployed segments of the adult female population into new jobs, these jobs have tended to become sex-typed as "female" jobs, and they constitute a part of the job market in which women largely compete with one another for employment. Unfortunately, the extent of a category of such jobs is not fully revealed in the data presented in Tables 7–4 and 7–5, as a consequence of the broad occupational categories which have been

Table 7–4

Women as a Percentage of the Labour Force, [a] by Occupation Division, Canada, [b] 1901–1961.

	Percentage				Difference
	1901 [a]	1921	1941 [c]	1961	1901-1961
White Collar	*20.1*	*29.5*	*35.1*	*41.3*	*+21.2*
Proprietary and managerial	3.6	4.3	7.2	10.3	+ 6.7
Professional	42.5	54.1	46.1	43.2	+ 0.7
Clerical	22.1	41.8	50.1	61.5	+39.4
Commercial, financial	10.4	25.6	32.1	40.3	+29.9
Blue Collar	*14.4*	*10.7*	*12.3*	*11.4*	*− 3.0*
Manufacturing and mechanical	24.8	24.1	19.0	16.8	− 8.0
Construction	0.0e	0.0e	0.1	0.2	+ 0.2
Labourers d	1.0	0.2	4.4	6.1	+ 5.1
Primary	*1.1*	*1.6*	*1.5*	*9.2*	*+ 8.1*
Agricultural	1.2	1.7	1.7	11.7	+10.5
Fishing, hunting, trapping	0.0 [e]	0.0 [e]	0.6	1.1	+ 1.1
Logging	— [f]	— [f]	— [f]	0.2	+ 0.2
Mining and quarrying	0.0 [e]	0.0 [e]	0.0 [e]	0.0e	+ 0.0e
Transportation and communication	*1.4*	*8.3*	*5.3*	*7.9*	*+ 6.5*
Service	*68.7*	*58.6*	*65.0*	*50.0*	*−18.7*

[a]   10 years and over in 1901.
[b]   Excluding Yukon and Northwest Territories; including Newfoundland in 1961.
[c]   Excluding those on active service, June 1941.
[d]   Except those in Primary.
[e]   Less than 0.05% but not empty category.
[f]   Empty category.
Source: Computed from Ostry (1967: Table 3).

used. That some three-quarters of those persons working in jobs in medicine and health are female obscures the fact that this occupational category comprises a number of different jobs, some of them almost entirely female, such as nurse and nurse's aide, and the remainder, including physician, and surgeon, almost entirely male. In the teaching category, day care, nursery school and primary school teachers are mostly female, while the majority of secondary school teachers are male. Among clerical jobs, the same principle holds true: over nine-tenths of all secretaries/stenographers, tellers and cashiers, typists and clerk-

Table 7-5

Women as a Percentage of the Labour Force, by Occupation Division,
Canada, 1971.

	Percentage
Managerial, administrative, and related	16.0
Natural sciences, engineering and mathematics	7.3
Social sciences and related	37.3
Religion	15.7
Teaching and related	60.4
Medicine and health	74.3
Artistic, literary, recreational and related	27.2
Clerical and related	68.4
Sales	30.4
Service	46.2
Farming, horticultural, and animal husbandry	20.9
Fishing, hunting, trapping and related	_a
Forestry and logging	2.1
Mining and quarrying	_a
Processing	17.8
Machining and related	5.7
Product fabricating, assembling, and repairing	23.7
Construction trades	1.0
Transport equipment operating	2.4
Materials handling and related	19.7
Other crafts and equipment operating	12.4

[a] Too few women for reliable calculation, but not empty category.
Source: Derived from *1971 Census of Canada*, Cat. 94-723.

typists, and receptionists in Canada are female, while the majority of shipping
and receiving clerks are male. And, in the sales category, over two-thirds of all
sales clerks are female, while some five-sixths of all sales supervisors are male.
Table 7-6 shows the leading occupations of the female labour force and the percentage in each occupation who are female. As one can see, the majority of employed females in 1971 worked at a small number of jobs in which a majority of
the workers were female. The overwhelming majority of jobs, of course, are and
always have been "male" and, since men are much more evenly distributed
across occupations than are women, it is not possible to assemble a comparable
short-list of jobs in which the majority of men work.

There is a visible tendency, then, for jobs to be dominated by members of
one sex or the other and, consequently, for them to be sex-typed as "male" or

Table 7-6

Leading Occupations of the Female Labour Force, Canada, 1971.

	Per Cent of Female Labour Force in this Occupation	Females as Per Cent of Labour Force in Each Occupation
Secretaries/stenographers	8.1	97.4
Sales clerks	5.4	66.0
Bookkeepers/account clerks	4.6	67.6
Elementary school teachers	4.1	82.3
Waitresses	3.6	82.9
Tellers and cashiers	3.5	91.2
Farm workers	3.2	46.2
Nurses, graduate	3.1	95.8
Typists and clerk-typists	2.9	95.6
General office clerks	2.7	62.2
Sewing machine operators	1.9	90.1
Personal service n.e.c.	1.9	92.0
Janitors/cleaners	1.9	32.4
Nursing aids and orderlies	1.8	74.4
Secondary school teachers	1.7	44.5
Other clerical n.e.c.	1.5	62.0
Receptionists	1.4	92.6
Supervisors: sales	1.4	16.8
Chefs and cooks	1.3	50.2
Packaging n.e.c.	1.3	56.3
Telephone operators	1.0	95.9
Total	58.6	

Source: *1971 Census of Canada*, Cat. No. 94-723.

"female," and the question arises as to whether this tendency has increased or decreased over time. The evidence seems to be that it has slowly but steadily decreased since the turn of the century (Lautard, 1977:9). If men and women tend to be highly segregated within particular occupations today, they were even more highly segregated in the past. Still, the overwhelming majority of jobs remain identifiably "male" or "female," and marked changes in sex composition have been largely (although not exclusively) confined to a relatively small number of white-collar jobs. Moreover, these changes have tended to involve the movement of women into relatively low-paying "male" jobs (as in the case of the clerical category generally, and those of agricultural and other labourers) and of men into relatively high-paying "female" jobs (such as school teacher). If occupational sex segregation has declined somewhat in the twentieth century, this has not necessarily meant any overall improvement in the position of women in the occupational structure.

Approaching the relationship between gender and jobs from a slightly different angle, we might inquire as to how different overall the jobs are at which men and women work, and how the differences between them have changed over the years. Table 7-7 shows the distributions of males and females across major occupational categories for every other census year, 1901-1961, while Table 7-8 brings this information up to date using the broad occupational categories of the *1971 Census of Canada*.

As these data show, men and women differ substantially in their occupational distributions, and this has been the case throughout the past seventy years. In 1971, for the two distributions to have been the same, 45 per cent of the men (or of the women) would have had to have changed from one broad occupational category to another. In 1901, the comparable figure (keeping in mind that the number and types of categories used prior to 1971 are quite different, and this could affect the results obtained) was about 66 per cent, which suggests that the differences between men and women in their occupational distributions in that year were larger than they are today. By 1921, it had dropped slightly, to about 64 per cent, and by 1941 still further, to about 58 per cent. In 1961, the figure stood at about 47 per cent. Overall, the trend seems to have been in the direction of decreasing differences between men and women in their occupational distributions, and this conclusion is more or less borne out when more detailed occupational categories and sophisticated statistical procedures are used (Lautard, 1977:9).

In the world of work, the picture is one of rapidly rising rates of female labour force participation (especially among the married), enormous (but slowly decreasing) occupational segregation by sex, and also enormous (if also slowly decreasing) occupational differentiation by sex. Great changes have taken place in the sexual division of labour in the workplace over the years, but these changes and their effects have not all been in the direction of increasing sexual equality. True, the differences between men and women in their relative likelihood of working for a wage or salary have diminished sharply in the period surveyed. But the jobs which women have taken on have generally been different from those of men. Disproportionately, they have been the "dead end" jobs of secretary, stenographer, sales clerk, bookkeeper, account clerk, waitress, teller or cashier, farm labourer, typist, clerk-typist, general office clerk and the like, rathen than successive rungs on the ladder of an occupational career.

Occupations in the Technical Division of Labour[1]

For the most part, sociological studies of occupations rely upon the

---

[1]   The research reported here is part of a continuing programme conducted with Michael Manley. Additional results are reported below in connection with gender and ethnic differences in earnings.

Table 7-7

Percentage Distribution of the Labour Force, [a] by Occupation Division and Sex, Canada, [b] 1901-61.

Percentage

	1901[a]			1921			1941[c]			1961		
	Male	Female	Difference	Male	Female	Difference	Male	Female	Difference	Male	Female	Difference
White Collar	14.0	23.6	− 9.6	21.1	48.3	−27.2	20.5	44.7	−24.2	30.6	57.3	−26.7
Proprietary and managerial	4.8	1.2	+ 3.6	8.2	2.0	+ 6.2	6.2	2.0	+ 4.2	9.6	2.9	+ 6.7
Professional	3.1	14.7	−11.6	3.0	19.1	−16.1	4.5	15.6	−11.1	7.7	15.5	− 7.8
Clerical	2.9	5.3	− 2.4	4.7	18.7	−14.0	4.5	18.3	−13.8	6.7	28.6	−21.9
Commercial, financial	3.2	2.4	− 0.8	5.2	8.5	− 3.3	5.2	8.8	− 3.6	6.6	10.2	− 3.6
Blue Collar	27.5	30.1	− 2.6	27.2	17.9	+ 9.3	29.6	16.8	+12.8	32.4	11.1	+21.3
Manufacturing and	13.8	29.6	−15.8	10.3	17.8	− 7.5	16.2	15.4	+ 0.8	18.4	9.9	+ 8.5
Construction	5.4	—[e]	+ 5.4	5.5	—[e]	+ 5.5	5.8	—[e]	+ 5.8	7.1	—[e]	+ 7.1
Labourers [d]	8.2	0.5	+ 7.7	11.4	0.1	+11.3	7.6	1.4	+ 6.2	6.9	1.2	+ 5.7
Primary	50.5	3.8	+46.7	42.1	3.7	+38.4	37.5	2.3	+35.2	16.1	4.3	+11.8
Agricultural	45.9	—[e]	+42.1	37.9	3.7	+34.2	31.5	2.3	+29.2	12.2	4.3	+ 7.9
Fishing, hunting, trapping	1.8	—[e]	+ 1.8	1.1	—[e]	+ 1.1	1.5	—[e]	+1.5	0.8	—[e]	+ 0.8
Logging	1.0	0.0[f]	+ 1.0	1.4	0.0[f]	+ 1.4	2.3	—[e]	+ 2.3	1.7	—[e]	+ 1.7
Mining and quarrying	1.8	0.0[f]	+ 1.8	1.7	—[e]	+ 1.7	2.1	—[e]	+ 2.1	1.4	—[e]	+ 1.4
Transportation and communication	5.0	0.5	+ 4.5	5.9	3.0	+ 2.9	7.5	1.7	+ 5.8	9.7	2.2	+ 7.5
Service	2.9	42.0	−39.1	3.5	26.8	−23.3	4.6	34.3	−29.7	8.5	22.6	−14.1
Unknown	—[e]	—[e]	0.0	0.2	0.3	− 0.1	0.3	0.2	+ 0.1	2.7	2.5	+ 0.2
Total	100.0	100.0		100.0	100.0		100.0	100.0		100.0	100.0	

[a] 10 years and over in 1901. [b] Excluding Yukon and Northwest Territories; including Newfoundland in 1961. [c] Excluding those on active service, June 1941. [d] Except those in Primary. [e] Less than 0.05% but not empty category. [f] Empty category.
Source: Ostry (1967: Table 2).

Table 7-8

Percentage Distribution of the Labour Force by Occupation Division and Sex, Canada, 1971.

	Percentage		
	Male	**Female**	**Difference**
Managerial, administrative, and related	5.5	2.0	+ 3.5
Natural sciences, engineering and mathematics	3.8	0.6	+ 3.2
Social sciences and related	0.9	1.0	− 0.1
Religion	0.4	0.1	+ 0.3
Teaching and related	2.4	7.1	− 4.7
Medicine and health	1.5	8.2	− 6.7
Artistic, literary, recreational and related	1.0	0.7	+ 0.3
Clerical and related	7.7	31.7	− 24.0
Sales	10.0	8.4	+ 1.6
Service	9.2	15.1	− 5.9
Farming, horticultural, and animal husbandry	7.2	3.6	+ 3.6
Fishing, hunting, trapping and related	0.5	_a	+ 0.5
Forestry and logging	1.2	_a	+ 1.2
Mining and quarrying	1.0	_a	+ 1.0
Processing	4.9	2.0	+ 2.9
Machining and related	4.0	0.5	+ 3.5
Product fabricating, assembling, and repairing	8.5	5.1	+ 3.4
Construction trades	9.9	0.2	+ 9.7
Transport equipment operating	5.8	0.3	+ 5.5
Materials handling and related	2.9	1.4	+ 1.5
Other crafts and equipment operating	1.7	0.5	+ 1.2
Occupations n.e.c.	2.6	0.7	+ 1.9
Occupations not stated	7.4	10.8	− 3.4
Total	100.0	100.0	

a Less than 0.05% but not empty category.
Source: Derived from *1971 Census of Canada*, Cat. 94-717.

classification of occupations into sets of categories defined in terms of some combination of type of work and social standing (as in Tables 7–4 and 7–5), or upon the location of occupations relative to one another in a hierarchy of social standing (e.g., Blishen, 1967; Blishen and McRoberts, 1976). Although there is nothing inherently wrong with either of these practices, they do not exhaust the useful ways in which occupations can be described. In particular, they do not permit any clear analysis of occupations in terms of the kinds of tasks or skills which they involve and, thus, of their relative locations in the *technical division of labour*.

As an approach to the analysis of occupations in the technical division of labour, a typology was developed which takes as its basis judgments of the task or skill requirements of occupations originally provided by a panel of experts and made available in the *Census of Canada Directory of Occupations*, using the statistical technique of factor analysis (Manley and Hunter, 1980; Hunter, 1980a). This typology allows occupations to be described relative to one another in terms of eight distinct, but related, dimensions of the requirements of work. These dimensions are:

1. *Cognitive skills:* the extent to which an occupation requires its incumbents to exercise verbal, quantitiative, and general intellectual skills. This is close to what was referred to in Chapter 4 as "style/ability." (Sample occupation, i.e., one which ranks high on this dimension: lawyer.)

2. *Routinization:* the degree to which an occupation involves standardized, repetitive activities. (Sample occupation: assembly-line worker.)

3. *Authority:* the extent to which an occupation requires those in it to exercise legitimate power over others and to supervise their work. (Sample occupation: factory manager.)

4. *Verbal skills:* the degree to which an occupation involves talking and listening to others. (Sample occupation: social worker.)

5. *Physical skills and strength:* the extent to which an occupation requires those in it to move about, lift heavy objects, and so on. (Sample occupation: farm labourer.)

6. *Manipulative skills:* the degree to which an occupation requires physical (e.g., hand and finger) dexterity. (Sample occupation: tailor.)

7. *Social skills:* the extent to which an occupation involves sustained and complex dealings with people. (Sample occupation: realtor.)

8. *Artistic skills:* the degree to which an occupation requires creativity. (Sample occupation: musician.)

When men and women are compared in terms of the task requirements of their occupations, it turns out that there are real differences between them in the work which they do for pay. Specifically, the occupations of men rank higher on the average in physical skills and strength, while those of women rank higher in routinization and manipulative and social skills. Contrary to what one might expect, perhaps, they did not differ in terms of cognitive skills, authority, verbal skills, or artistic skills, although a more refined comparison might reveal some more subtle differences in these dimensions as well. Women are heavily concentrated in elementary school teaching and nursing, for example, which are both high on the authority dimension, although the authority involved in them is quite different from that involved in managing a business firm.

Income

On the average, Canadian men who are employed earn about twice as much as employed women earn, as the data in Table 7-9 show — in 1970 some $6,574 for men, as opposed to $3,199 for women (see, also, Ambert, 1976; Armstrong and Armstrong, 1978). There is little detailed historical information on male–female income differentials in Canada, although what evidence there is suggests that the gap between men and women in their real earnings has widened slightly in the period since World War II (Gunderson, 1976:120) — despite the advent of legislation in recent years whose manifest purpose it is to ensure equal pay for equal work.

Table 7–9

Average Incomes for Males and Females 15 Years and Over Who Worked in 1970, by Occupation Division, for Canada, 1971.

Occupation Division	Average Income		Female as Percentage of Male
	Male	Female	
Managerial, administrative, and related	$13,407	$6,135	45.8%
Natural sciences, engineering, and mathematics	8,905	4,750	53.3
Social sciences and related	10,971	4,441	40.5
Religion	4,738	3,065	64.7
Teaching and related	9,014	5,401	59.9
Medicine and health	14,175	4,135	29.2
Artistic, literary, recreational, and related	6,545	3,274	50.0
Clerical and related	5,823	3,391	58.2
Sales	7,120	2,285	32.1
Service	5,276	1,954	37.0
Farming, horticultural, and animal husbandry	3,321	1,541	46.4
Fishing, hunting, trapping, and related	3,340	1,669	49.9
Forestry and logging	4,544	1,668	36.7
Mining and quarrying	6,966	4,577	65.7
Processing	5,957	2,563	43.0
Machining and related	6,695	3,263	48.7
Product fabricating, assembling, and repairing	6,402	2,828	44.2
Construction trades	6,175	3,708	60.0
Transport equipment operating	6,190	2,722	44.0
Materials handling, not elsewhere classified	5,141	2,551	49.6
Other crafts and equipment operating	7,528	3,122	41.5
Not elsewhere classified	4,496	2,603	57.9
Not stated	5,418	2,794	51.6
Total	6,574	3,199	48.7

Source: Derived from *1971 Census of Canada*, Cat. 94–768.

One reason for the large difference between men and women in their incomes is, of course, that they work at different jobs. Large differences remain,

Table 7-10

Average Incomes for Males and Females 15 Years and Over Who Worked Full-Time in 1970, by Selected Occupational Title for Canada, 1971.

| | Average Income | | Female as Percentage |
Occupational Title	Male	Female	of Male
Physicians and surgeons	$28,896	$14,965	51.7%
Civil engineers	12,786	9,941	77.7
Secondary school teachers	10,100	8,529	84.4
Real estate salesmen	8,609	6,095	70.8
Secretaries and stenographers	8,562	4,884	57.0
Social workers	8,532	7,733	90.1
Sheet metal workers	7,582	4,862	64.1
Truck drivers	6,796	4,712	69.3
Telephone operators	6,315	4,379	69.3
Service station attendants	4,597	3,026	65.8

Source: *1971 Census of Canada*, Cat. 94-767.

however, when men and women are compared within broad occupational categories, as one can see from the third column of Table 7-9. Women in mining and quarrying and religious occupations fared the best relative to men in income, while women in medicine and health and sales jobs fared the worst. But these occupational categories contain a wide range of jobs which vary enormously in their incomes, and men and women are not equally distributed among the jobs within them. In addition, men are more likely to be employed full-time over the span of the entire year than are women, and this no doubt contributes to the differences between them in their incomes. Table 7-10 shows the average incomes for men and women working in full-time in a selected set of specific occupations in order to give us some idea of male–female income differentials for people in the same jobs who worked approximately the same amount of time in a year. While female income as a percentage of male income is considerably higher than in the previous comparison, it still varies from a low of slightly more than 50 per cent for physicians and surgeons to a high of around 90 per cent for secretaries and stenographers and social workers. There is obviously more to sex disparities in income than either occupation or time on the job. In fact, Podoluk argues full-time employment and occupation "are likely to explain away less than half of the gap that exists" (1968:69; also see Goyder, in press; Ambert, 1976: Chapter 7; Robson and Lapointe, 1971).

In a more recent analysis of men and women in the technical division of labour (Hunter, 1980a), an overall difference of $5,873 (or 54.6 per cent) was found in favour of men over women in annual earnings among a sample of Canadians employed full-time in 1977. A small part of this difference was a consequence of the difference between men and women in the skills involved in their occupations (see above). And a large part of it derived from the fact that equal skills did not always command equal pay. Specifically, the men were paid more for cognitive, verbal, and physical skills and strength, while the women were better paid for authority and manipulative skills. When men and women were compared as if the women had occupations identical in skills to those of the men, the income difference between them was only reduced to $4,144 (or a 47.8 per cent male advantage). It turned out, then, that a $729 annual earnings differential (i.e., $5,873-5,144) between men and women occurred from their having occupations with different skill requirements, while a $5,144 differential resulted from their being paid less for doing work of comparable skill.

Case Study: On Women in Electoral Federal Politics[2]

Canadian women first won the right to vote in elections and run for office at the federal level in 1918, and the general election of 1921 was the first occasion in which they exercised these rights. The result was the election of the first female Member of Parliament — Agnes McPhail, representing the United Farmers of Ontario. In the intervening years, however, very few women have followed in her path. Between 1921 and 1970, a total of only 18 women sat in the House of Commons, and the number elected in 1964 was exactly the same as that elected in 1921, namely, one. The trend has been in the direction of the increasing representation of women on the federal scene, with five elected in 1972, eight in 1974, 12 in 1979, and 14 in 1980 but, while it has been steady in recent years, it has been slow. And the situation in Canada has been broadly similar to that in the U.K., the U.S., and other western countries.

How is it that women have enjoyed so little success in electoral federal politics? Part of the reason may be that women are rarely nominated by the three major parties to contest seats in federal elections. In 1980, for example, only 23 of the 282 Liberal candidates were female, while the corresponding figures for the Progressive Conservatives and New Democrats were but 14 out of 282 and 33 out of 282, respectively. So, even in the improbable event that every single woman nominated to contest a seat in that year by one of these parties won, the House of Commons would still have been dominated by men by a ratio of 3:1.

What might account, then, for the fact that women are much less likely to be nominated to contest federal seats? This would appear to be partly because women are less involved than men in the central activities of the organizations of these parties, from riding associations to national conventions. Historically, for example, women have been involved in the Liberal and Progressive Conservative parties as members of separate, women's associations and, as a result, in a more

---

[2]   The research on this topic was carried out with Margaret Denton (see Denton and Hunter, 1980).

or less auxiliary capacity. And, while this has never been true of the New Democratic Party (or, formerly, of the Co-operative Commonwealth Federation), even here, as in the case of the Liberal and Progressive Conservative parties, women are vastly under-represented as delegates to national party conventions.

Beyond the fact of their peripheral involvement in the activities of the federal political parties, a further barrier to the nomination of women to contest seats is the belief that female candidates "lose votes." Among party regulars, that is, women tend to be seen as less attractive than men to the voters on election day. And this argument is apparently often used against women in their quest for nomination. But is it true? An attempt will be made to determine whether or not it is, using data from the 1979 and 1980 federal general elections.

A simple comparison of male and female candidates in the 1979 and 1980 Canadian general elections shows that the men considerably outdrew the women in the average number of votes received — 8,569 vs. 4,271 in 1979, and 7,995 vs. 3,515 in 1980. But this overlooks the fact that the women, far more than the men, were likely to have been the representatives of parties with little or no chance of winning, such as the Communist Party of Canada and the Communist Party (Marxist–Leninist). If we restrict our comparisons to the four parties with members elected to the House of Commons in 1979 (i.e., the three major parties, plus the Social Credit/Créditistes), the male–female contrast is considerably reduced. In 1979, the average was 12,007 vs. 9,429 votes; in 1980, it was 11,602 vs. 8,758 votes. Nevertheless, these are substantial margins in favour of men, and they require that we refine the analysis still further.

One refinement which might be made is to restrict our comparison to male and female candidates for particular political parties within each of several regions in the country. We know, for example, that the Liberal and Progressive Conservative parties are far more likely to elect members than either the New Democratic or Social Credit/Créditiste parties. For this reason, coupled with the fact that women are more likely to be nominated by the New Democratic Party than by any of the other three major parties, it makes best sense to compare Liberal men with Liberal women, Progressive Conservative men with Progressive Conservative women, and so on. Likewise, we know that the parties do not fare equally well across the country. The Liberal party, for example, generally sweeps Quebec, except for a couple of seats; the Progressive Conservatives tend to do best in the West; the New Democratic Party is most successful in Ontario and the West; and the Social Credit/Créditistes have only elected members from Quebec since the mid-1960s. Consequently, it would seem best to compare male and female candidates within particular party/region combinations (e.g., Liberal men in the Atlantic region with Liberal women in the Atlantic region, Progressive Conservative men in the West with Progressive Conservative women in the West, and so on). Finally, it turns out that women are much more likely to be nominated to contest seats in large, urban ridings than in small, rural ones. Since candidates in large ridings ought to receive more votes on the average than candidates in small ridings, the comparisons which follow have been adjusted to reflect this fact.

In 1979, four party/region combinations showed significant male-female vote differentials. These were Liberals/Ontario, Progressive Conservatives/Ontario, New Democrats/Ontario, and Progressive Conservatives/West. Moreover, in each of these cases, it was the male candidates who received more votes, ranging from an average of 7,830 more votes than their female counterparts for Progressive Conservative candidates in the West, to an average of 2,393 more votes for Liberal candidates in the West, to an average of 2,393 more votes for Liberal candidates in Ontario. In 1980, there were six party/region combinations which showed significant male-female vote differentials: Liberals/Ontario, Progressive Conservatives/Ontario, New Democrats/Ontario, Progressive Conservatives/West, and Social Credit/West. Thus, it would appear as if female candidates do operate at a considerable disadvantage relative to males in their vote-getting power. But, then again, does it?

While the female disadvantage indicated above is real enough, it does not take into account the possibility that females tend disproportionately to be nominated to contest so-called "suicide seats," that is, seats in which the party they represent has little or no chance of winning. If this phenomenon occurs, it could be that the pattern of male advantage which has shown up so far is in fact a self-fulfilling prophecy. That is, women may be being systematically placed in ridings where they can only fare poorly, but their poor showings are interpreted as instance where women "lose votes." In order to test for this possibility, the results for 1980 were re-analysed, taking into account the size of the margin of victory (or loss) in the 1979 election. This was done by adjusting the 1980 results to take into account that female candidates for the Liberal and Progressive Conservative parties (but not for the New Democratic Party) in the 1980 election were actually disproportionately nominated to contest ridings which their party had lost by large margins in 1979. When this adjustment was made, the pattern of male advantage disappeared, to be replaced by a pattern of two fairly strong female advantages (Liberals/Atlantic, Progressive Conservatives/Atlantic), three weaker male advantages (New Democrats/Ontario, New Democrats/West, Social Credit/West), and the remainder of the male–female differences apparently insignificant.

The evidence, then, seems to point to the organizations of the federal political parties as the immediate source of the extreme under-representation of women in the House of Commons, rather than to any sentiments in the electorate which are translated into votes for men rather than women on election day. In general, women are relegated to secondary roles within these organizations and this, reinforced by the belief that they lose votes, makes it especially difficult for them to secure party nominations. And, once nominated, they are much more likely than men to be sacrificed in suicide seats, with the significant exception of those women nominated to contest seats for the New Democratic Party.

Case Study: On Gender and Social Position in a Nineteenth-Century Roman Catholic Parish

Although data on a wide variety of different topics are fortunately available in carefully tabulated form in published sources or readily accessible on magnetic tapes in data banks, there are many subjects for which no information can be found in such places. Sometimes it may never have existed in the first place; sometimes it may have been lost or destroyed; and sometimes it just may not exist in a form which we easily recognize as "data." In these instances, a bit of extra effort can occasionally yield answers to questions which would otherwise be left only to speculation.

Cemeteries are a seldom-used data source in sociology, and yet they contain a wide variety of potentially useful information which may not be available elsewhere. Often, this information can be obtained from official cemetery files and, in any case, these files will generally provide the means to map the location of each plot, along with at least some information about the person interred there. Sometimes, however, the files will be incomplete or the kind of information desired will not be normally recorded, in which case it can sometimes be gotten only through a systematic inspection of each gravesite. As an illustration of this type of research, a small-scale pilot study was conducted in a cemetery.

One of the purposes of the pilot study was to assess the possibility of using a measure of the size of grave markers as an indicator of the social position of individuals in nineteenth-century Canada. The height of the marker was chosen to be used in this way, since it serves to show an important element of the overall size of a marker, and because relative height has a fairly general significance in social inequality. According to the aphorism, for example, the most desirable men are "*tall,* dark and handsome"; the rich often locate their homes so that they overlook those of the poor; and the very imagery of social "stratification" itself is one of some individuals, families, or groups standing higher or lower than others. At the same time, if it is found that socially dominant categories or groups in nineteenth-century Canada did tend on the average to have higher grave markers than others, this will be mainly useful for research into earlier historical periods, since modern cemeteries typically place restrictions on the size and shape of the plaques and stones which mark the places of the dead.

To simplify the analysis, a Roman Catholic cemetery was chosen, so that the data gathered would describe the members of a relatively homogenous population. And, to make the task somewhat more manageable, the cemetery selected was not very large, containing about one thousand gravesites. The cemetery is attached to the one Roman Catholic parish in a middle-sized (c. 20,000) city in southern Ontario. In the mid-nineteenth-century period under investigation, the parishioners were largely of German descent, with a sprinkling of eastern Europeans and Irish. Because the research was restricted to a single cemetery in a single city and involved Roman Catholics, no conclusions can be drawn which strictly apply to other people elsewhere, although the utility of the research would be greatly enhanced if the conclusions drawn can be shown to be more generally applicable.

Since women in nineteenth-century Canada, no less than in the twentieth, occupied a social position which was subordinate to that of men, perhaps this is reflected in the relative heights of the grave markers of men and women. Restricting the analysis to only those persons who died in or before the year of Confederation, it was found that these heights did differ in the predicted direction. On the average, the grave markers of women were 47.9 inches, while the corresponding figure for men was 51.5 inches, with a total of fifty-eight women and fifty-three men included in the study. This difference of 3.6 inches in favour of men is small overall, but it masks a pattern of male–female differences which appears to vary somewhat by ethnic group, although the number of non-Germans was quite small (twenty-seven of a total of one hundred and eleven). Among those with what appeared to be German surnames, along with those of apparent Slavic ancestry, the pattern of male advantage was replicated. Among those of apparent Irish background, however, it was not. On the average, the Irish women had *higher* grave markers than the Irish men. While the reason for this is not obvious, it could have to do with some combination of a more authoritarian family structure among continental Europeans, coupled with the very low status of the Irish in pre-Confederation Canada. Often women occupy an elevated position in disadvantaged racial and ethnic groups as, for example, in the case of black Americans.

Summing Up

In Canada, then, there is a pronounced and far-reaching system of gender inequalities in which men are favoured relative to women. Although men and women do not differ much overall in their levels of educational attainment and whatever changes there have been in this have been slow, they differ considerably (if decreasingly) in the kinds of education which they receive and in the likelihood of attending and graduating from university. Men are more likely to be educated to take on a job and to obtain university training, while those women who are trained to move into the labour force tend to specialize in a relatively small number of areas which are extensions of traditional household tasks, such as teaching, nursing, and the like. Men are much more likely to take on paid employment than women are, although the labour force participation rates of married women have risen sharply in recent decades. And, among those men and women who work for pay, there are large differences between the sexes in the kinds of jobs which they have. Men tend to be distributed across the entire spectrum of occupational possibilities, while women are highly segregated into a small number of sex-typed, "female" occupations, although the phenomenon of sex segregation in the occupational structure has slowly, but progressively, decreased in the period of the present century. Finally, women earn substantially less than men do, even when comparisons between the sexes are restricted to persons working full-time in identical jobs.

The fact of a system of gender inequalities such as that which obtains in Canada poses important issues for social theory. For one thing, what are the likely origins of this system? For another, what factors appear to maintain it or change it over time? Prior to attempting to answer such questions, however, it might prove useful to describe some other systems of inequalities which are often characterized as similar to the system of gender inequalities, most notably ethnic inequalities and inequalities arising out of people's social backgrounds. Thus armed, we may be in a better position to determine what it is that lies beyond merit.

Chapter 8

Ethnic Inequalities

"Much can be done with a Scotsman if he be caught young"
(Dr. Johnson).

"It isn't easy being green" (Kermit the Frog).

One of the most popular and evocative images of Canada is that of a society which is a "vertical mosaic" of ethnic groups (Porter, 1965). In the "melting pot" of the United States, successive waves of immigrants are typically portrayed as having entered the society at the bottom of the hierarchy of inequality, only to assimilate to the dominant culture over time and eventually to meld as individuals into its major institutions. The Canadian mosaic, on the other hand, is usually described as consisting of culturally distinct ethnic groups occupying different niches in the overall system of social inequality. First among these groups historically are those of French origin, who originally settled under the auspices of France in what is now Nova Scotia, and later established the French colony in Quebec which became the major locus of the Francophone group in Canada (Morris and Lanphier, 1977: Part II). Second among them are those of British origin, who originally came to Canada as part of Britain's effort to colonize and control this part of North America for itself, and who remain the dominant Anglophone ethnic group.

Confederation brought the French and the British charter groups together to form a single country with two official languages and two distinct, but inter-dependent, sets of institutions. The societies and cultures of the aboriginal peoples of Canada — the Indians and the Inuit — have been almost completely destroyed through contact with the dominant European groups, whose numerical, economic, technological, and military superiority left the Indians and Inuit dispossessed of their original lands, largely confined to isolated reservations with limited natural resources, and in a condition of impoverishment and economic dependence.

Unlike the U.S., where large-scale immigration ended in the 1920s, Canada has had a continuing, if uneven, stream of immigrants from many other countries which has transformed it into a diverse and multicultural nation (Richmond, 1967). The vast majority of these immigrants have either been from English-speaking countries or have taken English as their new tongue in the New World, leaving the Francophone group to grow largely through a surplus of births over deaths (Joy, 1972).

While immigration to Canada has never really ceased, it has varied in volume over time, with the two peak periods having been between 1901 and 1921 and between 1951 and the present. And there have been important changes in immigration policies over time as well which have led to very different mixtures of people entering the country in different periods (Bienvenue, 1975). Although there has historically been a strong preference for persons of British origin and from northern and western European countries as immigrants to Canada, the decision to open up and populate the agricultural areas of the West in the early years of the present century led to an influx of southern and eastern Europeans, most notably Ukrainians, Poles, and Russians. They were, for the most part, rural people with little formal education, and there was no requirement that they speak either French or English as a condition of their immigration. By contrast, immigrants to Canada in the period following World War II have tended to be better-educated and more highly-skilled, and have been required to have some prior knowledge of one or the other of the two official languages — consequences, no doubt, of the evolution of the Canadian economy over time from agricultural to industrial. And, even more recently, Canadian immigration policies have been revised to allow people entrance to the country on the basis of such criteria as education, occupation, and the likelihood of employment, without reference to such matters as citizenship. As a result of this change, increasing numbers of non-Europeans have come to Canada from India, Pakistan, Hong Kong, the West Indies, Uganda (the Ugandan Asians), (most recently) Cuba, and elsewhere, settling mainly in the three largest cities of Toronto, Montreal, and Vancouver. Although the number of persons with managerial, professional, and technical training has increased in this latter period, the overall skill levels of this most recent wave of immigrants seem to be somewhat lower than before (Canada, 1974b).

Through the changing processes of natural increase and in- and out-migration over the span of three hundred years, the ethnic composition of Canada has been continuously transformed (Kubat and Thornton, 1974:25–27). In 1901, the two charter groups accounted for about 88 per cent of the total population. By 1971, this figure had dropped to around 73 per cent, and it is likely to continue to drop. The French have more or less maintained their relative representation in the population in the twentieth century, dropping from 31 per cent in 1901 to just under 29 per cent in 1971. At the same time, their birth rate has fallen dramatically in recent years, and this, coupled with negligible immigration from French-speaking countries, is likely to result in a significant decline in their representation in the future. The British constitute a declining plurality of the Canadian population, falling from 57 per cent in 1901 to just under 45 per cent in 1971. Members of noncharter groups have, thus, increased their relative representation over the past seventy-five years or so from about 12 to 27 per cent. The largest of these groups are those of German origin, who made up just over 6 per cent of the population in 1971, followed in turn by Italians (between 3 and 4 per cent), Ukrainians (just under 3 per cent), and persons from the Netherlands (2 per cent). The remainder, about 13 per cent, belong to a large number of other groups, including Canadian Indians (just over 1 per cent) and the Inuit (about .1 per cent), no one of which makes up more than 2 per cent of the total population.

If Canada is a nation of diverse ethnic groups, it is not, however, a nation of immigrants, even though immigration has been and remains an important source of population increase, and there are currently more foreign-born persons in the country than ever before. In 1971, just under 15 per cent of the Canadian population were foreign-born. In 1901, the figure stood at 13 per cent, reached a peak of about 22 per cent in 1911, remained at about that level until 1931, dropped to just over 17 per cent in 1941, and has not changed much since that time (Kalbach and McVey, 1971:133).

Education

Members of different ethnic groups have continued to differ over the years in their rates of educational participation, as the data in Table 8–1 show, with Jews standing above, and Indians and Inuit standing below, the other groups considered here. At the same time, all of these groups have shared in the overall process of educational upgrading which has taken place in Canada in the post-war period, although not all to the same extent. In general, there has been a diminution in the differences among these groups over time, with those in the relatively disadvantaged groups (most notably Indians and Inuit and Italians) making higher gains than the others, and those in the relatively advantaged groups (especially Jews and the British) making the lowest gains of all. This

Table 8–1

Number of Persons 5 Years and Over Attending School Full-Time as Percentage of Persons 5–24 Years for Selected Ethnic Groups, Canada, 1951 and 1971.

	1951	1971	Change: 1951–1971
British	56.1%	71.0%	+14.9%
French	49.0	66.4	+17.4
German	53.7	70.6	+16.9
Italian	46.2	67.4	+21.2
Jewish	61.3	71.8	+10.5
Ukrainian	52.8	70.5	+17.7
Indian and Inuit	42.1	65.3	+23.2
Total	52.8	69.4	+16.6

Source: Derived from *1951 Census of Canada*, vol. II. Table 51 and *1971 Census of Canada*, Cat. 92–742

Table 8–2

Percentage of the Population 15 Years of Age and Over Not Attending School by Highest Level of Schooling and Ethnic Group, Canada 1971

	British	French	German	Italian	Jewish	Ukranian	Indian and Inuit
Less than 9 Years	27.0	48.4	37.0	66.0	25.6	44.1	69.1
9-13 Years	61.9	44.5	53.8	29.4	49.5	47.8	29.0
Some University	5.9	3.7	5.0	2.9	11.1	4.4	1.4
University Degree	5.2	3.4	4.2	1.7	13.8	3.7	0.5
Total	100.0	100.0	100.0	100.0	100.0	100.0	100.0

Source: Derived from *1971 Census of Canada,* Cat. 92-743.

pattern largely reflects the fact that the relatively disadvantaged groups have improved their rates of educational participation at the primary and secondary school levels, whereas the relatively advantaged ones have had high (but still increasing) rates of primary and secondary school participation throughout this period. The improvement registered by members of the latter has disproportionately occurred at the level of post-secondary education, and Indians and Inuit, in particular, have yet to find their way in any numbers into post-secondary educational institutions. In 1970/71, for example, full-time university enrolment as a percentage of the age group 15-24 for Canada as a whole was about 7.5 per cent, while the corresponding figure for Indians and Inuit was 3.3 per cent. For this reason, the data in Table 8–1 may not provide the most sensitive measure of differences in educational participation among these groups, since the most important differences are probably those among the higher age groups.

The levels of educational attainment of the various ethnic groups shown in Table 8–2 can be seen to be largely the consequence of the changing patterns of educational participation observed above, except that the Italians place slightly lower than one might otherwise expect. At the top are the Jews, followed at some distance by the British. Next come the Germans, with the French and the Ukrainians somewhat lower down, and the Italians considerably behind all three. Last are the Indians and Inuit.

Employment and Occupations

Of the groups considered here, the Jews were least likely to report having no income in 1971, followed in turn by the British, Ukrainians, Germans, Italians, French, and Indians and Inuit. The first four groups fell below the national unemployment average, while the Italians matched it, and the last two fell considerably above it. While the Ukrainians fared rather better in this regard than one would have expected, the major anomaly here would seem to be the relatively poor showing of the French.

Members of the several ethnic groups considered here differ, as well, in the kinds of jobs they have. In general, Jews, along with the British, are over-represented in white-collar jobs, while members of the other groups are under-represented in varying degrees. This basic pattern has been maintained over a period of many years, as the data in Table 8–3 show, although the historical trend has been in the direction of *decreasing* intergroup differences (Darroch, 1979). Still, Jews and those of British origin have increased over time their hold on white-collar jobs at the expense of the other groups. Table 8–4 brings these data up to date using the occupational categories of the *1971 Census of Canada.* If we use Jews as a kind of baseline group for 1971, since they are the most favoured in their occupational distribution, the differences between them and the British are such that, in order for the two distributions to match, a minimum of 32.8 per cent of the British (or of the Jews) would have had to move from one occupational division to another. Continuing the comparison, and retaining Jews as the point of reference, the corresponding figures for the remaining groups turn out to be 42.4 for the Germans, 50.4 for the Italians, 41.3 for the Ukrainians, and 61.0 for the Indians and Inuit. Relative to the group with the firmest grip on what are generally the better jobs, then, the British have the most similar occupational distribution, followed in turn by the French, the Ukrainians, the Germans, the Italians, and the Indians and Inuit.

This occupational ordering is essentially the same as the ordering for the seven groups on educational attainment, which suggests that at least some of the differences among the groups in their occupational distributions can be traced back to differences among them in their levels of education. In a comparative analysis of the relative positions of the British and the French in the occupational structure, the Royal Commission on Bilingualism and Bicultur-alism observed that, if the labour force of French origin had a level of education equivalent to the British, the differences in the occupational distribution of the two groups would be reduced by about 60 per cent (Canada, 1969:47). Unfortunately, no comparable estimates exist for the other groups, although it is reasonable to assume that differences among them in education do account for some part of the differences among them in their occupational distributions. Even so, it is also reasonable to assume that, as in the case of the British and the French, equivalence in education does not always yield equivalence in occupation. If educational differences explain 60 per cent of the differences between the British and the French in their occupational distributions, this leaves a further 40 per cent unaccounted for.

Finally, it would be useful to analyse the contemporary positions of Anglophones relative to Francophones in terms of the skill requirements of their occupations, as was done earlier with men and women (Hunter, 1980a). When this is done, a pattern of very small differences emerges, with Anglophone men

Table 8-3

Occupational Distributions of Selected Ethnic Groups, Male Labour Force, Canada, 1931, 1951, and 1961.

	British	French	German	Italian	Jewish	Ukrainian	Indian and Inuit	Total
1931								
Professional and financial	6.4%	4.0%	2.6%	1.5%	7.0%	—	0.3%	4.8%
Clerical	5.3	3.0	1.6	1.3	3.9	—	0.1	3.8
Personal service	3.2	3.2	2.3	5.6	2.3	—	0.4	3.5
Primary and unskilled	13.1	21.0	12.2	43.8	3.2	—	63.0	17.7
Agriculture	31.0	34.1	55.0	6.4	1.6	—	29.1	34.0
All others	41.0	34.7	26.0	41.4	82.0	—	25.1	36.2
Total	100.0	100.0	100.0	100.0	100.0	—	100.0	100.0
1951								
Professional and financial	7.5	4.4	3.7	2.8	10.1	2.9%	0.7	5.9
Clerical	7.5	5.1	3.4	4.2	5.9	3.2	0.7	5.9
Personal service	3.1	3.2	2.2	5.4	2.0	5.4	2.8	3.4
Primary and unskilled	11.1	16.3	9.6	22.9	1.8	13.9	50.3	13.3
Agriculture	16.2	19.1	38.5	4.7	0.7	35.3	11.6	19.4
All others	54.6	51.9	42.6	60.0	79.5	39.3	23.9	52.1
Total	100.0	100.0	100.0	100.0	100.0	100.0	100.0	100.0
1961								
Professional and financial	10.6	6.7	6.8	3.4	16.0	5.8	1.1	8.6
Clerical	8.2	6.7	5.1	3.7	6.8	5.7	1.0	6.9
Personal service	3.4	4.1	3.6	7.2	1.9	7.3	5.6	4.3
Primary and unskilled	7.7	12.8	7.9	21.5	1.1	9.4	44.7	10.0
Agriculture	10.7	10.8	21.0	2.7	0.5	22.9	19.1	12.2
All others	59.4	58.9	55.6	61.5	73.3	48.9	28.5	58.0
Total	100.0	100.0	100.0	100.0	100.0	100.0	100.0	100.0

Sources: *1931 Census of Canada*, monograph 4, Table 67, and Vol. 7, Table 49; *1951 Census of Canada*, Vol. IV, Table 12; and *1961 Census of Canada*, Vol. 3.1-15, Table 21.

Table 8-4

Percentage of Male Force 15 Years and Over by Ethnic Group and Occupation Division, for Canada, 1971.

	British	French	German	Italian	Jewish	Ukrainian	Indian and Eskimo
Managerial, administrative and related	6.9	4.6	4.5	2.3	14.2	3.8	1.6
Natural sciences, engineering and mathematics	4.4	2.5	3.7	1.7	3.5	3.6	1.4
Social sciences and related	1.0	0.8	0.5	0.3	3.6	0.6	1.3
Religion	0.4	0.4	0.5	0.1	0.3	0.2	0.1
Teaching and related	2.5	2.5	2.3	1.1	3.5	2.4	0.7
Medicine and health	1.4	1.5	1.1	0.5	5.1	1.2	0.5
Artistic, literary, recreational and related	1.1	1.0	0.8	0.7	2.2	0.8	1.1
Clerical and related	8.6	8.1	5.6	4.8	8.8	6.7	3.0
Sales	11.1	9.3	9.0	6.9	27.5	8.3	2.3
Service	9.1	9.1	7.3	11.2	4.9	9.0	7.3
Farming, horticultural and animal husbandry	6.7	5.3	14.3	2.1	0.5	13.2	7.5
Fishing, hunting, trapping and related	0.6	0.4	0.2	0.0 a	0.0 a	0.1	3.0
Forestry and logging	0.9	1.9	0.7	0.3	0.0 a	0.6	8.9
Mining and quarrying	0.9	1.3	1.0	0.6	0.0 a	1.3	1.5
Processing	4.1	6.1	4.7	6.7	1.8	4.8	4.8
Machining and related	3.4	4.0	4.9	6.9	0.8	4.0	2.6
Product fabricating, assembling and repairing	7.7	9.0	9.4	12.0	7.8	8.7	4.1
Construction trades	8.6	10.2	11.8	22.2	2.6	10.0	13.7
Transport equipment operating	6.3	6.6	5.2	3.7	2.6	5.7	4.7
Materials handling, not elsewhere classified	3.1	2.6	2.9	3.2	0.9	3.6	3.9
Other crafts and equipment operating	2.0	1.7	1.4	0.9	0.8	1.4	0.9
Not elsewhere classified	2.3	3.0	2.1	4.4	1.3	2.7	4.4
Not stated	6.8	8.2	6.1	7.4	7.2	7.3	20.7
Total	100.0	100.0	100.0	100.0	100.0	100.0	100.0

Source: Derived from *1971 Census of Canada*, Cat. 94–734.
a Less than 0.0%, but not empty category.

tending to have occupations which are somewhat higher on the average in cognitive and artistic skills than those of Francophone men (author's own calculations, using data from a national sample gathered in 1977). In general, though, the two groups do not differ much overall in their relative locations in the technical division of labour and, although strictly comparable data do not exist on this issue for earlier historical periods, it is likely that this represents a real change from the (even fairly recent) past.

Income

The ethnic groups considered here also differ in their average income levels, as the data in Table 8–5 show. In terms of income, the Jews stand clearly above the rest, the Italians, the British, and the Germans are bunched together at some distance behind them, the French and the Ukrainians are next, and the Indians and Inuit trail far behind. While these ethnic income differences vary from province to province, the general pattern is everywhere similar.

Table 8–5

Average Incomes for Selected Ethnic Groups, Canada, 1971.

British	$5,162.06
French	4,710.59
German	5,087.67
Italian	5,219.32
Jewish	7,630.97
Ukrainian	4,636.63
Indian and Inuit	2,976.41
Total	5,033.27

Source: *1971 Census of Canada*, Cat. 99-709.

To a considerable extent, these ethnic differences in income can probably be explained in terms of differences among the various ethnic groups in their levels of educational attainment and occupational distributions. The evidence suggests, however, that, even when a large number of objective explanatory factors such as these are taken into account, some income differences may yet remain. Data from the early 1960s used by the Royal Commission on Bilingualism and Biculturalism (1969:77) showed, for example, that when people were equated in terms of levels of educational attainment, occupational distributions, under-employment (number of weeks worked in a year), age, region of residence, and industry, those of English–Scottish, Irish, and Northern European origins still seemed to get more than one would have otherwise expected; persons of French, Italian, and Eastern European origins got less; and Jews and Germans got about what one would have anticipated. Since the collection and analysis of the above data, Lanphier and Morris (1974) and Beattie (1975) have studied Anglophone–Francophone income differentials using more recent information. Lanphier and Morris found evidence to suggest that the overall gap has probably diminished somewhat over time, although the income disparities for workers in some occupations, most notably the lesser skilled, seem actually to have increased (see also Raynauld et al., 1967; Morris and Lanphier, 1975; Raynauld et al., 1975). In commenting on the effect of the Quiet Revolution, the authors conclude that:

> although it is now a commonplace that the middle class, and perhaps the skilled workers, are the main beneficiaries in terms of fresh employment opportunities, our data support the further argument that reductions in income inequality have been restricted to these same groups (Lanphier and Morris, 1974:65).

Beattie, on the other hand, found that the Anglophone–Francophone salary differential for his sample of middle-level bureaucrats in the federal public service during this same period had actually increased (1975:188).

Finally, in a more recent analysis, modest earnings gaps between full-time employed Anglophones and Francophones were found by the author (own calculations). Among men, the overall difference in annual income from employment was $1,104 (or 6.9 per cent) in the Anglophones' favour, while the comparable figure for women was $1,222 (or 12.3 per cent) — also in the Anglophones' favour. These differences can be seen to stem from differences between Anglophones and Francophones in the skill requirements of their occupations and in how they are remunerated for their skills. If Francophone men had occupations comparable in skills to those of Anglophone men, the Anglophone advantage in earnings would have been an insignificant $300 per year, while for women it would have been about $720 — significant, perhaps, but not substantial. At the same time, there were differences between the two groups in rates of pay for skills. Among the men, Anglophones got paid less for cognitive and physical skills and strength, while they were not penalized as heavily as Francophones for manipulative skills (which received negative rates of return!). Among the women, Anglophones got higher rates of pay for authority, while they were actually penalized for artistic skills and Francophones were not.

Case Study: Ethnic Background and Wealth

Although ethnic background may no longer be of profound significance for income, noting the exceptions mentioned above, the mechanisms by which great wealth is generated are not the same as those by which income is determined, so that there may be a relationship between ethnicity and wealth in the absence of any strong connection between ethnicity and income. Table 8-6 shows the cross-tabulation between ethnic background (British vs. French vs. Other) and estimated amount of wealth (100 million and over, 50–100 million, and 20–50 million) for families and individuals in Canada in the mid-1970s. In the case of wealth, the data have been taken directly from Newman (1975, 1979) and, since he does not document his sources, they should be regarded as tentative. As for ethnic background, the classification was based upon the ethnic origins of the people's names, using name dictionaries (e.g., Black, 1946; Reaney, 1958; MacLysaght, 1972; Cottle, 1978) since no other means were available for this purpose. If it were very accurate, this procedure would almost certainly over-estimate the number classified as British, given the tendency in this country for people to anglicize their names. On the other hand, name dictionaries are never complete, so that some unknown percentage of British or French names undoubtedly ended up in the Other category. Since the data are intended to be more illustrative than definitive, however, and only large ethnic differences will be treated as possible findings, it is likely that this imprecision is more an annoyance than a source of errors in interpretation.

Table 8–6

Wealth by Ethnic Background, Canada, c. 1975.

Wealth	Ethnic Background			Total
	British	French	Other	
100 million and over	56.0%	4.0	40.0	100.0
	(14)	(1)	(10)	(25)
50–100 million	60.5%	9.3	30.2	100.0
	(26)	(4)	(13)	(43)
20–50 million	52.6%	6.9	40.5	100.0
	(61)	(8)	(47)	(116)
Canadian population, 1971	44.6%	28.7	26.7	100.0

Source: Derived from Newman (1975, 1979) and *1971 Census of Canada.*

These data show a pattern of moderate British and Other over-representation among the very wealthy in Canada, along with considerable French under-representation. Relative to their numbers in the general population, the British are over-represented among the very wealthy by between 8 and 16 per cent, while the comparable figures for the Others are between about 3 and 14 per cent. And the French are under-represented by between 19 and 25 per cent.

Case Study: Ethnic Background and Social Position in a Nineteenth-Century Roman Catholic Parish

While the results of the earlier analysis of gender and social position suggested the potential utility of using the height of grave markers as an indicator of the latter variable, in studies of earlier historical periods, our confidence in this approach would be at least somewhat enhanced if more apparently successful examples of its use could be found. To that end, an attempt was made to replicate the analysis for ethnic groups. Since only people of apparent German, Irish, and Slavic descent were represented in any numbers at all in the small cemetery which was used to gather the data, only the results for these groups could possibly be meaningful. And the small numbers of Irish (sixteen) and Slavic (eleven) people represented render even comparisons among these three groups highly tentative. With this warning, however, we will proceed.

In pre-Confederation Canada, the Irish stood far below most of the other European groups in the system of social inequality. In southern Ontario, this included the Germans, but it is unclear where persons of Slavic origin would have been located in the hierarchy, as they were few in number. Consequently, if the grave marker measure is a fairly reliable and valid one, it should place the Irish measurably below the Germans and, if it does, we should have some small confidence that, whatever the results it yields for the Slavs, it is at least an indication of how they might have been located relative to the other two. For the Germans, their average grave height turned out to be 51.9 inches. The corresponding figure for the Irish was 36.9 inches. And the average for the Slavs was 46.1 inches. These would seem to be large average differences and, in the test case of the Germans vs. the Irish, in the predicted direction, with an average difference of fully 15 inches in favour of the Germans.

Case Study: Ethnicity and Home Ownership in Metropolitan Toronto

Using data originally gathered for a study by Richmond (1972), Hayward (1980) attempted to assess the extent to which ethnic differences in the probability of home ownership in Metropolitan Toronto reflected disparities among the various groups in economic resources or represented noneconomic, lifestyle or status group differences. Briefly, Richmond had earlier reported fairly large differences in the relative frequency of home ownership among five broad ethnic categories which he studied, although he attempted no detailed analysis of the factors involved in these. Expanding the number of ethnic groups, Hayward found that, of the groups included in the analysis, the Italians ranked highest in the probability of home ownership, followed, in turn, by the Poles, Ukrainians, Dutch, Other Slavic, Greeks, Portuguese, Jews, Germans, British, Hungarians, Scandinavians, and French Canadians. Some of these differences were small, however, although the Italians, Poles and Ukrainians clearly stood out above all the rest. When these groups were equated in terms of income, the differences among them in home ownership were to some extent magnified, rather than reduced. The reason for this was that, although families with high incomes were generally more likely to own homes than were families with low incomes within each ethnic group, it was the ethnic groups with the lowest incomes which were typically the most likely to own homes. Although the data were insufficient to test the hypothesis, Hayward speculates that home ownership is importantly a function of lifestyle differences. In the case of ethnic groups, it was the southern and eastern European groups which ranked highest in the probability of home ownership, and she suggests that this may be due to some combination of the influence of coming from cultures with rural, agrarian (perhaps peasant) traditions which emphasize the importance of the extended family as a social unit.

Summing Up

Three centuries of immigration, war, and politics have helped to create in Canada a diverse and multicultural country with a continuously changing system of ethnic inequalities. In terms of education, occupation, and income, it is generally the Jews who stand out above the rest *of the groups studied here* (an important qualification, since information is not always available for the full range of ethnic groups), while the Indians and Inuit lag far behind. And, in terms of wealth, the fact which stands out most prominently is the relatively poor position of Francophone Canadians. Still, the clear trend has been in the direction of progressively decreasing ethnic inequalities over time, although it can only take generations (as opposed to years or decades) for the system of ethnic inequalities in Canada to disappear altogether, if ever it will.

Chapter 9

Social Background and Social Inequality

"From clogs to clogs in four generations" (old Dutch proverb, cited in Goyder and Curtis, 1977).

Among the major concerns of Western sociology over the past several decades has been to identify the mechanisms by and to measure the extent to which the life-chances of parents span the gap of the generations to influence those of their children. In particular, there has been special interest in the question of the importance of an individual's socio-economic background for his or her subsequent educational and occupational attainment. The present chapter explores this question, along with a number of related issues involved in the accumulation of great wealth.

Some Basic Concepts

Let us begin by imagining a continuum along which all societies might be located in terms of the extent to which the positions in the overall system of social inequality occupied by people resemble those once occupied by their parents. This we will refer to as the continuum of *social inheritance*, and it is anchored at one end by those (undoubtedly hypothetical) societies in which everybody occupies exactly the same positions as their parents did (i.e., in which there is perfect positive inheritance) and at the other end by those societies in which everybody occupies positions which are as different as they can be from those their parents occupied (i.e., in which there is perfect negative inheritance). This continuum is represented by the horizontal line in Figure 9–1.

Having defined the continuum of social inheritance, even if only simplistically, it is fairly straightforward to introduce two additional concepts which are useful in characterizing certain aspects of systems of social inequality. The first of these is *social mobility*, or the amount of vertical movement which occurs in a system of social inequality from one generation to another. This is represented by the diagonal line in Figure 9–1. As this schematic representation shows, the amount of social mobility in a system decreases as the amount of social inheritance approaches the perfect positive (i.e., +1.0) end of the continuum. When inheritance is perfect and positive, social mobility is zero; when inheritance is perfect and negative, social mobility is maximized. And the second of these is *permeability* (Svalastoga, 1965), or the extent to which the locations

Figure 9-1   SCHEMATIC REPRESENTATION OF THE RELATIONSHIPS
AMONG STATUS INHERITANCE, SOCIAL MOBILITY, AND
PERMEABILITY

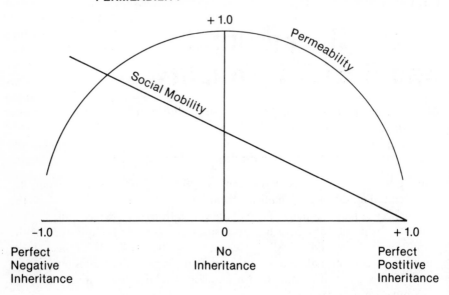

−1.0	0	+ 1.0
Perfect	No	Perfect
Negative	Inheritance	Postitive
Inheritance		Inheritance

of people in a system of social inequality are determined by the prior locations of
their parents in that system. This is represented by the parabola in Figure 9-1. As
the representation indicates, permeability reaches its maximum under
conditions of no social inheritance, and approaches zero as social inheritance
approaches the perfect (positive or negative) ends of the continuum.

Figure 9-1 shows something very useful about the inter-relationships
among social mobility, permeability, and social inheritance, namely that they do
not constitute three, independent pieces of information. In particular, if we
know how much social inheritance there is in a society, we can tell by that fact
alone how much social mobility is present and how permeable the society is.
Thus, under conditions of perfect, negative inheritance, mobility is maximized
and permeability minimized. This is a set of circumstances which corresponds to
no known societies current or past, but which might sometimes be approximated
in revolutionary situations where having come from a favourable social background is a source of stigma after the revolution and the low-born replace the
high-born. Where there is no social inheritance, social mobility is intermediate in
volume and permeability is maximized. This would occur, for example, where
people are randomly assigned to positions in the system of social inequality or
where people routinely rotate through the system (as on a volleyball team or in
sandlot baseball). And, finally, where there is perfect, positive social inheritance,
mobility and permeability are both minimized. Again, this set of circumstances
corresponds to no known societies, although it may sometimes be approximated
in certain countries ruled by small, hereditary elites. Because social mobility,

permeability, and social inheritance are related one to another by definition, as opposed to empirically, and because the first two can be expressed in terms of the third, the discussion which follows will largely be couched in terms of social inheritance in order to avoid confusion.

Societies in which people compete with one another under rules which apply equally to all and are rewarded according to their accomplishments (i.e., universalistic-achievement or meritocratic societies) would be highly permeable ones with intermediate levels of social mobility. Societies in which there are some rules for some people and other rules for others and people are rewarded not for their performances but for certain qualities which they may or may not possess (i.e., particularistic-ascription societies) would be highly impermeable, but may have very high, moderate, or low levels of mobility. Consequently, meritocracy is associated with permeability, rather than with mobility, although the assumption often made in the literature is that high levels of social mobility imply a meritocratic society. And maximum permeability implies an absence of social inheritance.

Educational and Occupational Inheritance

The few studies of social inheritance conducted in Canada have reported that anywhere from about one-sixth to about one-quarter of the differences among men (there being no studies published to date on women) in their levels of educational attainment can be shown to derive from differences among them in their socio-economic backgrounds (Turrittin, 1974; Cuneo and Curtis, 1975; McRoberts et al., 1976; also see Tepperman, 1975). The particular fraction varies from sample to sample and subgroup to subgroup, and should not be considered an important finding in and of itself. It also varies with the number and kind of variables used as indicators of socio-economic background, which sometimes makes it difficult to compare the results obtained in one study with those obtained in another. In general, the larger the number of socio-economic background variables taken into account, the stronger the relationship will be between these variables and one's level of educational attainment.

This inter-generational determination of educational attainment means that persons from relatively advantaged backgrounds tend to attain higher levels of education than persons from relatively disadvantaged backgrounds. In general, the data show that men whose fathers are well-educated and/or who have high-paying jobs with high educational requirements go farther on the average in school than do men whose fathers are less well-educated and/or who have lower status jobs. Where mother's education has been included in the analysis (e.g., Cuneo and Curtis, 1975), it has been found to have an additional effect upon educational attainment which is similar to that of father's education. These relationships, along with certain others to be discussed below, are often portrayed in path diagrams such as Figure 6–1.

With regard to the status of a man's first job upon entry into the labour market, father's education is related to occupational status, but only indirectly through its effect upon the individual's level of educational attainment

(Turrittin, 1974; Cuneo and Curtis, 1975; McRoberts et al., 1976). That is, men whose fathers are well-educated tend to move into the labour market in higher status jobs than do those men whose fathers are less well-educated, but the reason for this is that the former are themselves better-educated on the average than the latter. The status of the father's occupation, however, is related to the status of the individual's first job, both indirectly, through its effect upon the individual's level of educational attainment, and directly. That is, men at a certain level of education whose fathers have good jobs tend to move into better first jobs than do their equally well-educated counterparts whose fathers have lower status jobs. Still, the most important single variable influencing the status of an individual's occupation is his or her level of educational attainment. Taken together, father's occupational standing, father's education, and the individual's own education usually explain between one-quarter and one-half of the differences among men in the status of their first jobs.

When the status of a man's present job is considered, the most important determinants of this are his level of educational attainment and the status of his first job (Cuneo and Curtis, 1975; McRoberts et al., 1976). But socio-economic background is still important. The educational level of the father is related to the status of the son's present job, but only indirectly via its effect upon the educational level of the individual himself and the status of his first job. The status of the father's occupation, however, continues to have an impact, both indirectly and directly. When first job is added to a model of this kind to explain differences in present occupational status, the model usually explains anywhere from one-third to nearly two-thirds of the variation in present occupational status.

The facts of the inter-generational determination of inequality as they are revealed in such models are, then, undeniable. Even so, it is likely that they are underestimated in studies of the sort discussed here — incorporating, as they do, only a limited number of explanatory variables relating to family background. Anywhere from three-quarters to five-sixths of the differences among individuals in their levels of educational attainment, for example, are typically left unexplained in such studies, suggesting that they may either be caused by socio-economic background factors which have not been incorporated into such models (e.g., father's income, mother's education, occupation, and income — to name but a few of the more obvious ones) or that they are the consequence of other, nonsocio-economic family variables which have not been taken into account (e.g., inherited cognitive abilities, birth order, family size, parental values, etc.). When status of first job is considered, again, anywhere from one-half to three-quarters of the differences among individuals are not explained by the variables included in the models, and it could be that they, too, have causes which lie in people's family backgrounds and which will be uncovered when these models are expanded to include additional explanatory factors. And much the same could be true of that one- to two-thirds of the differences among men in present occupational standing which these models typically do not account for.

Some further reasons why the inter-generational determination of social inequality could be underestimated in status attainment models have to do with the manner in which the central variables of educational and occupational attainment have been conceived and measured. The focus in this research tradition has been on *level* of educational attainment and the status of occupations, even though there are other, perhaps equally important, aspects of education and occupation which could be studied. In the case of education, it is likely that the *type* of education which an individual receives (e.g., vocational, technical, or academic and, within each of these categories, still further distinctions) is determined in part by social background factors and, in turn, operates as an important element in the market signals which help locate people in jobs. As for occupation, very little attention has been paid to such matters as the task requirements of people's occupations, or the location of a person's occupation in the technical division of labour (e.g., the extent to which his or her occupation involves mental vs. manual labour, the amount of authority involved in the occupation, and so on), even though social background factors, such as the location of parental occupations in the technical division of labour, and the type of education a person has, could be important determinants of this. Occupations can be characterized in a large number of different ways, of which their status is only one, so that the tendency of sons and daughters to inherit high status occupations from their parents is only one kind of inheritance.

There are, as well, some problems in the measurement of occupational status which probably cause its inheritance from one generation to another to be underestimated and, more generally, which could result in occupation appearing to be more weakly tied to many other variables than is actually the case. Specifically, the status of occupations is generally measured using a procedure which begins with information concerning the average judgments of people of the desirability of each of a relatively small number of occupations. The evidence is, however, that there is often substantial disagreement among people on just how they see different occupations. To use but one typical example, a registered nurse received a national score of 64.7 in Pineo and Porter's (1967) study. This was, however, simply the average score across all of the respondents in the sample, whereas the data which Pineo and Porter present suggest that perhaps as many as one-third of the respondents gave this occupation a score of 86 or more or 44 or less.[1] Moreover, since Pineo and Porter's study included only about two hundred occupations, it cannot be used directly to provide scores for the full range of occupations. In order to do this, a technique is used which generates status scores for a large number of occupations based on the *average* educational and income levels of the persons in these occupations (e.g., Blishen, 1967; Blishen and McRoberts, 1976). But, since people in any occupation vary quite considerably in terms of their levels of education and income, a further source of error is introduced. As a consequence of these averaging errors, it is likely that the procedures used to characterize the status of occupations in most studies do not reflect very accurately people's perceptions of their status.

---

[1]   Assuming a normal curve.

While educational and occupational inheritance in Canada are real and probably under-estimated in existing studies, they are apparently strongest between adjacent generations and tend rapidly to weaken over time (Goyder and Curtis, 1977). In the case of occupational status, for example, having a well-placed father is a distinct advantage for a son. Having a well-placed grandfather, however, confers only small benefits. and having a well-placed great grand-father is of little or no advantage. At the same time, this is probably true of the bulk of the population, but not of the very wealthy and the most highly placed (Tepperman, 1975).

Inheritance of Wealth

Table 9–1 gives the names of those Canadians (sometimes families) in 1979 who had in excess of $100 million in wealth, the location of their Canadian base of operations, their probable present major source of wealth, and whether or not they received business inheritances at some time in their careers.

These data show that only a minority of the very richest people in Canada can easily be described as entirely "self-made." Of the twenty-one individuals and families listed in Table 9–1, fully fifteen are known to have been aided in their careers by business inheritances of one size or another. Some of these inheritances made their recipients instant millionaires (apparently including Howard Webster, the Eatons, Charles Rathgeb, Tomas Bata, W. Galen Weston, Kenneth Thomson, David Stewart, Maxwell Meighen, the Molsons, Nelson Davis, Charles Bronfman, George Richardson, and William Siebens). But others were much more modest (as in the cases of E.P. Taylor and Paul Demarais). Kenneth Thomson, for example, inherited the estate of his father, Lord Thomson of Fleet, upon the latter's death in 1976, including *The Times* of London, about two hundred other newspapers, and North Sea oil interests, among other things, while Paul Demarais was given a bus line with sixteen old buses by his father, debts of $340,000, and a franchise for transportation between Sudbury and the International Nickel Company operations (see Newman, 1975, 1979 for details).

Rich dad buys club for girl
By Marty York

Vancouver millionaire Nelson Skalbania, who bought the Atlanta Flames yesterday, has also purchased a Major Junior A hockey club for his 20-year-old daughter to run.

Mr. Skalbania, who will move the National Hockey League club to Calgary, recently placed a down payment of about $25,000 on New Westminster Bruins of the Western Hockey League.

The $325,000 purchase, to be completed on June 15, already has been ratified by the WHL's board of governors.

"Rosanda is as sharp as a whip and she has one of those crazy photographic memories," her father said from his Vancouver office yesterday. "She deserves the opportunity. She has always been interested in the operations of hockey organizations and it will be a learning experience for her."

He added that he may make his daughter

Table 9-1

Canadians with Wealth in Excess of $100 Million, Canadian Headquarters, Probable Present Major Source of Wealth, and Business Inheritance, 1979.

Name	Canadian Headquarters	Probable Present Major Source of Wealth	Business Inheritance
Tomas Bata	Toronto	Bata Ltd. (footwear)	Yes
Samuel Belzberg	Vancouver	First City Financial Corporation Ltd.	Unknown
Poldi Bentley	Vancouver	Canadian Forest Products Ltd.	Unknown
Charles Bronfman	Montreal	Distiller's Corporation-Seagram's Ltd.	Yes
Nelson Davis[1]	Toronto	N.M. Davis Corp. Ltd. (Arrow Leasing, etc.)	Yes
Paul Demarais	Montreal	Power Corporation (Montreal Trust, etc.)	Yes
Eaton Family	Toronto	Eaton's of Canada Ltd., T. Eaton Co. Ltd.	Yes
K.C. Irving	St. John	K.C. Irving Ltd. (oil refining, etc.)	Yes
Maxwell Meighen	Toronto	Canadian General Investments Ltd.	Yes
Molson Family	Montreal	Molson Industries Ltd. ("Molson Golden," etc.)	Yes
Charles Rathgeb	Toronto	Comstock International Ltd. (construction)	Yes
Reichmann Family	Toronto	Olympia and York Developments Ltd. (real estate developer)	Unknown
George Richardson	Winnipeg	James Richardson & Sons Ltd. (securities, etc.)	Yes
Stephen Roman	Toronto	Denison Mines Ltd. (uranium)	No
William Siebens	Calgary	Family sold Siebens Oil and Gas interest	Yes
David Stewart	Montreal	Sold Macdonald's Tobacco ("Export," etc.)	Yes
E.P. Taylor	Toronto	International Housing Ltd. (real estate developer)	Yes
Kenneth Thomson	Toronto	Thomson Newspapers Ltd. (*Globe and Mail*, etc.)	Yes
Howard Webster	Montreal	Burns Foods Ltd., Quebecair	Yes
G. Van Wielingen	Calgary	Sulpetro Ltd. (oil and gas)	Unknown

From *The Canadian Establishment* by Peter C. Newman. Reprinted by permission of The Canadian Publishers, McClelland and Stewart Limited, Toronto.
[1] Deceased, 1979.

an assistant administrator with his NHL operation.

Rosanda said she will attend all the WHL meetings as a member of the board of governors. "It's my intention to oversee the operation of the Bruins. I don't anticipate any difficulties."

"Remember," Mr. Skalbania said,

"Rosanda is only 20 so she won't be handling the actual hockey personnel. She won't be making any actual deals or trades.

"But I think I will be expecting her to look after the nickel-and-dime things. In other words she'll be in charge of the finances."

Rosanda said she will hire and fire managers and coaches. She offered the coaching job to the father of Edmonton Oilers' superstar Wayne Gretzky a few weeks ago but he turned down the offer.

"I'm seeking to have competent and professional help to assist Rosanda," Mr. Skalbania said.

Actually, Miss Skalbania will not be a raw rookie in a governing role of a hockey club.

"She was involved quite a bit in the operation of our bad team too," her father noted.

The "bad" team was the defunct World Hockey Association's Indianapolis Racers, where Rosanda, then a teen-ager, was employed as a front-office assistant.

WHL chairman Ed Chynoweth said he doesn't foresee any difficulties with Miss Skalbania as the only female governor in the league.

Chances are she will have a right-hand man of her own in New Westminster by retaining Ernie (Punch) McLean, team coach for the last decade. Mr. McLean was also co-owner of the Bruins. He and partner David Shinskie sold the club to Mr. Skalbania.

The New Westminster club was the Memorial Cup national junior hockey champion in 1977 and 1978.

The Globe and Mail, Toronto, May 24, 1980.

Educational and Occupational Inheritance by Ethnicity

At least prior to the Quiet Revolution, it was generally assumed that French Canada was a more traditional society than English Canada — late to industrialize, slow in rationalizing its system of education, less secular generally, and less mobility-oriented (Dofney and Rioux, 1964). In their study of Anglophone–Francophone mobility in Quebec, de Jocas and Rocher (1957) report evidence consistent with this characterization. They conclude that the channels and barriers of mobility that we have observed for the French-speaking are not the same as for the English-speaking Canadians. The former go up the scale step by step, while the latter seem to move more rapidly to the top occupational levels. It seems obvious that in the time since these data were gathered this situation has changed both within Quebec and without it, but the research necessary to demonstrate the change remains to be done. In general, the process of intergenerational inheritance seems broadly similar for Anglophones and Francophones. There is some suggestion in the available data that social background may be more strongly related to level of educational attainment among Francophone than among Anglophone males, and that, in particular, the impact of father's on child's education may be relatively greater among Francophones than among Anglophones (Cuneo and Curtis, 1975; McRoberts et al., 1976). But, beyond this, there seem to be no differences of consequence which have been found to obtain in more than a single study.

Changes Over Time

There is little evidence which might be used to make judgments as to changes over time in Canada in levels of social inheritance. McRoberts et al. (1976) present data which suggest that the relationship between father's occupational standing and son's occupational standing may have decreased somewhat over time for both Anglophones and Francophones, although it is likely that this change has come about largely as a function of changes in the occupational structure (see, for example, Hauser et al., 1975). As white-collar jobs have grown in relative importance and agricultural jobs have shrunk, a certain amount of mobility must necessarily occur since the sons of farmers have increasingly had to seek nonagricultural jobs, and persons have had to be recruited to fill the newly-opened white-collar jobs.

Comparisons With the U.S.

In comparing their results with those reported in a major study conducted in the U.S. (Blau and Duncan, 1967), Cuneo and Curtis (1975) were not able to conclude that the level of inter-generational inheritance in Canada was significantly different from that in the United States. The nature of the data, however, and the difficult problems involved in making precise comparisons of this kind prevented a more definitive statement. At the same time, Turrittin (1974) was led to conclude that Ontario, at least, had higher levels of social inheritance than were revealed in the Blau–Duncan data, although the data are actually ambiguous on this point. Finally, a comparison between the reported by Blau and Duncan and those reported by McRoberts et al. (1976) seems to reveal no real differences of consequence in levels of inheritance. There would seem to be no clear basis in this, then, to conclude that there are any differences in these matters between Canada and the U.S.

Summing Up

Although the data are not richly detailed, they show Canada to be characterized by a significant measure of positive social inheritance in education and occupational status and, hence, by low to intermediate levels of social mobility and less than maximal permeability (see Figure 9-1). Although these figures undoubtedly underestimate the amount of social inheritance and, thus, can be considered lower bounds to the true estimates, the findings are that between about one-sixth and one-quarter of the differences among men in their levels of educational attainment are inherited, while the corresponding figures for status of first job were between one-quarter and one-half. Although more precise analyses may subsequently show this to be otherwise, there is no good evidence to suggest that the phenomena of social inheritance are different among Anglophones than among Francophones or in Canada as compared with the U.S. Finally, it is clear that a disproportionate number of the very rich in Canada did not accumulate their fortunes entirely by themselves but, rather, received significant business inheritances along the way, although the data are insufficient to determine much more than simply that about the role of inheritance of wealth in this country.

Chapter 10

Beyond Merit:
Some Interpretations

We have seen that inequalities by gender, ethnicity, and social background all exist in Canada (Chapters 7–9). And we have also seen that these phenomena cannot be given easy interpretation in terms of a simple model of merit in many cases. Men and women with equivalent educational preparation, for example, do not on the average have equivalent occupations, and substantial income differences between the sexes remain, even after the influences of education and occupation have been accounted for. Although they have progressively diminished over time, some large gaps still exist among at least certain ethnic groups in educational, occupational, and income attainment. And coming from a privileged social background appears to confer real benefits upon people in terms of education, occupation, and wealth. To what extent, then, do these phenomena lie beyond merit? And, to the extent that they do, what is there beyond merit which might give rise to them and cause them to persist? The present chapter attempts to give at least some tentative answers to these questions.

On Gender Inequalities

Education, Occupation, and Income

An important element underlying the different educational experiences of men and women is that, from an early age, males and females are socialized to very different roles (Ambert, 1976: Chapter 5; Fischer and Cheyne, 1978). Most young girls are prepared for an adulthood in which their major functions will involve household work and child care and, while they may increasingly realize that they are likely to be employed both before and after they marry and have children, they learn to think of themselves as future wives and mothers, with attachments to family more important for them than attachments to career (Canada, 1977:128; Breton, 1972a:129; Porter et al., 1973:Chapter IV), although this may be somewhat more true of girls from lower than from higher socio-economic backgrounds (Gaskell, 1975). Most young boys, however, are raised in anticipation that they will be employed throughout much of their adult lives, and that this employment will be the major source of the income required to maintain themselves and their families in a comfortable style of life. For them, family will be important, to be sure, but career may be even more so. Consequently, parents less often think that their female children ought to or will go on to higher education, and they are less often willing to provide financial assistance for them to do so. In light of this, it is hardly surprising to find that girls tend to have lower educational aspirations and expectations than boys (Porter et al., 1973:Table 4.2). Moreover, when the time comes, girls probably find it more difficult to obtain part-time and summer jobs which pay well, and which might be a source of funds to assist them in education beyond high school. And, since they marry at an earlier age than men, and they are expected to take the major responsibility for household work and child care in the sexual division of labour within the family, many more women than men must tailor their educational participation to fit their family lives, rather than the other way around.

Because of the different roles males and females learn to take on, too, it makes sense that they would tend to pursue rather different courses of study in the later years of high school, in community college, and in university. Those areas in which women have long been over-represented relative to men are most often extensions into formal education of the traditional household tasks of helping to satisfy the social, emotional, and maintenance needs of other people. As family functions have been progressively taken over by outside institutions, and as women have been increasingly employed outside the home, the jobs which they have been seen as best equipped to do have been extensions into the marketplace of such traditional household tasks as taking care of children. So it is understandable that women would be over-represented in courses of study leading to such occupations as nursery and elementary school teacher, home economist, librarian, and nurse.

In terms of employment, two related phenomena loom large: the increasing labour force participation of women, and their large-scale movement into white-collar, especially clerical and sales, jobs. Concerning the former, single women have had a long tradition of employment in Canada, and their labour force participation rates have not changed markedly over time. Consequently, the rapid rise in female labour force participation has for the most part involved married women, who have increasingly sought paid employment despite the historical prejudice against their doing so. While it is clear enough that men and single women most often work for pay out of economic necessity, this may be increasingly true of married women as well (Armstrong and Armstrong, 1975; Gunderson, 1976; Armstrong and Armstrong, 1978). Among married women with a husband present, the lower the husband's income, the more likely the wife is to be employed outside the home. And, as well:

> There is evidence to suggest that in recent years wives have replaced unmarried children as the most important secondary contributors to family income. This has resulted from the growing employment of married women, the lengthening of the years of schooling for children, and the drop in the age at which children leave home to marry (Podoluk, 1968:11).

Perhaps, then, married women have to some extent moved in to play a role once played by unmarried sons and daughters living at home, enabling families to gain or maintain a style of life otherwise beyond their means.

Still, the increase in the labour force participation of married women seems larger than might reasonably be explained by this factor alone, and another possibility might be that it has also occurred in response to shifts over time in the distribution of income (Armstrong and Armstrong, 1978:Chapter 6). As the higher-income groups have taken an increasing share of the total income available, more and more middle- and lower-income families may have found themselves in a position whereby more than just the husband must work for pay in order for them to live as they have been living or aspire to live. And this may have meant that the wife has left the home for paid employment. "Obviously, the presence of the wife in the labour force is, for many families, the means by which families can move into middle-income brackets (Podoluk, 1968:132–33). Overall, families with employed wives actually had about 13 per cent more income on the average in 1961 than did families without employed wives, for example.

As for the movement of women into white-collar jobs, and the transformation of clerical jobs from male- to female-dominated, these are processes which are not entirely understood. Probably they are attributable in part to the changing character of these jobs over time (Glenn and Feldberg, 1977; Braverman, 1974; Crozier, 1974; Lockwood, 1958). The increasing bureaucratization and mechanization of clerical work seem at least partly to have eroded away the craft-like components it had in earlier times, and to have caused a proliferation of relatively low-skill, low-paid office jobs whose most important single requirement is literacy. As the demand for clerical labour has risen, and as clerical work has been progressively robbed of its skill requirements and financial benefits, the most likely source of labour was, first, single women and, later, as this pool was absorbed, married women. With the increasing scale and productivity of the industrial sector of the economy, the distribution and sale of manufactured (especially mass-produced) products has become an increasingly important element in the Canadian economy, creating a rising demand for a force of salespersons with basic verbal and quantitative skills. Again, women — especially married women — were perhaps the most obvious source of new workers for these new jobs, since they typically had the skills required, and they were available for employment.

How is it, finally, that men and women working at similar jobs for roughly equal amounts of time in a year do not earn about the same amount of money? Differences between them in their levels of educational attainment do not seem to be importantly involved here; in general, women are not less well-educated than men within specific jobs, but the economic returns to education within jobs tend to be somewhat lower for women than for men, at least among those who have higher than average levels of educational attainment. One reason why one would expect such a male–female income differential is that, relative to men, women are more likely to have discontinuous careers and, thus, to accumulate experience on the job more slowly than men do, and to be seen more often by employers as workers with weak commitments to their jobs. Married women in the labour force tend to see themselves and to be seen by others as secondary income earners whose first responsibility — especially when there are young children involved — is to manage the household and to work for pay only when they can accomplish both jobs and when they are not in competition with men for employment. Because of this, labour force turnover is much higher for women than for men (Canada, 1977:115). Moreover, "female turnover usually arises because women quit their jobs in order to leave the labour force, which lowers wages.... Men, in contrast, tend to leave their jobs to obtain better-paying ones. Consequently, turnover has a differential effect on male than on female earnings" (Gunderson, 1976:119; also see Goyder, in press).

Origins of Sex-Role Differentiation

To show that males and females *are* socialized to very different adult roles, of course, does not explain the basis for this practice. Perhaps it has something to do with differences between males and females in their intellectual abilities. The evidence is that males tend to score higher on the average than females on tests of quantitative and visual-spatial ability at all ages, and that females perform better on the average on tests of verbal ability, at least up to their teens (Maccoby and Jacklin, 1974; Ambert, 1976; Armstrong and Armstrong, 1978). And males enjoy an advantage in measured I.Q. which increases slightly through the school years. Could it be that these differences account in part for the relative over-representation of males in science and commerce and business administration courses in university, and the relative over-representation of females in such fields as arts and education? This seems unlikely, since these are *small, average* differences — hardly large enough to account for the large differences between males and females in such things as specialization in particular fields of study. Moreover, it is not at all clear whether these differences are causes or effects of differences in sex-role socialization. Perhaps they are innate differences which have led over time to differences in the manner in which males and females are raised and regarded. But perhaps they are the consequences of differences in sex-role socialization.

If not cognitive differences between the sexes, then what? Men and women also differ physically in a number of ways, most notably in their average body size and strength, and in the fact that it is the women who bear and suckle the children. And studies quite consistently find that it is the males who are the more aggressive. Body size and strength are, of course, clearly irrelevant for education as such, and largely irrelevant for most jobs in the labour force today, especially those which require any advanced educational preparation. Although physical capacity might once have been an important criterion for a significant number of jobs and, thus, might once have determined to some degree the physical attributes of those who undertook the training for them, few jobs in the modern world place physical demands upon their incumbents that women cannot meet as well as men. Too, the differences in body size and strength are only average differences, with much overlap between the sexes. As for the fact that it is the women who bear and suckle the young, this could presumably account for some small part of the differences between men and women in university attendance, part-time study, and the like. It could also explain at least a measure of their over- and under-representation in different fields of study as a consequence of the physical demands of the jobs these fields provide preparation for. Women are for a time curtailed in their activities as a consequence of pregnancy and giving birth, and the children are often physically dependent upon them for awhile. Still, even these differences between men and women are relevant only once or twice for short spans of time in the life of the average woman, so they could scarcely account for many of the large differences between them in their educations, occupations, and incomes.

When viewed from the perspective of a time and place where the number and spacing of children can be determined by the parents and the birth rate is at a historic low, formula feeding can release mothers from extended nursing, day-care facilities are available to most middle- and upper-income families, compulsory school attendance laws require all able children between the ages of about six and sixteen to be in school most of the day for most of the year, and few jobs have any real physical requirements, the very different circumstances of men and women in Canada may seem especially hard to apprehend. First, conventional male and female sex roles are not inviolate packages, such that the person who bears and suckles the young must also be the one who washes the dinner dishes, defers in important family decisions to the spouse, and works as a retail sales clerk, or the one who does the impregnating is also the one who mows the lawn, punishes the children, and operates a service station. Second, there is no necessary connection between biological technology and most "male" and "female" tasks. So what might account for these differences between men and women in the roles to which they are socialized and the rewards which they receive?

Historically, it seems likely that there has always been at least some sexual division of labour in human populations based not upon biologically-grounded differences between males and females as such but, rather, upon the extra-ordinary (for animal species) dependence of human infants upon their mothers (Ambert, 1976). Although the particular forms which this division has taken have varied enormously over time and from society to society, there has been a fairly constant element in the fact that the dependence of the young upon their mothers has tended to restrict women's activities to the home and its immediate environs, whereas men's activities have been more widely distributed in space. This may help explain how it is that child care and the everyday household tasks came together in the female role, at least in the past. But the conditions which originally gave rise to this no longer apply, so that the next task is to account for how it is that it persists today, and that the role of women is subordinate to that of men in status and power.

Persistence of Gender Inequalities

In certain modes of production, such as tribal hunting and gathering, the household is an economic unit, even though the greater mobility of men seems generally to mean a sexual division of labour in which (in this case) the men specialize in the hunting and the women in the gathering. In others, such as industrial capitalism, however, there is a separation of the domestic and the industrial units, such that economic activities occur largely outside the household (Armstrong and Armstrong, 1978). Under conditions of such separation, and where women tend to be tied to the home for significant periods in their lives, as in nineteenth- and early twentieth-century Canada, it is the men who must be employed outside the home, for the most part. Consequently, it is the male role which is the dominant one, since it is the men who control the economic resources of the family. But, if so, it remains to be seen how this situation is reproduced in the present, when the conditions which gave rise to it have largely disappeared.

One factor which probably plays some role in maintaining the system of gender inequalities is the existence of an ideology of male dominance. Since social arrangements based directly upon differences in power are inherently unstable, social groups and categories must find means more subtle than simply force and coercion in order to maintain both their dominance and smooth relationships with those subordinated to them. One such means is the development and dissemination of a belief system or ideology which portrays one group or category as rightfully dominant and the other(s) as rightfully subordinated to them (Kemper, 1976). Where this effort is successful, power is said to be transformed into authority, or *legitimated*. What seems likely in the present case is that the historical circumstances which gave rise to the system of male dominance also provided the basis for the development and dissemination of an ideology of male dominance, which ideology has helped to maintain a system of gender inequalities in which males are the favoured sex.

Situations in which members of one social category tend to be preferred over members of others involve an element of *ascription*, that is, the treatment of people on the basis of their category memberships, rather than in terms of their individual abilities to achieve. The criteria which distinguish members of one social category from another may be entirely unrelated to capacity to perform (e.g., secondary sex characteristics) or related only in the sense that there are small, average differences in performance-related capacity between the categories but, in either case, ascription can lead to large differences between the categories in how they fare in systems of inequality. In the labour market, for example, men tend to be preferred for high-paying jobs. As a result, they are placed first in the labour queue and hired before women. Even though men may be no more capable of doing these jobs, the outcome is a large difference between men and women in their incomes. Depending upon the number of available jobs and the number of qualified applicants, the results could be as extreme as all those men who have applied being hired and none of those women who have applied being taken on. Processes such as this, in which small, initial differences, perhaps entirely unrelated to performance capacity, are magnified into large, later ones, are sometimes described using models of *statistical discrimination* (Thurow, 1975) or *catastrophe theory* (the results being catastrophic in the sense that they are dramatically different, as in being hired for a job or not; see, for example, Zeeman, 1976). And they suggest something of the mechanisms by which far-reaching and profound inequalities can persist long after any initial causes for them have disappeared and, perhaps even, in the presence of only a very "mild" set of prejudices.

On Ethnic Inequalities

Education, Occupation, and Income

A crucial element underlying ethnic inequalities in Canada seems to inhere in the intersection of ethnicity and place of residence. All ethnic groups are not evenly distributed across the socio-economic landscape of the country. All places of residence do not offer equal opportunities for obtaining a good education, landing a good job, or earning a good income. And there is at least a broad association between how favoured an ethnic group is in these respects and how favoured the places are in which they tend to be concentrated. It should be useful, therefore, to indicate something of how ethnicity and place of residence combine to create and maintain ethnic inequalities.

The history of Canada has been that of the uneven development of regions within a larger context of uneven development among the capitalist countries of the West and an even larger world system. Thus, it is fairly common to speak of "metropolitan" (or "core") countries (e.g., the U.S.) and "hinterland" (or "peripheral") ones (e.g., Canada, although perhaps not so obviously as the countries of the Third World), as well as of metropolitan regions (e.g., Central Canada) and hinterland ones (e.g., the rest of Canada) within countries (Davis, 1971). In general, the metropolis is the locus of economic development and power, and uses the hinterland as a source of raw materials, (often relatively unskilled) labour, and markets for manufactured goods.

The National Policy of the immediate post-Confederation period set the stage for the development and maintenance of a regional system in Canada in which an industrialized Central Canada found raw materials, workers, and markets in the Atlantic provinces, the West, and the North, while the metropolis itself straddled the two nations of French and English Canada (Bercuson, 1977). The outcome of this has been the emergence of large and persistent regional inequalities and the ascendance of Ontario over Quebec within the metropolis (Phillips, 1978). By and large, people in the hinterland are less well-educated, more likely to be unemployed, less well-placed occupationally, and less affluent than are those in the metropolis, although some parts of the hinterland (e.g., Alberta and British Columbia) are so well-endowed with valuable natural resources that their hinterland status is not clearly reflected in these ways, and others (e.g., Manitoba and Saskatchewan) have managed to combine some economic growth with fairly high levels of out-migration, which has kept unemployment quite low. The Atlantic provinces and the North, however, more consistently display the effects of their hinterland positions. Figure 10–1 shows the historical trends in unemployment in the regions (but see Stirling and Kouri, 1979), while Table 10–1 contains some selected indicators of regional economic disparities.

In general, the phenomena of the uneven development of countries and

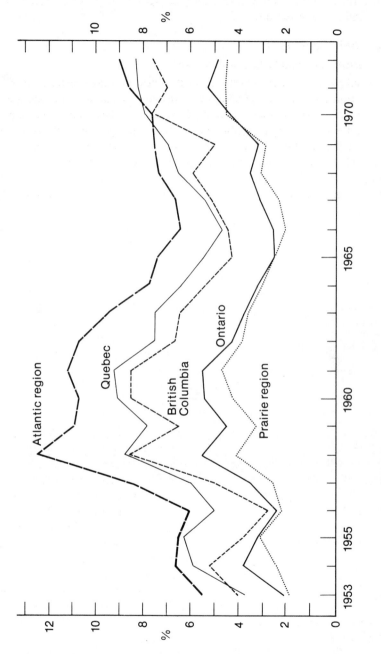

Figure 10-1 UNEMPLOYMENT RATES BY REGION

Source: Canada (1974a: Chart 6–13).

regions are not easily explained in terms of the concepts and precepts of either neoclassical or Keynesian economics, except as fairly short-run occurrences

Table 10-1

Some Selected Indicators of Regional Economic Disparities, Canada, Various Years.

Indicator	Atlantic Provinces	Quebec	Ontario	Prairie Provinces	British Columbia	Yukon and Northwest Territories
Infant mortality rate, 1972–1974, Canada=15.9 deaths per 1,000 live births	15.6– 19.3*	16.5	14.2	15.6– 19.3*	16.5	22.7– 42.8*
Family disposable purchasing power including housing cost differential, 1970, Canada=100	75– 87*	102	106	85– 101*	97	70
Percentage of males aged 16 attending elementary and secondary schools, 1974–75, Canada =84.3	62.1– 76.9*	81.5	88.7	82.6– 85.3*	86.5	63.8– 74.5*

* Range within the region across provinces.
Source: Economic Council of Canada (1977: Tables 4–8 and 4–11).

(see, for example, Armstrong, 1970). The regional system in Canada, however, can hardly be seen as an ephemeral economic disequilibrium. Rather, it is an enduring feature of the social, political, and economic organization of the country and, as such, requires analysis in its own right. There have been a number of attempts among Marxist scholars (e.g., Frank, 1969) to provide this kind of analysis and, although they are not fully developed or easy to summarize, the unifying theme is generally that uneven development occurs and continues because it is in the interest of the capitalist class (Cuneo, 1977). Briefly, it is their commercial and industrial establishments which populate the metropolis and which require the raw materials, labour power, and markets for manufactures available in the hinterland. Also, a major preoccupation of an earlier generation of Canadian political economists was an attempt to analyse Canadian development and uneven development in terms of what is known as *staples theory* (see Easterbrook and Watkins, 1967). According to the staples approach, the fortunes of regions are tied to their supplies of marketable natural resources, so that regions with ample supplies are characterized by high wages, low unemployment and, as a consequence, high rates of in-migration from other regions, where exactly the opposite prevail in regions with a scarce supply. Because it was developed to fit one case (i.e., Canada), staples theory lacks the kind of generality required of scientific explanations, and it has largely fallen into disuse. It is not possible for a theory to explain the facts used to generate it in the first place, so that a revival of the staples approach would seem minimally to require that it be adapted to analyses of other times and places (but see Clement and Drache, 1978).

On this background of regional inequalities in Canada, we can overlay information about the regional distribution of certain ethnic groups and observe the coincidence of regional and ethnic inequalities. Of the groups considered here, the Jews are probably the most highly concentrated in urban areas, especially the major urban centres of Central Canada, and most notably in Montreal and Toronto. Over time, in Canada, the British have become more evenly distributed among the regions, and they are not especially distinctive in terms of rural–urban residence. The French, of course, are largely concentrated within Quebec, along with neighbouring regions in Ontario and New Brunswick and they, too, are neither especially urban nor especially rural in their residence. The Germans and the Ukrainians tend disproportionately to be rural people engaged in agriculture, with the former concentrated in southern Alberta and Saskatchewan, and the latter in south-central and south-western Manitoba. The Indians and Inuit are overwhelmingly located in rural, nonfarm areas in the northern and western parts of Canada. While some regions are poorer than others, rural areas are typically poorer than cities, and rural, nonfarm areas are the poorest of all. And, finally, the Italians stand as something of an exception to the principle elaborated here, since they are at once concentrated in the major cities of Ontario and Quebec and tend to lag behind in education, occupation, and income.

It is likely, of course, that there is more to the system of ethnic inequalities than just region of residence. Differences in school attendance at various levels among ethnic groups, along with related inequalities, are often given explanation in terms of ethnic differences in attitudes and values toward education. Jews, in particular, are typically singled out as placing an especially high value on education, while the Indians and the Inuit are often identified as peoples who have not acquired this trait, and the French in Canada have been held to have suffered in some measure from the importance which they have placed upon a distinctly classical education ill-adapted to equip a labour force for participation in a modern, industrial economy. At the same time, the Jews have historically been an urban, commercial people, the Indians and Inuit are largely confined to regions wanting in educational facilities and occupational opportunities, and urbanization and industrialization in Quebec have only arrived in the past three or four decades. Thus, it is unclear to what extent attitudes and values toward education can be shown to have an effect on ethnic inequalities apart from the material circumstances of these groups' lives.

In French Canada, there has always been a class of lawyers, physicians, and clergymen produced by a small-scale, elitist, educational system with a strong classical emphasis (Hughes, 1943: Chapters XI and XII). As Quebec has become increasingly urbanized and industrialized in the period since World War II, however, its educational system remained ill-equipped to meet the labour force demands of the emergent new society. Consequently, Francophone Canadians lagged behind in their educational participation, especially at higher levels, and especially in commerce and the sciences (Quebec, 1966; Canada, 1968). Over the past two decades, however, the educational institutions of the province have been overhauled and vastly upgraded, with the result that Francophone Canadians have rapidly begun to close the gap between themselves and the more advantaged groups (Denis, 1975).

Just what the future holds for Francophone Canadians, though, is difficult to say (Morris and Lanphier, 1977: Part III). Concentrated in Quebec with a French-language educational system, comparable at all levels to any other educational system in Canada, future changes in the levels of educational participation and attainment would seem to depend importantly upon future changes in the demand for educated labour among Francophone Canadians. This, in turn, hinges in part upon the evolution of relations between Quebec and the rest of the country, since the federal government's language and employment policies have created a continuing demand for well-educated Francophones in the public sector. And it hinges, as well, upon the economic future of Quebec and the role of the Francophones in this future. To the extent that the Parti Québécois is successful in making French the language of business in the province, the employment possibilities for well-educated Francophones might be expected to increase, except that success in this venture holds the already visible prospect of an exodus of business and industry from Quebec which could more than counterbalance these gains.

Although they continue to lag behind, the Italians and the Indians and Inuit registered the greatest gains of all in educational participation between 1951 and 1971. The Italians are among the newer of the immigrant groups in Canada, and it seems likely that the increase in their case can be best viewed as an aspect of their acculturation to and integration with the larger society over time (Danziger, 1975). As for the Indians and Inuit, the federal government has moved increasingly into the field of education, replacing the earlier system of denominational boarding schools with a system of its own local schools, with teachers and curricula largely imported from the urban, industrial, white culture (Canada, 1972a). The express purpose of this effort has been to acculturate and integrate the aboriginal peoples, and the rising rates of educational participation among the Indians and Inuit can be taken as an indicator of the results of this policy (Economc Council of Canada, 1968). While the educational policies of the federal government seem likely to draw more and more Indians and Inuit into primary and secondary schools, community colleges, and universities, there would seem to be real limits to how far this process will go. Life in the rural and northern areas of Canada, where the Indians and Inuit are concentrated, holds relatively little promise of future opportunities for employment in high-skill, high-paying jobs. The reservation system has had the effect of keeping Indians out of the economy and in a state of poverty and economic dependence upon the government. And resistance among the aboriginal peoples to acculturation and integration seems likely to become stronger in the decades ahead, rather than weaker.

A further element in the system of ethnic inequalities is the history of immigration policies and practices. In general, the members of the various ethnic groups who are native-born are better educated than the foreign-born members who immigrated to Canada prior to World War II, and less well-educated than post-war immigrants to this country. Even so, the only groups considered here with a high proportion of post-war immigrants are the Italians, and the levels of educational attainment of pre-war and post-war immigrants of Italian descent are at once both lower than for the native-born and slightly higher among the pre-war than among the post-war immigrants (Kalbach and McVey, 1971:210). This is probably due to the relatively high demand in the post-war period for unskilled labourers, particularly in the construction industry, at a time when large numbers of poorly-educated men in the south of Italy were willing and able to emigrate.

With rates of educational participation for the Jewish, British, German, and Ukrainian groups now roughly comparable, differences among them in their overall levels of educational attainment should effectively disappear within a generation or two. And there would seem to be no obvious reasons why, as Italians become increasingly acculturated and integrated, their levels of educational participation and attainment will not rise eventually to the levels of these other groups, although it will clearly take a period of two or three or more generations for this to happen.

Finally, it is likely that, at least for certain groups, a process of ascription operates such that their occupations are not commensurate with their educations, and occupations and educations do not combine to yield the levels of income that one would otherwise predict, as a consequence of the aggregated prejudices of members of more favoured groups. Although fine-grained studies of this phenomenon are largely lacking, it is obvious that Indians, particularly in the smaller communities in the north and the west of Canada, fit into this category, as do blacks and immigrants from the Indian subcontinent. Canadian Indians are new to the industrial system and tend to be perceived as not having those habits of work which are required to adapt to it, while many black, Pakistani, and other Canadians are recent immigrants with habits of speech and dress and other cultural accoutrements which are not part of middle- or upper-class Canadian culture. In such cases as these, it is probable that, other things being equal, the members of these groups are seen as lacking in the levels of style/ability (see Chapter 6) that their educational preparation would otherwise guarantee and that, consequently, they tend to be placed further down in employment and promotion queues than otherwise they would. Unfortunately, the groups to which this happens tend not to be numerous enough to be studied using data from national surveys, and official government statistics almost never contain detailed information about them, so that it is not possible to provide much of an account of their experiences.

Wealth

As we saw in Chapter 8, those of British background in Canada are considerably over-represented among the wealthy, while those of French origin are very under-represented. What are the likely reasons for this difference? In order to attempt an answer to this question, we must first consider the more general one of how it is that some people are able to collect millions of dollars worth of assets while others are not. Unfortunately, the processes involved in this are not well understood, although Thurow (1975) presents a provocative argument in favour of the *random walk*. Briefly, Thurow notes that a theory of the accumulation of great wealth must take into account a number of facts. First, anybody who puts together a fortune is no doubt very intelligent but, since most intelligent entrepreneurs never manage to do this, intelligence (or any other such personal quality, for that matter) provides no very useful clues to the explanation. Second, large fortunes are almost invariably made in the course of a few years and, once made, grow quite slowly. Third, people who put together one fortune doing one thing are almost never successful at assembling another fortune doing something else. So how do individuals become wealthy? This depends upon the fact that, contrary to the dicta of neoclassical economics, some investments earn much better than average returns over fairly long periods of time. To become wealthy, one must invest in these. But, since which investments these are cannot be known beforehand, whether one invests and becomes rich (e.g., rolls the dice and wins) or goes broke (rolls and loses) is essentially a random process — hence the name random walk. At the same time, it is the walk itself which is random. Whether or not one takes it in the first place and, if taken, how much he or she invests, are clearly influenced by the amount of a person's initial wealth, however acquired.

From this account of the random walk, it seems safe enough to conclude that British-French differences in wealth in Canada do not derive importantly from ethnic differences in entrepreneurial ability as such but, rather, from historical and contemporary differences among these groups in the relative likelihood of involvement in entrepreneurial pursuits with sufficient capital to strike it rich. Taylor, for example, has pointed to the considerable under-representation of the French in Quebec in entrepreneurial occupations, which he attributes to the "relatively low status accorded to business as a profession in French-Canadian society" 1964:273), although Hunter (1977) was unable to find any differences between the two groups in their evaluations of entrepreneurship. More likely, differences between the two groups in entrepreneurial involvement are to be found in an historical analysis of the development of capitalism in Canada. After the Conquest, the British dominated economic activity in the colonies, while the former French elite in Lower Canada departed en masse to the home country. Throughout the nineteenth century, this British dominance was maintained, aided by the privileged access of Canadians of British origin to the rapidly growing money markets in the U.K. In regard to the U.K. capital, Myers observes that, in the period prior to World War I:

> Aside from the consideration of native Canadian capital, the amount of British capital put in Canada has been stupendous. In 1911, Sir George Paish, one of the editors of the London *Statist,* estimated that £372,541,000 of British capital had gone to Canada, chiefly in the form of investments; of that sum £223,740,000 was represented by investments in Canadian railways. Since 1911, at least £120,000,000 more of the British capital has been placed in Canada. The total of British capital in Canada is, therefore, more than $2,000,000,000. Capital in Canada from various Continental countries of Europe is computed at about $140,000,000. Of the $500,000,000 of United States capital active in Canada, $180,000,000 is represented in 300 factories which, to a great extent, are branches of the American Trusts (1972:xxxiii).

Up to the Depression of the 1930s, U.K. capital provided the major source of investment funds in Canada and, in contrast to the U.S. pattern of direct ownership and active control of branch plants, it typically came in the form of portfolio investment (i.e., minority stock ownership without real involvement in management or loans to Canadian entrepreneurs).

Background and Inequality

As we saw in Chapter 9, men whose fathers are relatively well educated and well-placed occupationally tend to end up better educated than those from less favoured social backgrounds, and they tend to do better occupationally, as well, even after their educational advantages have been taken into account. In addition, although the evidence for it is less well established, the mother's education may also have effects on the son's education independently of the father's educational and occupational achievements.

It has proven very difficult to unravel just how it is that educational and occupational advantages in the parents' generation are to some extent passed on to their children, and very little research on this matter has been conducted in Canada. First, it no doubt helps to come from a family in which there are sufficient financial resources to fund one's education, not only in the sense that a person so favoured need not be concerned to help fund his or her own education, but also in the sense that neither the person himself or herself nor the parents are likely even to think of lack of money as a problem (Porter et al., 1973). Second, it can hardly be a disadvantage to come from a family in which the parents place much store in education, encourage their children to have effective study habits and high educational aspirations and expectations, and themselves possess the kinds of cognitive skills and values (or high style/ability — see Chapter 6) which are rewarded by good grades in school (Breton, 1972a: Part II; Gilbert, 1977; MacKinnon and Anisef, 1979). Third, well-placed people tend to live in suburban areas in close proximity to others of their kind, which means that their children will tend to have friends and classmates with high style/ability, so that parental influences are reinforced by the peer group. Fourth, and finally, it remains possible that the inter-generational transmission of educational advantages or disadvantages involves not only environmental influences such as those discussed here, but genetic ones as well, as in the inheritance of certain cognitive abilities (Williams, 1977).

As for advantages to occupational achievement which come from a favoured social background independently of the effects of an individual's own education, the mechanisms which might operate here are quite unknown, although we can speculate as to what certain of them might be. In particular, high style/ability was earlier identified as a factor of some potential importance for people in gaining access to desirable jobs. Now, while style/ability is doubtless fostered in and certified by school systems, it probably originates, more than anywhere else, in the family. If so, this could help account for how a person's social origins affect occupational achievement above and beyond the influence of formal education as such.

Although the process of social inheritance often has elements of pure ascription in it, as in countries and cultures where noble titles, for example, are literally handed down from generation to generation, this is largely absent in Canada today. It did probably exist to some extent in much earlier times, and it probably persists in some measure amongst the most monied or prestigious circles, but it does not seem especially important as a general social phenomenon. Social inheritance probably does play a role, however, in some systems of inequality which do involve a degree of ascription, such as the system of ethnic inequalities in Canada. To the extent that a system of ethnic inequalities obtains in one generation and the phenomenon of social inheritance persists, then that system will necessarily be at least partially reproduced in the next generation. Thus, the relatively favoured positions of Jews and persons of British origin in Canada, and the relatively disfavoured positions of the Indians and Inuit, clearly derive in part from the inheritance of inequalities from previous generations, rather than just from the system of regional inequalities and the operation of ascriptive processes which allow some groups to benefit at the expense of others.

Finally, we saw in Chapter 5 that enormous inequalities in wealth exist in Canada and, in Chapter 9, that most of the wealthiest Canadians for whom the information was available received substantial business inheritances at some point in their careers. Moreover, the relationship between the amount of income a person receives and the amount of his or her wealth is such that, at least for the wealthiest of Canadians, it is clearly impossible for them to have accumulated their wealth through a process of saving from income. The theory of the random walk presented earlier in this chapter suggested one mechanism by which fortunes are made initially. Since we do not have the necessary detailed data on the careers of the Canadian rich, it is not possible to apply the theory of the random walk to examine how those of them who made their own fortunes actually did it. But a reading of Myers's *A History of Canadian Wealth* shows something of this process for the period prior to World War I, although Myers himself was inclined to the more conspiratorial view that behind most

Canadian fortunes was an equally big crime or two. And it is nicely illustrated in the early career of the Bronfman family in Canada, of which Newman notes that:

> Their business past could be construed as a series of lucky accidents, with the bounce of each experience leading to another and the angle of the bounce (or in the Bronfmans' case, the nature of the latest twist in government anti-liquor legislation) determining the direction of their various ventures (1978:151).

If the random walk helps explain how it is that initial fortunes are made, inheritance contributes further to existing inequalities in wealth and ensures that inequalities in one generation are to some extent reproduced in the next. We can identify, then, three processes by which people come to possess at least some wealth: saving from income, the random walk, and inheritance. Since the rate at which people save from income is higher for those with high incomes than for those with low, it follows that the relationship between income and wealth will not be a simple, proportional one, and that inequalities in the distribution of wealth will be at least somewhat greater than corresponding inequalities in the distribution of income. If the theory of the random walk is correct, it implies still greater disproportionalities between income and wealth. And the mechanism of inheritance guarantees even greater disproportionalities yet. Many questions, however, remain to be answered, including the following. First, just how do the three mechanisms of saving, the random walk, and inheritance combine to produce the existing distribution of wealth? Second, how is it that people seek to accumulate great wealth in the first place and, once having got it, generally keep it until death and then pass it on to their spouses or children — even though they could never conceivably spend it all, and would typically pass more wealth on to their heirs if they began to de-accumulate it at some point prior to death?

Social Ascription and Social Theory

To Marx and Engels, "the workingmen have no country" (1959:26), and they seem generally to have regarded ethnic ascription as of relatively minor historical moment. (Engels (1959:457–58) did point, however, to ethnic divisions in the U.S. as at least a temporary impediment to the development of a large socialist party in that country, and contemporary Marxists have analysed ethnic inequalities and the subordination of the Third (entirely nonwhite) World to the First (mainly white) World in the context of capitalist development (e.g., Genovese, 1965; Leggett, 1968; Horowitz, 1966). As for gender inequalities, Marx himself wrote almost nothing, although Engels (1972) did discuss them in a Marxist framework, and these themes have been increasingly picked up and elaborated upon by latter-day Marxist writers (e.g., Seccombe et al., 1975; Armstrong and Armstrong, 1978). To the extent that there is a common Marxist argument underlying the analyses of ethnic and gender inequalities, it is that disadvantaged ethnic groups and women in capitalist society serve to cut the costs of labour and, in so doing, serve the interests of the capitalist class. This point may be illustrated, for example, in the labour practices of many west coast fishing companies, where native Indian men and Indian and white women provide cheap sources of seasonal labour for unskilled and semi-skilled jobs, and the management and other year-round jobs belong almost solely to Caucasian men. While capitalism is usually seen by Marxists as the principal source of ethnic and gender inequalities, however, these two sets of phenomena are in some important ways quite different, since ethnic groups can be differentially distributed across class boundaries, but men and women cannot. Or, as Anderson puts it:

> ...women as such are not a class. Women are members of families, families of the ruling class, the working class, the lumpenproletariat. The family is the social-unit basis of the system of class inequality, not individual men, women, and children (1974:317).

Weber, of course, was especially concerned to emphasize the importance of status along with that of class, and the prototypic status groups for him were ethnic groups. These are, he argued, normally communities characterized by a distinctive style of life which seek to monopolize economic and other opportunities for their members. As such, they represent intrusions of the irrational into the rational marketplace and, thus, the principle of social organization along the lines of status is inherently antagonistic to that of social organization along the lines of class. As the one comes into ascendance, the other goes into eclipse. This is a view apparently at some odds with the Marxist one that racial-ethnic distinctions and inequalities typically serve the interests of the capitalist class and, thus, of class society, although Weber did not go on to develop a full-fledged theory of class, status, and power, and he seems ultimately to have felt that the future lay neither with status nor class but, rather, with increasing rationalization and state bureaucratic control. Status has no place in the rational society; and the important feature of capitalism is not so much class domination, but the rationalization of economic life. Finally, Weber himself had little to say about sex-role differentiation and gender inequalities.

There are several related versions of the operation and mechanisms of racial-ethnic and gender ascription in the human capital theory and structural-functionalist literatures. While it is difficult to summarize and analyse them briefly and neatly, they all orbit around some conception of efficiency, both narrowly economic and otherwise. Thus, when the economic returns to human capital are found to be less for some racial-ethnic groups than for others, or less for women than for men, it is often assumed (rather than shown) that this occurs because of some unmeasured sources of racial-ethnic or gender differences in productivity (e.g., Becker, 1964). The reason for this is most likely that, according to the principles of marginal productivity theory, the distribution of marginal products *is* identical with the distribuion of earned income (Thurow, 1969:20, emphasis — a view which Thurow has since recanted). And one naturally hesitates to remove one of the cornerstones from the edifice of modern microeconomics on grounds of a few tenants who apparently cannot be accommodated.

In functional theory, ascription makes sense and survives to the extent that it is an efficient principle of social organization which contributes to the maintenance of the larger social whole. Males and females are differentially socialized from birth, for example, because this maximizes the time available for them to be tutored in their adult roles, and "the earlier ... training for status can begin, the more successful it is likely to be" (Linton, 1936:115). And Mayhew characterizes ascription as socially useful because "it is cheap" (1968:110). Since most people can be trained to the requirements of most jobs, for instance, it is less expensive for a business firm to assign people to positions on the basis of their membership in certain ascriptive categories than to allocate them in terms of their competitive excellence.

None of the major theoretical traditions surveyed appears to provide an entirely satisfactory analysis of the phenomena of racial-ethnic or gender ascription, although each can be seen to make some contribution to our understanding of them. A Marxist analysis holds some promise in each case, since it points to the likely role of power in the establishment and maintenance of racial-ethnic and gender inequalities, indicates some of the possible mechanisms by which differences in power among social categories and groups occur (i.e., control over the means of production in society, control over the economic resources of the family), and suggests the role of ideology in maintaining systems of racial-ethnic and gender inequality. Still, it is as yet insufficiently developed, and yields no ready clues as to how it is that, for example, some racial-ethnic inequalities are rapidly on the wane and others are not, while changes in the system of gender inequality have been uneven and slow, but generally in the direction of increasing equality between the sexes. Although Weber never elaborated his ideas at any length, at least part of his contribution can be seen to lie in his assertion of the importance of status in general, and of race-ethnicity in particular, as an organizing principle of social life. And the progressive diminution of racial-ethnic distinctions and inequalities in the twentieth century in Canada is quite in line with his expectations, even if it is not clear that he correctly identified its causes. To the human capital theorists and functionalists, finally, we owe some debt for the observation that ascription arises and persists because it is efficient or cheap, although, as Kemper (1976) observes, it is necessarily cheap for some and expensive for others.

The Canadian Meritocracy

Among social scientists, Canada is often described as standing somewhere between the United States and Great Britain in its emphasis on equality of opportunity and its tolerance for positional inequality, with the U.S. highest on the former and lowest on the latter (e.g., Lipset, 1964; Naegele, 1964).

> ... there is *less emphasis in Canada on equality than there is* in the United States .... In Canada there seems to be a greater acceptance of *limitation*, of hierarchical patterns. There seems to be less optimism, less faith in the future, less willingness to risk capital or reputation. In contrast to America, Canada is a country of greater caution, reserve and restraint (Naegele, 1964:501).

Or as Lipset phrases it, "Horatio Alger has never been a Canadian hero" (1964:327). At the same time, "... Canadian frontier conditions were just as destructive of traditional social relations as were those on the American frontier" (Lipset, 1964:326–27). Pressures toward egalitarianism and individualism resulted, Lipset continues, but there were counter-forces which prevented individualism of the American type from becoming the accepted way of life on the Canadian frontier (1964:327). These counter-forces included, most importantly, the respect for law and order which developed in Canada as a consequence of the early role of the North West Mounted Police in protecting the frontier from incursions from the south, and from the threat to Canadian unity posed by the distinctly American values of egalitarianism and individualism.

This characterization of Canadian values relative to those of the U.S. and the U.K. is admittedly impressionistic (Lipset, 1964:326), and entirely omits any consideration of French Canada. Moreover, it has come under real attack (e.g., Truman, 1971; Davis, 1971), and the subsequent evidence which has been brought to bear on the issue of the intermediacy of Canada's value position (e.g., Fearn, 1973; Crawford, 1975; Archibald, 1978) lends, at most, only limited support to it. For his part, Truman points to Lipset's heavy reliance upon secondary sources, and comments that "he creates rankings which are *his* estimate of *their* estimate"(1971:498). Moreover, he is able to cast doubt upon a number of Lipset's more important conclusions by showing that other — certainly no less valid — data than Lipset used often lead to precisely the opposite conclusions.

In his response to the intermediacy thesis, Davis is especially critical of the description it contains of the U.S.:

> ...the conception of the United States as a universalistic, achievement-oriented, equalitarian society — a conception so deeply rooted in three centuries of ideological expressions and verbal ritual that a majority of American social scientists automatically affirm it — needs severe revision. Judged by the evidence of historical fact rather than by the liberal rhetoric, the United States is a hierarchical, racist society — contrary to the long-nourished American middle-class, liberal self-image (1971:16).

Debate on these issues is lively and interesting, and far from ended. It sometimes suffers, however, from a certain confusion between abstract values relating to what the nature of inequality *ought* to be and *actual* patterns of inequality themselves. Lipset, for example, was especially concerned to show that relatively small differences among the three societies (he also considered Australia) in their values have had profound and enduring effects on their social structure and organization. For the most part, however, the only evidence he has on the former are data about the latter, so that differences in values (the cause) are inferred from information about social structure and organization (the effect). In order to make a convincing case, though, information must be obtained on both cause and effect independently of one another.

However the dominant ideology of Canada may compare or contrast with those of other nations in its emphasis on equality of opportunity and its tolerance for positional inequality, the issues are also less than completely clear at the level of Canadians' perceptions of inequality in their own society. For example, while a majority of young Canadians apparently agree that getting good grades in school, working hard, having a nice personality, and getting a university education are very important in achieving material success, a significant minority apparently do not (Johnstone, 1969:8). Moreover, fully half of those included in Johnstone's national survey for the *Royal Commission on Bilingualism and Biculturalism* felt that knowing the right people was very important for material success, while a significant minority endorsed coming from the right family, coming from the right religious group, and being born in Canada as being very important. As for positional inequality, many Canadians believe in the existence of social classes, and most who do can place themselves as members of a particular social class (e.g., Pineo and Goyder, 1973). And, although the evidence in this case comes from a single, small-scale survey of a southern Ontario city, many Canadians seem also to believe that big business in Canada holds effective sway over the federal government (Rinehart and Okraku, 1974). At the same time, it is unlikely that the real character and range of inequality is very clearly apprehended by the majority of people, most of whom probably see it in the context of their own personal experience as relatively minor, personal, and accidental, rather than as major, social, and systematic (see, for example, Runciman, 1966).

In a society where equality of opportunity is valued and a measure of positional inequality is regarded as just, real inequalities in the material conditions of people's lives are to be expected as a consequence of merit having received its just reward. If members of such a society come to feel that merit is too often not properly rewarded, however, some criticism of the system of distributive inequality will result. And if this criticism becomes widely disseminated throughout the society and given organized expression in a social movement or a political party, this can lead to some reform of the system or, perhaps, even revolution. In societies such as Canada, though, such developments have limited potential. First, given the emphasis on individualism in this country, the tendency is to interpret failures to achieve material success — one's own or those of others — as the consequence of individual inadequacy, rather than of some problem in the systems of distributive inequality. Thus, poverty is often explained in terms of poor individuals being either lazy or unintelligent or, in a more sophisticated version, of their having been raised in a culture of poverty where they have acquired inappropriate values and their capacity to learn has remained undeveloped (Lewis, 1961). Instead of the system being blamed, the victims themselves are blamed (Ryan, 1971). Second, given the likely lack of knowledge on the part of most people of the nature and extent of social inequality and their own locations in the system, it is probably often difficult for them to judge whether or not their own or others' merit is, in fact, appropriately rewarded.

Part IV

On Class in Canadian Society

Chapter 11

On the Historical Development
of Class Formations in Canada

*"A Guide to the Peaceable Kingdom" (subtitle to a prose
anthology of Canadian writing edited by William Kilbourn,
1970).*

In North American sociology, the term *social class,* or alternately, *socio-economic status (SES) group,* tends to be defined in one of two ways. Sometimes it denotes a *statistical category,* where families or individuals are grouped together for largely descriptive purposes in terms of some distributive attribute (see Chapter 1), such as education, income or occupational standing (e.g., Blishen, 1970). People might be classified together on the basis of their incomes, for example, so that those with the highest incomes would constitute the "upper class" and those with the lowest incomes the "lower class," with as many intermediate classes arrayed between these two as one might choose to recognize. In defining these categories, however, a sociologist would claim nothing for the reality of one such set of social classes or socio-economic groups as against any other, since each set is quite arbitrary with regard to the lines which separate the categories from one another.

Sometimes social class refers less arbitrarily to an *empirical aggregate* of people who share a similar lifestyle as, for instance, in the work of Kahl, who states that:

> A family shares many characteristics among its members that greatly affect their relationships with outsiders: the same house, the same income, the same values. If a large group of families are approximately equal to each other and clearly differentiated from other families we call them a *social class* (1957:12, emphasis in original).

Still, he notes that "the classes that we talk about are *ideal-type constructs. They are intellectual inventions* based on observation of reality..." (1957:13, emphasis in original). And a similar conception informs the work of many North American stratification theorists and researchers, such as Warner et al. (1960, 1963) in the Yankee City series, Hollingshead in *Elmtown's Youth* (1949), Hollingshead and Redlich in their well-known *Social Class and Mental Illness: A Community Study* (1958), and others.

Notions of class-as-statistical-category and class-as-empirical-aggregate are both distributive definitions. By contrast, social class in the European tradition tends to be relationally defined. That is, social classes are typically defined vis à vis one another by reference to their respective locations in the social division of labour. Thus, in Marx, the bourgeoisie are those who own and control the means of production and purchase the labour power of others to appropriate surplus value, while the proletariat are those who have only their own labour power to sell and exchange it for a salary or a wage with members of the bourgeois class. Here, it does not matter that members of a particular social class might vary widely in their possession of one or more distributive attributes. What matters is that institution of private property creates the basis for a set of social classes which stand in relation to one another as exploiters and exploited. The present chapter will be concerned primarily with classes as relational phenomena.

Class Divisions and Internal Class Differentiation

Perhaps in an earlier time the major Marxian class categories of bourgeoisie, petty bourgeoisie, and proletariat could have been applied to Canada in a relatively straightforward and illuminating way. Marx and Engels, however, wrote in a period and about places far removed from contemporary Canada and, as each subsequent generation of Marxist scholars has discovered, the evolution of capitalist relations of production in the different areas of the world has required a progressive refinement and continuous reformulation of the concepts and theories of the founders. Thus, the changing character of Canadian capitalism has brought forward several categories of people who do not stand in unambiguous relation to the traditional three classes which figure most prominently in Marx and Engels's work, but who have assumed an importance which cannot be easily denied in any modern class analysis. One problem, however, is that there are often apparently serious disagreements among Marxist scholars as to just where these categories ought to be located relative to the original three classes or, indeed, if their emerging importance might not even call into serious question aspects of the traditional trichotomy of classes itself. Consequently, no definitive class analysis can be presented here, although an effort will be made to show what the beginnings of such an analysis might look like.

Bourgeoisie

One of the potentially major developments in Canadian capitalism has been the emergence of the joint-stock corporation, in which ownership resides in the possession of publicly-traded stocks potentially available for purchase to anyone. In such corporations, it is not possible to make a simple distinction between owner-operators and their employees, since the functions of owning and operating are not necessarily combined in a single position. Initially, we can distinguish between *ownership* of stocks in a company and *control* of a company's investments, resources, and day-to-day operations. Then, among those who own stocks in a company, we can differentiate between those who only have some claim on a company's dividends as a right of stock ownership and those who own sufficient numbers of stocks to have controlling interest in the company. And, finally, in the case of control, we can distinguish between those who exercise active control over a company and those who do not. (See Poulantzas, 1975, and Wright, 1978, for essentially similar, but more elaborate, typologies of ownership and control).

In place of the (admittedly over-simplified) dichotomy of owner-operator and employee, then, we have in this (over-simplified, as well) typology four possibilities including, most importantly, "Finance Capitalist" and "Top Executive." The emergence of these two categories as a consequence of the separation of ownership and control has stimulated a lengthy debate which is far from ended and difficult to summarize quickly or neatly (Dahrendorf, 1959:41–48). Central to it, however, is the issue of whether separation has produced two new categories of people, finance capitalists (or "capitalists without function") and top executives (or "functionaries without capital"), whose interests differ fundamentally from those of industrial capitalists, as well as from one another, or whether this separation has occurred along lines which leave an essential harmony of interest among the three categories. That is, do these three categories differ sufficiently to be regarded as three distinct classes, or are they most usefully treated as class fractions within the bourgeoisie?

Those who hold the former view often tend to see the joint-stock corporation as an important transformation of capitalism, in which control resides in top executives who are delegated authority by a large number of small shareholders, but whose powers are circumscribed by the capacity of those subject to their commands to deny them legitimacy (e.g., Dahrendorf, 1959) and by pressures from the community (e.g., Berle and Means, 1932). Those who adopt the latter position, however, often regard the joint-stock corporation as more of an innovation in capitalism, whose major consequence has been that businessmen can aggregate the investments of many small stockholders for their own use and control the activities of companies through ownership of only a small proportion of their shares (e.g., Miliband, 1969).

In Canada, the tendency toward the separation of ownership and control may have been less pronounced than is sometimes thought. First, the family firm has remained very important (see Newman, 1975, 1979 and Newman, 1978).

> Only such dominant firms and upper class families as ... the Molson's Eaton's, Woodward's, Weston's, the Bronfman's of Seagrams or the Jeffrey's of London Life among many others, need to be mentioned here to illustrate their importance (Clement, 1975:19).

Second, ownership in many companies has become dispersed, but we saw earlier that stock ownership is largely that confined to a small minority of well-to-do Canadians, and large numbers of stocks are owned by only a small minority of them. As a result, the phenomenon of a small number of stockholders holding only a minority of the stocks in a company, but nevertheless having an active, controlling interest in it, has become fairly common as illustrated in the case of Argus Corporation — a large, Canadian company which exercises controlling interest in many other companies through the device of minority ownership (Newman 1975, 1979).

If the separation of ownership and control in Canadian business is far from complete, it may also be that the separation which has taken place has not created three distinct categories of top executives and industrial and finance capitalists whose interests stand in basic opposition to one another. For one thing, top executives often sit on the boards of directors of the companies who employ them but, in any case, they must normally share their employers' concerns with profits and growth in order to keep their jobs. For another, as Anderson observes, "the potential and existence of conflict between bankers and industrialists is historically factual, just as conflicts of interests exist within banking and industry" (1974:207), but it may be that overriding class interests bring these two categories together in the long run, despite short-term conflicts between them (Porter, 1965; Clement, 1975). On the whole, it seems reasonable to conclude, along with Miliband, that:

> This "elite pluralism" *does not ... prevent* the separate elites in capitalist society from constituting a dominant economic class, possessed of a high degree of cohesion and solidarity, with common interests and common purposes which far transcend their specific differences and disagreements (1976:45, emphasis mine).

While it may often make sense to speak of the bourgeoisie as a single, relatively undifferentiated category, it may often be useful to distinguish among members of this class in terms of the relative size of their holdings. Those who control Power or Argus corporations may stand in similar relation to capital as those who control some much smaller company, and they may all have like goals of profits and growth, but they do not deal with one another as equals, their contacts across class boundaries (e.g., with employees) often seem quite different, and they do not relate to their markets in the same way. Thus, modern researchers working in the tradition of *elite theory* (e.g., Mills, 1956; Porter, 1965; Clement, 1975; also see Bottomore, 1964; Stanworth and Giddens, 1974) distinguish between those few owners and top executives who command considerable economic resources and those who do not, often referring to the former as an *economic* or *corporate elite.*

Although elite theory is most frequently associated with the writings of Mosca and Pareto, who were concerned with developing a theory of politics in direct opposition to Marxism, contemporary researchers who study elites generally owe little allegiance to the original advocates of this approach, whose specific theories have long since been left to languish in libraries. Moreover, there have really been no new elite theories which have emerged to take their place. As Mills observed, ". . . I don't really understand what is meant by 'the elite theory.' There is no such thing. Merely to study elite groups is not automatically to accept some one definite theory of elites" (1968:147). Today, elite "theorists" are usually either "plain Marxist" or eclectic, that is, willing to use bits and pieces of different systems of theory as they appear useful, but wedded to no particular theoretical approach. Work in this area, then, tends to adapt its theory from several sources and to take on a descriptive flavour.

If the concept of an economic elite can be dissociated from any particular theory of elites, then it may be possible to assimilate it to the concept of the bourgeoisie as a way of distinguishing among the members of this class in their relative economic importance (Miliband, 1969: Chapter 2; Stanworth and Giddens, 1974:3–4). Or, as Clement puts it:

> Because of their relationship to ownership and control of property, all members of the corporate elite are also members of the bourgeoisie, but all members of the bourgeoisie are not members of the corporate elite. . . . the elite is defined as the uppermost positions only within dominant corporations. The corporate elite may then be said to correspond to the "big bourgeoisie" 1975:5–6).

Finally, members of the economic elite or big bourgeoisie control the activities of large-scale corporate structures with huge assets, enormous work forces, and national or international markets, while nonelite members of the bourgeoisie are connected to much smaller concerns. This implies at least a loose correspondence between the economic preserve of the corporate elite and what *dual economy* writers often refer to as the *monopoly sector* of the economy (e.g., Averitt, 1968; Bluestone, 1970; O'Connor, 1973) and the holdings of the nonelite members of the bourgeoisie and the *competitive sector* of the economy. Briefly, firms in the monopoly sector differ from those in the competitive sector in the relative size of their market shares. Because of this, monopoly firms tend to be stable and well-capitalized, with high profit margins. Given their strong market position and great resources, they are relatively immune from market fluctuations, and typically attempt to control the markets for their products through advertising and an ideology of consumerism. Competitive firms, by contrast, tend to be less stable and less well-capitalized, with lower margins of profit, and their weaker market position and smaller resources make them more dependent upon fluctuations in the market.

It may also be useful in a country such as Canada, where major elements of the means of production are owned or controlled from outside the national borders, to distinguish between members of the bourgeoisie who are associated with Canadian firms and those who are involved in foreign businesses (Bowles and Craib, 1979). As Clement remarks:

> From the perspective of the nation being studied, it is important to distinguish between national or *indigenous elites* who may operate primarily within the particular nation or the based in the nation but operate internationally through multinational corporations, satellite or *comprador elites* who operate branch plants of foreign multinational corporations and may be either nationals or imports from the headquarters and, finally, the foreign or *parasite elites* who are the heads of multinational corporations outside the host country (1975:36, emphasis in original).

These distinctions may be useful not so much because nationality as such matters, or even because there are cultural differences which come with differences in nationality, but mainly because the relationships between members of these three kinds of elites and the kinds of companies which they head differ systematically, and because these different kinds of companies do not play quite the same roles in the Canadian economy (see Perry, 1971). The reader might notice that this typology implies a fourth, unmentioned category — those who manage the branch plants of companies located outside the country ("external," as opposed to "internal" comprador elites, perhaps), although such people may not be especially important "from the perspective of the nation being studied." At the same time, whether internal or external, it may be a contradiction in terms to refer to compradors as "elites," given the definition of elite offered above, since they are necessarily limited in ownership and control.

Petty Bourgeoisie

There are several distinct sectors among the modern petty bourgeoisie, including the "old" petty bourgeoisie of independent commodity producers and small businessmen and the "new" petty bourgeoisie of self-employed, fee-for-service professionals. Within the old, as well, one can distinguish between the commodity producers (e.g., the fishermen, farmers, independent artisans, and the like), on the one hand, and the businessmen (e.g., the small shopkeepers, self-employed salesmen, and so on), on the other. In the original Marxian tradition, these fractions all belong in the same class by virtue of their common location in the relations of production, but the differences among them are such that it may often be necessary to take them into account.

While it could be that, in the long run, they share a common "class enemy" in the bourgeoisie, and that they ultimately risk the shared fate of losing their independence and, thus, of dropping into the ranks of the proletariat, this does not preclude serious rifts between different sectors of the petty bourgeois class. Something of this sort seems to have happened, for instance, in the evolution of the politics of Saskatchewan, where the Co-operative Commonwealth Federation (CCF) first came to power in 1944, largely on the strength of the farmers' vote and in the face of opposition from urban professional and business groups (Silverstein, 1971). Moreover, the introduction of medicare in that province on July 1, 1962, along with the twenty-three day doctors' strike which followed, can perhaps be best understood against a historical background of conflict which set different factions of the petty bourgeoisie in opposition to one another (Krueger, 1971).

Working Class

The classical proletarian of Marxist theory does not participate in the ownership or control of the means of production, but sells his or her capacity to work in exchange for a salary or a wage. In this role, he or she lives off value created through labour, and contributes to the production of surplus value by putting in surplus labour time. The model of the proletarian is the factory worker, who fits each of these criteria quite well. He or she is a propertyless, powerless, exploited person. There are several categories of people in modern capitalist society, however, who do not seem to fit all of the defining criteria of proletarian or working-class status, even if they fit some of them, and it may matter a good deal for interpretations of class relations in Canada just how these people are located in the class system.

Recently, Poulantzas (1975) has offered an interpretation of the Marxist analysis of classes in capitalism which bears importantly upon the issues of the present section. Briefly, Poulantzas begins his discussion by distinguishing between productive and unproductive labour, supervisory and non-supervisory personnel, and mental and manual work as criteria for the structural determination of social classes. The first of these three distinctions — that between productive and unproductive labour — is a fairly strict one in his scheme. Productive labour is that which contributes directly to the creation of surplus value through *direct* involvement in the production of material commodities. With these criteria in hand, Poulantzas then proceeds to locate the modern proletariat as those productive, nonsupervisory workers who do not have access to critical knowledge about the production process (or who perform *manual*, as opposed to *mental*, labour).

This is a rather restrictive definition of the working class relative to most — excluding , as it does, all managers, supervisors, and foremen, all engineers and technicians, and all white-collar workers generally. In fact, if our concept of the proletariat is confined in this fashion, it would constitute a fairly small and fast-shrinking fraction of the work force in Canada today — probably no more than about 20 per cent (see Wright, 1978:53–58 for relevant U.S. data). This is not in itself a criticism of Poulantzas's argument, but it underscores the point made above concerning the importance of how classes in capitalism are to be construed. If the proletariat is a small and shrinking class, then its importance in the Canadian system of class relations is likely to be small and shrinking as well.

Poulantzas's position is not one to be dismissed out of hand. Still, it is hard to see his definition of the proletariat as anything but arbitrarily narrow in its exclusion of all positions which cannot be seen to generate surplus value through direct involvement in the production of physical commodities (see Giddens, 1973:128–29). Even if one accepts the view that surplus value is something which is only created via the production of material commodities — and many would say, for example, that it can also be created by managers, supervisors, foremen, engineers, technicians and white-collar workers generally, as well as through services produced for the market — the bulk of white-collar workers do put in unpaid labour time which is useful to capitalists. That this labour time may sometimes create surplus value and may sometimes merely assist in its appropriation would hardly seem to matter to the individuals involved who, in either case, are not paid for their time (Wright, 1978:46–50).

Also, to say that white-collar workers must be excluded en masse from the working class on grounds that they have access to privileged knowledge of the production process which is used to dominate the working class or that, if not, they at least participate subtly in this domination through their proximity to mental labour does not sound very convincing. Many skilled workers have knowledge of the production process which is not widely disseminated, even while remaining part of the proletariat, and many white-collar workers are far removed from anything resembling mental labour in Poulantzas's sense of the term. At the same time, there is a small stratum of true technical experts, including certain engineers and technicians and some other very highly-educated professionals, who do appear to have a monopoly over critical knowledge of the production process, and they could perhaps be excluded from the working class in terms of the mental vs. manual labour criterion.

Poulantzas also excludes from the working class all persons in supervisory positions. This would include, of course, all industrial capitalists and top executives, along with all managers, line supervisors, and foremen. Since authority is either exercised by or on behalf of those who control the means of production, it would seem reasonable to differentiate between those who exercise it and those who are merely subject to it. At the same time, there is disagreement as to just where the line ought to be drawn. Do most white-collar, as opposed to blue-collar, workers "participate" in the exercise of authority (Giddens, 1973:182–83)? Or is it more useful to distinguish between those who are in positions of manifest, legitimate authority — whether delegated or not — and those who are not (i.e., between the industrial capitalists, top executives, managers, line supervisors, and foremen, and those who take their direction from such people), even if the latter are not necessarily without either power or influence (Wright, 1978:78)? Rather than resolve this issue prematurely and inconclusively, only persons in actual positions of authority will be excluded from the working class in the analysis which follows, leaving open the possibility that they may be joined by others with some proximity to authority as future developments in theory and research further our understanding of these problems.

The working class is internally differentiated in terms of a variety of educational, income, occupational, lifestyle, and related differences. Many of these differences are often either summarized in or attributed to the distinction between *white-* and *blue-collar* workers, depending upon the particular purpose and theoretical orientation of the sociologist. To some (e.g., Lipset and Bendix, 1959:13–17), the white- and blue-collar dichotomy is a useful summary device, since the former tend to enjoy greater status, pay, job security, pension and other fringe benefits, opportunities for advancement, quality of working environment, autonomy in work, and freedom from supervision than the latter (Parkin, 1972:24–26). To others (e.g., Giddens, 1973:179–86), however, the dichotomy is explicitly drawn out of a belief that it demarcates a major division in modern society. As Giddens remarks:

> It is perfectly clear that, since the first origins of the modern large-scale factory, there has come into being a generic disparity between white- and blue-collar labour — suggested by those very terms themselves, as well as

by the terminology of "nonmanual" and "manual" work — in terms of task attributes in the division of labour (1973:182).

Perhaps, then, the distinction between white- and blue-collar workers provides the basis for a class division.

The distinction between blue- and white-collar workers, as Giddens and others like him draw it, derives from the *technical division of labour* in society in which some people work at manual and others at nonmanual jobs. This differs from the Marxist distinction between manual and mental labour, which is anchored in the *social division of labour* in society in which some do not have critical knowledge of the production process and others do, which knowledge the latter use to dominate the former. While it may be true that there is a "generic disparity" between blue- and white-collar work — a disparity which is seen most clearly, perhaps, in the modern factory where the two are physically separated, and white-collar workers tend to identify with and to be identified by blue-collar workers with management — the majority of both blue- and white-collar workers seem to fit the model of the proletarian fairly well, that is, that of the propertyless, powerless, exploited person. For this reason, the distinction between blue- and white-collar workers will occasionally be retained in the discussion which follows, but only as shorthand way of referring to differences within the working class in a variety of distributive, socio-economic attributes.

Although they have tended to concentrate on issues of structure, organization, and process in the sphere of production, dual labour market theorists (e.g., Averitt, 1968; Bluestone, 1970; O'Connor, 1973) often suggest that there is a grand divide in the working class between those who labour in the monopoly or state sectors of the economy on the one hand, and those who work in the competitive sector on the other. In particular, it is argued that workers' incomes are especially sensitive to sectoral location, and Bibb and Form (1977) and Beck et al. (1978) have found income differences across economic sectors in the U.S. which are broadly in line with these arguments. Specifically, workers in the *core* sector (roughly to monopoly and state sectors combined) do seem to earn significantly more than do workers in the *peripheral* (or competitive) sector. At the same time, the analysis of labour markets provided in this literature is, at most, rudimentary, and much more work needs to be done to replicate these findings, refine the social and economic concepts used, and identify the mechanisms at work.

In a different but related approach — even if they are sometimes apparently confused with one another (e.g., Tolbert et al., 1980) — a number of economists and sociologists have seen what they identify as *dual* or (sometimes) *segmented labour markets* (e.g., Piore, 1975). In this perspective, the major distinction usually drawn is between *primary* and *secondary jobs*, in which the former differ from the latter principally in their better pay, superior working conditions, greater stability of employment, and more favourable opportunities for promotion through a hierarchy of connected jobs. Often, as well, an upper tier is distinguished from a lower tier of primary jobs and, again, the difference between them lies primarily in the relatively greater desirability of the latter as compared with the former. Beyond the fact of differences between these labour markets in working conditions and job benefits, it is often suggested, the distinction between them is important because it marks a major barrier to worker job mobility and, hence, a decisive division within the working class. Or so it is argued.

Although dual labour market theory does focus directly on the analysis of labour markets, its present utility for illuminating issues of the internal differentiation of the working class appears limited. The principal reasons for this seem to lie in the fact that it is largely atheoretical and descriptive. Moreover, it is plagued by some persistent problems of definition. Thus, the several labour markets are typically distinguished from one another partly in terms of workers' incomes, even though the location of workers in one labour market or another is sometimes used in an attempt to *explain* the differences among them in their incomes. To say, for example, that "engineers earn more than labourers in some degree because the former are employed in upper-tier primary jobs while the latter are working in secondary jobs" is to make a circular argument, *if* upper-tier primary jobs are *defined* as being better-paying than secondary ones. And sometimes they are.

In a somewhat more theoretically ambitious effort than either economic sector or dual labour market theory, several radical (mainly Marxist) economists (e.g., Gordon, 1972; Edwards et al., 1975) have attempted to analyse the relationship between sectors of production and labour markets in order to show how segmented labour markets have developed historically as a consequence of the uneven development of economic sectors in capitalism. Thus, the monopoly and state sectors of the economy are seen as requiring reliable and well-trained workers, and this is regarded as important in the creation of the primary labour market. The competitive sector, however, requires workers with only weak attachments to their jobs and minimal skills, and this is viewed as lying importantly behind the development of the secondary labour market. Although this approach seems to hold good promise to reveal and account for divisions within the working class, it is as yet insufficiently developed and, like the dual or segmented labour market perspective, it is not entirely free of conceptual confusions.

Even if there may be no entirely firm foundations in economic sector, dual or segmented labour market, or radical economic analyses upon which to rest any very thorough-going discussion of divisions within the working class, there are some suggestive convergences in this literature which should probably be noted. Allowing for the fact that definitions in the study of labour markets are still being refined, and that they vary somewhat from source to source, there seems to be some agreement that there is (by whatever name) a primary labour market consisting of jobs characterized first by relatively high levels of productivity which vary from job to job and substantial skill requirements which demand (more or less) lengthy training and on-the-job experience. These jobs tend to be organized into hierarchies graduated in terms of skill requirements and pay in which workers are offered real job security and opportunities for promotion on the basis of personality factors and accumulated expertise. Typically, these hierarchies are part of *internal labour markets* (Doeringer and Piore, 1971) organized by business firms, labour unions, or occupational groups in which the workers are protected from external competition. In the primary labour market, finally, income is determined by job level, amount of training, and on-the-job experience. And there seems to be some agreement, as well, that there is something resembling a secondary labour market of jobs in which productivity is generally low, varies little from job to job, and is largely independent of training or experience. These jobs have uniformly low skill requirements, differ little from one to another in their rates of pay, offer few opportunities for advancement, and are usually won or lost in open competition in the market. In the secondary labour market, differences among workers in their incomes are largely determined by differences among them in their hours of work.

Without necessarily accepting the argument that there are sharply-defined primary and secondary labour markets separated by considerable barriers to mobility, the suggestion seems to be that jobs differ in terms of the extent to which productivity and, therefore, pay are determined by *expertise* and *labour time* (see Chapter 4; also see Blackburn and Mann, 1979). These would seem to be very different criteria and, although there may be no strict division between those jobs in which expertise is the most important factor and those in which labour time is, they suggest the possibility of a potentially important distinction between two fractions within the working class. The mechanisms by which a worker is paid, the amount of pay received, and the conditions of employment, among other things, are determined in large measure by what the worker sells to his or her employer — expertise or labour time.

Others

Omitted from the three major classes — bourgeoisie, petty bourgeoisie, and proletariat — have been a number of categories of employed people, most notably top and middle managers, line supervisors and foremen and engineers, technicians, and certain other highly-educated professionals. Moreover, there is little consensus in the literature as to how these categories ought to be dealt with. Sometimes one or more of them is assigned to one of the major class categories as, for example in Poulantzas's (1975) analysis, where top managers are treated as part of the bourgeoisie, and engineers, technicians, and other highly-educated professionals (along with the remainder of white-collar workers) are classified as part of the petty bourgeoisie. Sometimes one or more of these categories is taken to define a newly emergent class, such as Touraine's (1971) elite cadre of true technical experts. And sometimes one or more is seen as occupying a "contradictory class location," as in the writings of Braverman (1974) and Wright (1978). In Wright's analysis, for example, each of the categories mentioned above is located somewhere between the bourgeoisie and the proletariat. In defense of his decision not to locate every category of person in the workforce in a single class, Braverman argues that "this problem cannot always be solved neatly and definitively, nor, it should be added, does science require that it must be so solved" (1974:409).

Given the variety of views as to how different levels of management and types of technocrats ought to be incorporated into a class analysis, it is probably not worthwhile to undertake any very detailed discussion of the several positions which various writers have adopted. Nevertheless, a brief overview of the arguments of the more prominent contemporary class theorists will give the reader a sense of the extent of disagreement which reigns on this issue, as well as to indicate some of the possible directions which future theoretical developments could take.

Mallet (1963) envisions the emergence of a *new working class* of employed engineers and technicians who, under conditions of increasing rationalization in the workplace, can be expected more and more to see their jobs become specialized, routinized, and eroded in their skill requirements. Well-trained, they will find themselves performing tasks "beneath" their professional training. Ambitious, they will see their aspirations for challenging and creative careers thwarted. And highly paid, they will emerge as a revolutionary model for other workers. Gorz (1968) casts his net over the more inclusive category of employed professionals generally, along with students, in his conception of the new working class. Apart from this, his argument broadly parallels Mallet's thesis of progressive bureaucratization and de-skilling under capitalism, leading to heightened worker dissatisfaction and, ultimately, to a revolution led by the new working class to wrest control of the means of production from the capitalist class. Touraine (1971) identifies what he sees as an emergent class of true technical experts on a trajectory to dominance in the post-industrial society of the future replacing the traditional working class as the vehicle for far-reaching social change. Instead of experiencing progressive specialization, routinization, and de-skilling in their conditions of work, the power which the members of this class will have by virtue of their abstract, theoretical knowledge can be expected to provide them with satisfying careers and abundant benefits. Although he sees the university replacing industry as the major institution for the production and distribution of new techniques and the dominant ideology of the new era, Touraine anticipates that students will tend more to be critics of, than an integral part of, the new technocratic class, since they are articulate representatives of the socially subordinate and culturally manipulated groups.

Since each of these analyses, as it might be applied to Canada, is projected to some point in the indefinite future, there is no way of evaluating just how prophetic any one of them might ultimately prove to be. Mallet's argument points to the phenomenon — already apparent — of dissatisfaction among engineers and technicians arising out of the general process of the rationalization of work (Miller, 1967; Greenbaum, 1976). At the same time, it is not obvious that this process necessarily affects technicians and engineers any more than it does other employed professionals under capitalism, and it is not clear, therefore, why technicians and engineers might be expected to form a class unto themselves. Perhaps more plausibly, then, Gorz identifies the well-educated, that is, those with the highest expectations for creative and satisfying careers, as the ones most likely to suffer acutely from the increasing rationalization of work. But here again, it is not clear why they should emerge as a class separate from other classes, since the capitalistic-bureaucratic master-trends which Gorz singles out as responsible for the deteriorating conditions of their work also affect the traditional proletariat. And, finally, one might ask of Touraine just what it will be about the post-industrial society of the future which will transform the human repositories and creators of the most advanced theoretical knowledge of the age into a class and elevate them to power. First, as Giddens (1973:Chapter 14) points out (following Weber), industrialism is characterized before anything else by the application of science to production, and the notion of post-industrial society appears more to be an extension of this principle, rather than some wholly new principle altogether. Second, there have always been "experts," Giddens continues (again, following Weber), and they have in the past almost invariably put their knowledge at the command of the ruling groups of their time. This was true of the pre-industrial age as well as of the industrial one, and there are no obvious reasons which Touraine identifies which would give us cause to believe that the post-industrial era will be fundamentally different in this respect.

The Historical Development of Classes in the Twentieth Century

Interpretation of the structure, organization, and course of change of Canadian society from a class perspective exist largely in scattered articles and books, and much of the basic research remains yet to be done (Clement and Drache, 1978). In the absence of any large body of original scholarship in this tradition, then, no thorough-going analysis of Canada from this point of view can be attempted here. Consequently, what follows is a highly-abbreviated overview of a changing class structure which can now only be dimly seen, but which should be more clearly revealed in the writings of current and future generations of scholars.

Bourgeoisie

A major historical trend in Canadian capitalism has been the increasing accumulation and centralization of capital in a relatively small number of dominant corporations whose presence defines the monopoly sector of the economy. Evidence for this extends back to the pre-Confederation period, and it appears as if the highest levels of *overall* corporate concentration were reached by the early 1920s, with relatively little change since that time, although this has not been true of all sectors (most notably the industrial) of the economy (Canada, 1978). Ryerson (1968) for example, reports that 1,618 sawmills produced some 400 million board feet of lumber in Upper Canada in 1851, while comparable levels of output were achieved by only six mills in 1971. And "Myers dates the beginning of corporate concentration in 1879 with the absorption of a series of small railways by the Grand Trunk and later by the Canadian Pacific" (Clement, 1975:69; also see Myers, 1914, 1972). The accumulation and centralization of capital continued in the period from the 1880s to World War I, which saw the emergence of the factory system, along with the phenomena of the joint stock corporation and the foreign-controlled branch plant. As part of this, there was shift away from an entrepreneurial capitalism of many small, independent businessmen to a corporate capitalism of relatively few wealthy investors whose practice it was to consolidate smaller companies into larger ones and to exercise control of their enterprises through stock holding, rather than through outright ownership. And, alongside an indigenous commercial elite who had earlier established themselves in transportation, trade and banking (Creighton, 1937, 1956), there grew up an internal comprador industrial elite of persons heading up the branch plants of (increasingly) U.S.-based manufacturing and resource firms (Levitt, 1970), while the Canadian-owned industrial sector never developed sufficiently to support an important indigenous elite (Naylor, 1975; but see Ryerson, 1976).

Historically, foreign investment has always been a prominent feature of the Canadian economy, and Canada currently has the highest levels of foreign investment of any developed country (Canada 1972b). Since the Conquest, the two major sources of foreign investment have been the United Kingdom and the United States. Prior to World War I, British investments in Canada were much greater than were those from the U.S., and they differed in type. The British were generally concerned to make long-term, low-risk profits, and so tended to invest their funds in securities, largely "government and financial institution bond and debenture stock without voting rights" (Naylor, 1972:22). This is known as portfolio investment, and can be contrasted with the propensity for U.S. investors in Canada to put their funds into more high-risk, *direct* investments in branch plants which they control. Both U.K. direct and U.S. portfolio and direct investment in Canada increased in the years during and after World War I, although U.K. portfolio investment in Canada decreased during the war. In this period, the United States supplanted the United Kingdom as Canada's most important economic "partner"; after the war, the majority of Canadian exports were destined for the United States, and U.S. investors held the bulk of foreign investments in Canada.

In the decades immediately preceding and following World War I, the pattern of mergers continued (Canada, 1978). According to Myers:

> From January, 1909, to January, 1913, there were 56 industrial mergers or amalgamations ⸱which absorbed 248 individual companies. The total capitalization of 206 of these individual companies was about $167,000,000; this amount was increased with the amalgamating process. The authorized capitalization, including bonds, of these 56 industrial mergers was... $456,938,266 (1972:xxxii-xxxiii).

As a consequence, many important industries came to be dominated by a smaller number of large firms (Clement, 1975:80–83). Pulp and paper, which accounted for almost one-sixth of all exports in the latter years of the 1920s, was a good example of this, as was automobile manufacturing, in which Canada became second only to the United States (Laxer, 1973:32–33). The concentration of capital, however, was probably most evident in the banking system. "Perhaps nowhere in the world can be found so intensive a degree of close organization as among the bank interest in Canada," Myers (1972:xxxii) wrote in reference to the pre-war period. And, by the late 1920s, the three largest Canadian banks — the Royal Bank, the Bank of Commerce, and the Bank of Montreal — held among them over 70 per cent of all bank assets in Canada (Clement, 1975:83; also see Canada, 1978:221–23).

Heavily dependent upon world markets for wheat, pulp and paper, and mineral exports, Canada generally, but especially the prairie provinces, was especially hard hit by the collapse of the world economy in the period of the Great Depression, 1929–1939, as export prices plummetted (Easterbrook and Aitken, 1956). These events, along with an overall decline in foreign investment, retarded the development of industrialization but, even as U.K. investments declined, U.S. investments, particularly in manufacturing and mining, actually increased in this decade, and the influx of United States-based branch plants continued. One apparent result seems to have been increased levels of industrial concentration. The major bankruptcy and merger victims of the Depression appear to have been the smaller Canadian-controlled firms which constituted the competitive sector of the economy; whether Canadian- or United States-controlled, enterprises in the monopoly sector seem generally to have survived this period quite well (Reynolds, 1940).

World War II rejuvenated the industrial sector of the Canadian economy, as manufacturing plants produced the machinery of war and related industries — most notably steel, aluminum, tool-making, electronics, and chemicals — prospered and grew (Easterbrook and Aitken, 1956). The government set up the Wartime Industries Control Board, presided over by C. D. Howe, and the Wartime Prices and Trade Board, headed by Donald Gordon. Together, these two men mapped out the development of the Canadian economy and oversaw the transformation of Canada from a predominantly staple-exporting, commercial economy into one which, while still heavily dependent upon the export of staples and the import of manufactured goods, had a modern industrial component to serve large sectors of the (albeit modest) domestic market (Canada, 1972b; Bourgault, 1972; Drache, 1975). Led and manned in the upper echelons by many of the most influential figures in business and government (the legendary "dollar-a-year" men), these two boards assumed almost total control of economic activity within the country during the period of their existence. By the time the two boards were phased out after the war, many of the corporations important in the Canadian economy today (e.g., Massey-Ferguson) had risen to dominance. And many of those men who were to become Canada's business leaders (e.g., E. P. Taylor) had spent a valuable apprenticeship in their employ, developing useful contacts and acquiring inside information about business and government in Canada (Park and Park, 1962, 1973; Clement, 1975; Newman, 1975, 1979).

The processes of accumulation and centralization of industrial capital seem to have continued in the years following World War II, with the result that the levels of corporate concentration in Canada are high relative to the past and to other nations. For example, "... the 50 largest manufacturing enterprises in the United States held 25% of total manufacturing value added in 1963/72, whereas in Canada their share increased by 0.2 percentage points to 33.6% in 1965/1972..." (Marfels, 1976:xxii). And comparisons between Canada, on the one hand, and Australia, West Germany, France, Japan, Sweden, Switzerland, and the United States for nine manufacturing industries "gave Canada a clear overall lead in terms of high concentration both for 1965 and 1972" (Marfels, 1976:xxiii). At the same time it should be noted that "Canadian" companies are relatively small by international standards. In 1975/76, for instance, it is estimated that "only four Canadian corporations (George Weston Limited, Ford, General Motors of Canada Limited and Imperial Oil Limited), were on a list of the 100 largest nonfinancial corporations in the world" (Canada, 1978:25). This figure, though, does not take into account that some corporations (such as Argus and Power) are larger than they seem, since they control a number of large corporations via minority ownership, and that some others (such as Ford, General Motors, and Imperial Oil) are branch plants of foreign-controlled multinationals. As for financial corporations, The Royal Bank of Canada — the largest in the country — ranked 23rd in the world in 1975/76 (Canada, 1978:25).

Since levels of concentration vary widely across the different sectors of the economy, it would be useful to know which sectors are highly concentrated and which are not. Marfels notes that:

> A classification of the eight divisions of the Canadian economy with regard to asset concentration levels and levels of inequality in the size distribution of assets designates Utilities, Finance, and Mining as highly concentrated divisions, and Services and Agriculture/Forestry/Fishing as divisions of low concentration; Manufacturing, Trade, and Construction assumed intermediate levels (1976:xix).

These are, of course, rather broad categories, and any very satisfactory analysis of changing concentration levels would necessarily have to move to a more detailed system of classification. Within the manufacturing sector, for example, there are real differences in concentration levels, even though the sector as a whole is not highly concentrated:

> Highly concentrated industries are mainly found in the following industry groups: Tobacco Products, Rubber Industries, Textiles, Primary Metals, Transportation Equipment, Petroleum and Coal, and Misc. Manufacturing Industries. Low concentration has its domain in Knitting Mills, Clothing, Printing and Publishing, and Metal Fabricating (Marfels, 1976:xx).

Over time, there has been little change in the pattern of Canadian control of the financial sector of the economy. As for the nonfinancial sectors, Table 11-1 documents something of the changing patterns of U.S. control in the period after World War I (also see Levitt, 1970). Clement summarizes these data in the following way:

> The steady pattern of an increasing share of control in manufacturing and in mining and smelting is readily apparent, while fluctuations in petroleum

and natural gas mainly reflect other foreign interests (Britain and the Netherlands). Much lower levels of control in transportation and utilities are also evident (1977:91).

For the most part, what is not controlled by United States-based companies in controlled from within Canada, although it is important between public and private control. Table 11-2 provides a more detailed breakdown of the last column in Table 11-1, showing those economic sectors which are Canadian-controlled and, of those, which tend to be public and which private. Briefly, the Canadian-controlled sector consists of railways and other utilities, which are largely publicly owned, and merchandising and construction, which are mostly privately held.

Table 11-1

Percentage of U.S. Control of Canadian Nonfinancial Industries, Selected Years, 1926–70.

Sector	1926	1930	1939	1948	1954*	1960	1965	1970
Manufacturing	30	31	32	39	41	44	46	47
Petroleum and Gas	—	—	—	—	67	64	58	61
Mining and Smelting	32	42	38	37	49	53	52	59
Railways	3	3	3	3	2	2	2	2
Other Utilities	20	29	26	24	7	4	4	4

* Petroleum and natural gas included in manufacturing and mining and smeling before 1954.
From *Continental Corporate Power* by Wallace Clement. Reprinted by permission of The Canadian Publishers, McClelland and Stewart Limited, Toronto.

Combining the information on corporate concentration with the data on ownership provides an overview of the major components of the monopoly, state, and competitive sectors of the economy, and of the extent of U.S. penetration into different parts of the Canadian economy (also see Park and Park, 1962, 1973). Briefly, there is the Canadian-controlled, state sector which consists, most importantly, of railways and other utilities. In the historical development of Canada, government has taken a leading role from the very earliest days in developing this sector on its own or helping to finance the networks of transportation necessary to an economy based on the staples trade (Easterbrook and Aitken, 1956). There is, a well, a Canadian-controlled monopoly sector centering around the banks and other financial institutions, and a U.S.-dominated monopoly sector located prominently in petroleum and gas, mining, and certain kinds of manufacturing (most notably tobacco, rubber,

Table 11–2

Percentage of Control of Non-Financial Industries in Canada, 1970.

Sector	Canada Government	Private	United States	Other Foreign	Total
Manufacturing	2	37	47	14	100
Petroleum and Gas	2	22	61	15	100
Mining and Smelting	1	29	59	11	100
Railways	73	25	2	—	100
Other Utilities	69	24	4	3	100
Merchandising and Construction	1	87	8	4	100
Total	22	42	28	8	100

From *Continental Corporate Power* by Wallace Clement. Reprinted by permssion of The Canadian Publishers, McClelland and Stewart Limited, Toronto.

textiles, primary metals, transportation equipment, and petroleum and coal). Here, again, one can see in this the cumulative results of the several trends in the Canadian economy which have already been touched upon. The competitive sector is largely Canadian-controlled, and includes services, agriculture, forestry, and fishing, along with certain manufacturing (e.g., knitting mills, clothing, printing and publishing, and metal fabricating). Merchandising and construction are also largely Canadian-controlled, with some elements (e.g., department store retailing) in the monopoly sector, and others not.

Within the broad category of the bourgeoisie, then, there is an indigenous elite who head up the major commercial enterprises in the Canadian economy, and an internal comprador elite who occupy the commandposts of the important, largely United States-based, industrial branch plants. Although the historical data on the Canadian bourgeoisie in general, and elites in particular, are relatively sparse, information for the period following World War II is more systematic and detailed, including studies by Park and Park (1973), Porter (1965), Clement (1975, 1977), and Newman (1975, 1979). Each of these works merits an analysis in itself. The brief discussion below, however, is based largely on Porter (1965) and Clement (1975), and is confined for reasons of space to only certain of their more important findings and conclusions.

Referring to the period of the early 1950s, Porter identified the "economic elite of Canada . . . as the 985 Canadian residents holding directorships in the 170 dominant corporations, the banks, insurance companies, and numerous other corporations" (1965:274). The 760 (or 77 per cent) of these persons for whom

relevant additional information was available held 82 per cent of the directorships in the dominant corporations held by Canadian residents. Following
Porter's lead almost twenty years later, Clement located the Canadian economic
elite in those 946 directors and senior executives who

> ... preside over the corporate world, using as their means of power, the
> central institutions of the Canadian economy — 113 dominant corpora-
> tions, their subsidiaries, affiliates, investments, interlocking directorships
> with smaller corporations, family ties and shared class origins" (1975:167).

The 775 (or 82 per cent) of those for whom biographical data were available held
88 per cent of the directorships in the dominant corporations held by Canadian
residents.

Of the 907 elite members for whom the relevant data could be obtained,
Porter found that about 22 per cent held directorships in more than one
dominant corporation, and most sat on the boards of other corporations not
classified as dominant. One person held ten directorships. The majority of those
sitting on the boards of the nine chartered banks were also directors of dominant corporations. Likewise, there was considerable overlap in membership
among the boards of directors of dominant corporations and the major life
insurance companies. In aggregate, this evidence suggests a high degree of potential coordination among members of the economic elite 1965:578–80). Indeed, Porter concludes that "the boards of the dominant corporations ... are
... woven by the interlocking directorship into a fabric not unlike the web of
kinship and lineage which provides cohesion to primitive life" (1965:304).
Twenty years later, Clement reports of the 964 members of the elite for which
he could obtain the information that fully 29 per cent held more than one
directorship in a dominant corporation, and that this 29 per cent held among
them 54 per cent of the total number of directorships, with one member
holding a total of eight. In comparing these findings with Porter's, Clement
concludes that "there has been ... an increasing centralization and concentration of capital into fewer and larger firms" (1975:168), and that there has been
"a further concentration of power at the top of the economic elite over the past
twenty years" (1975:168). It should be pointed out, however, that differences in
the manner in which Porter and Clement define such critical terms as
"dominant corporation" and, consequently, "economic elite," do not permit
any precise comparisons between the two studies.

Porter points out two striking aspects of the careers of members of the
economic elite in the early 1950s: almost all of them achieved their positions
within established corporations, rather than having founded their own firms
and built them up themselves; and a very high proportion had fathers who were
members of the elite before them. Like Porter's, Clement's elite was disproportionately "upper class" (i.e., high SES) in background. Indeed, "three-fifths of
the present elite came from upper class origins. This was an increase of almost
10 per cent from ... twenty years ago" (1975:219), an apparent change which he

attributes partly to the decline of banking as a mobility route for the middle and working classes and the emergence of new financial sectors with exclusive recruitment patterns (1975:220). Persons who have made their way into the inner circles of the corporate world, he suggests, have done so largely through "Canadian-controlled corporations in the finance sectors. . . . The only notable exceptions were 15 per cent who made it through U.S.-controlled resource and manufacturing corporations" (1975:220). Not only were a majority of the economic elite of high SES origin, but those holding multiple directorships were much more likely to be high SES in background than holders of single directorships were. And "more than one-quarter of the present elite . . . inherited important positions from previous generations" (1975:220).

The homogeneity of social background which Porter found among the members of the elite was remarkable. Not only did many come from elite or (more broadly) high SES backgrounds, but the majority were university-educated, Protestant, Anglophone males, and better than one-third had attended private schools, such as Upper Canada College. Virtually absent were Jews and Francophones. Totally absent were women. As he was able to show, "economic power belongs almost exclusively to those of British origin" (1965:286). Even though over 30 per cent of the Canadian population were Francophone, they made up only 6.7 per cent of the economic elite. Jews made up 0.78 per cent of the elite and 1.4 per cent of the population as a whole. Given the over-representation of Jews in upper-level, white-collar occupations, their under-representation among the elite is all the more notable. In 1972 (the year of Clement's data), the economic elite was still almost exclusively a male preserve (99.4 per cent), but perhaps even more the preserve of persons with university degrees and post-graduate training than it was earlier (1975:241). The vast majority of elite members received their training in Canadian institutions, with fully 42.8 per cent having obtained their undergraduate training at the University of Toronto or at McGill. As in the earlier period, Anglophones are vastly over-represented in Clement's elite, with Francophones and members of most "third" ethnic groups grossly under-represented. In the interim, the Anglophone hold on elite positions may have relaxed somewhat, with Francophones and Jews gaining slightly, although this is not the interpretation which Clement makes of his data (see Clement, 1975:234, Table 35; also see Himelfarb and Richardson (1979:233–34) who, in an otherwise careful book, follow Clement's misinterpretation, which derives from some misleading arithmetic which suggests that *all three* groups have either maintained or increased their relative representation — an impossible outcome).

Consistent with what one would expect from knowledge of the historical development of the Canadian economy (Easterbrook and Aitken, 1956), persons born in central Canada were over-represented among Clement's elite by about 8 per cent, while those born in the Atlantic provinces were under-represented by approximately 3 per cent, and those from the West by some 5 per cent (1975:224–30). Furthermore, elite members from the West were found to be more often from middle- and working-class backgrounds than were those from other parts of the country, and more likely to be United States comprador elite as well.

In both the early 1950s and early 1970s, then, control of the major financial and industrial institutions in the Canadian economy appears to have been disproportionately vested in a relatively small number of very powerful people. As unrelated individuals, each controlled enormous economic resources. The evidence is, though, that they did not at all operate as totally uncoordinated aggregates. The high degree of homogeneity of social background among elite members in his study, Porter argues, produced a group of persons very similar in belief and attitude. It is a similarity reinforced through informal social contact, kinship, and membership in certain exclusive clubs, as well as through the mechanism of the interlocking directorship. Clement, too, attempts to unravel the tangled network of associations among his small, select, and socially homogeneous elite. Associations first developed in childhood are often reinforced and multiplied through attendance at one of Canada's few and "finer" private schools.

> After attending private school and typically going on to the University of Toronto, or possibly McGill, the sons of the upper class are ready for the corporate board rooms. Like their fathers, they then enter another private world — the exclusive men's clubs (1965:247).

And they enter other private worlds as well, many of which contribute directly to internal coordination with other elites in Canada and elsewhere (1965:243-69).

Blacks invited 'people we're fond of' to party
Zena Cherry

Mr. and Mrs. Conrad Moffat Black were married in July in Grace Church on-the-Hill; she is the former Shirley Hishon Walters of Montreal.

Their first large party was held recently at the York Club and the bride looked lovely in a simple plum-shade silk blouse and silk paisley-patterned skirt, mid-calf length with a side slit to the knee.

Among the first to arrive were Lieutenant-Governor Pauline McGibbon, who was on her way to speak at a dinner in Barrie. Others who left early were the Roland Micheners and the Sydney Hermants — they went on to cocktails with Mr. and Mrs. C. Halim Harding in their Rosedale home. The Blacks and the Hardings had each invited the other to the coinciding parties.

As explained by Shirley Black, "We asked the people we're really fond of." And so one saw Rev. John E. Erb, who officiated at their wedding, with Mrs. Erb. And some of the Old Guard like Mr. and Mrs. J. Harold Crang, Joseph Sedgwick, the Terence Sheards, Maj. Conn Smythe, Mr. and Mrs. Charles B. Stewart, Mr. and Mrs. Douglas H. Ward and the E.P. Taylors.

Mr. Taylor told me he's lost 60 pounds, and had to cart all his suits to London to be taken in.

"You look wonderful," I told him, "How did you lose?"

His answer, "I didn't do anything. I think it's age. I'm outliving everyone."

Col. and Mrs. Kenneth L. Campbell came with their house-guests Mr. and Mrs. J. Barry O'Brien of Ottawa; Mrs. Charles

L. Gundy was escorted by photographer Ken Bell, and with their wives were Mr. Justice Charles Dubin, Donald C. Early, Deputy Crown Prosecuting Attorney Stephen C. Leggett, John C. Lockwood and Charles Rathgeb. Also there were Mr. and Mrs. John H. Taylor with their son-in-law and daughter Mr. and Mrs. John Craig Eaton.

The Blacks used to live back-to-back to the Eatons — also present were Mrs. John David Eaton, Mr. and Mrs. George R. Eaton and Mrs. Thor Eaton. Other long-time friends were Fruma Bell, Mr. and Mrs. Robert Dale-Harris of Uxbridge, Mr. and Mrs. Leighton McCarthy, David F. Jewell and Mrs. Jewell, Mr. and Mrs. Morton Simcoe and Mr. and Mrs. Thomas McMahon, who've recently moved from Montreal to Toronto.

Conrad Black is the author of Duplessis, which came out one year ago. His publisher, John G. McClelland, was at the reception and others in the publishing world who attended were Douglas G. Bassett, St. Clair Balfour, Floyd S. Chalmers, J. Douglas Creighton, George N. M. Currie, Michael C. de Pencier, Gordon N. Fisher and Michael C. Sifton.

Other authors there were Peter Charles Newman, Richard Rohmer and Madeline Kronby.

Members of the media there included John W. H. Bassett, Anthony F. Griffiths, Betty Kennedy and her husband G. Allan Burton, Adrienne Clarkson, Philippe de Gaspe Beaubien, Barbara Frum and her husband Dr. Murray Frum, Fraser Kelly, Frederick Langen with his fiance Helen Meyer, Edward S. Rogers, and Morton Shulman with Mrs. Rogers and Mrs. Shulman.

Relations present included Mr. and Mrs. Bruce E. Brymer, Mr. and Mrs. Robert Gillan and their daughter Janice, the Gordon P. Oslers with their daughter and her husband Mr. and Mrs. Robert Beverly (Biff) Matthews, Mrs. Conrad S.

Riley, Nancy Riley, and Mrs. W. Culver Riley and her daughter Mrs. Robert de Langley.

From the political arena were the following with their wives — Edwin A. Goodman, Senator John M. Godfrey, Jerahmiel S. Grafstein, Donald S. Macdonald, Rob Parker, recently elected Conservative MP for Eglinton; John P. Robarts, David Smith, John Napier Turner and two Liberal candidates for the next federal election, Roy MacLaren and James S. Peterson.

Also there was Michael Arthur Meighen, the former national president of the Progressive Conservative Party of Canada. He's now a consultant to TV Guide magazine. He was with his wife, the former Kelly Dillon. They were married in the spring and are living in Rosedale. She's the daughter of Richard M. Dillon, Ontario's deputy provincial secretary for resource development, and Mrs. Dillon. Kelly is head of the personnel department at General Foods.

Conrad Black and his brother G. Montegu Black 3rd, with associates, recently took over Argus Corp. Ltd. This includes control of Dominion Stores, Domtar Inc., Hollinger Mines, Massey-Ferguson and Standard Broadcasting.

Business friends with their wives were Thomas Bolton, Albert L. Fairley, Anthony S. Fell, Henry R. Jackman and his son H. N. R. Jackman, Igor Kaplan, Douglas W. Maloney, Donald A. McIntosh, Victor A. Rice, Albert A. Thornbrough and William O. Twaits. Bankers there included R. Donald Fullerton, Russell E. Harrison, Hartland Molson MacDougald, Richard M. Thomson and J. Page R. Wadsworth.

And after the hulabaloo in the financial world about the dispute relating to the valuation of the Ravelston Corp. shares between the Meighen group and the Blacks, all has been settled.

The Globe & Mail, Toronto, November 14, 1978.

The Parks cover much the same ground as do Porter and Clement, and for a period of time which overlaps with Porter's work. Their analysis, however, was carried out from a Marxist point of view, and addressed the question of "who owns Canada?" They discuss in detail what they see as "the structure of Canadian monopoly and the alliance of Canadian and U.S. capital that is bringing about U.S. domination of Canada" (Park and Park, 1973:xv). Beginning with the premise that "control is based on ownership and that without ownership control vanishes" (1973:11), they attempt to identify the members of Canada's dominant class "that owns and controls the mines and mills and factories of Canada" (1973:10). These persons, they argue, form a tightly-knit group who, on the basis of an ideology of corporate internationalism, are selling the country out to United States financiers. They note that "at the centre of this financial and industrial corporate structure lie the chartered banks, the members of whose boards of directors make up the 'Who's Who' of the dominant financial groups" (1973:71), and then try to show how the same group of financiers dominates both industry and the banks through the mechanism of overlapping board memberships.

In general, the picture of the economic elite which the Parks paint is similar to Porter's, although it tends to be rather more narrowly economic — something which they regret in retrospect.

> Class was defined in economic terms without reference to the role of class consciousness; nationalization was discussed with only a passing reference to Canada as a bi-national state. And while we saw economic growth as something more than an increase in per capita gross national product, the problems of development in Canada as in the Third World were seen mainly as turning on the growth of manufacturing industry and not in their wider social-political context (1973:ix–x).

If they did not weight the "wider social-political context" as heavily as did Porter, they did focus on the extensive and increasing penetration of the United States-based multinational corporations into the Canadian economy, where Porter is largely silent on this issue.

If Porter paid insufficient attention to issues of foreign capital in the Canadian economy, not so Clement, whose major works, *The Canadian Corporate Elite* (1975) and *Continental Corporate Power* (1977), provide historical and contemporary data on indigenous, internal comprador, and parasitic elites and the inter-relations among them. As Clement argues, it is probably a mistaken view which sees the indigenous Canadian elite as simply dependent upon or as engaged in "selling out to" foreign (largely U.S.) financial interests. Rather, it seems more accurate to say that the indigenous economic elite or big bourgeoisie presides over an "overdeveloped financial and transportation/utilities system in Canada" (1977:291), the continuing prosperity of which seems largely to have been generated through a practice of "stable, long-term, interest bearing investments" (1977:292). "... since the U.S. industrial system was further advanced in technology, management, and marketing, the U.S. companies were often favoured as more secure investments" (1977:292).

In other words, the process of compradorization has been sector specific and took place in the presence of traditionally powerful Canadian capitalists rather than displacing them. The effect on weak capitalists in production was, of course, to bring about their downfall (1977:293).

The research of Porter, Clement, the Parks, and others has furthered by a large measure our understanding of issues of classes, elites, and power in Canada. And the "rediscovery of political economy" which some (e.g., Drache, 1978) have seen in the work of such scholars as Clement seems to hold promise to advance it still further. Yet the odyssey is only just begun, and it is still not obvious that it will lead us to real discovery. First, the new political economy seems to represent an advance over the earlier tradition of elite studies (e.g., Mills, 1956; Porter, 1965; and, to some extent, also Clement, 1975) in that it is theoretically informed — in particular by various varieties of Marxism. But this may pose as many new problems as it solves old ones, partly because the history of Marxist scholarship has so often been the history of internecine paper warfare (see, for example, Ryerson, 1976 and Watkins, 1977). Second, at least in its worst forms, the "new" political economy seems occasionally to eschew the careful methodology of the best of the "old" in favour of an anti-quantitative stance and reversion to the methodology of "demonstration by overwhelming example" characteristic of many earlier elite studies (e.g., "Mr. W is married to the daughter of Mr. X who shares membership on a board of directors with Mr. Y who is the godfather of Mr. Z who plays polo with Mr. W. . . ."). While there is clearly some value in extended examples to make a point, they are no substitute for a careful mapping of interconnections among members of an elite. Third, the sum of individual power, common backgrounds, and corporate, family, and other connections among people adds up to less than a demonstration of whether and how members of an elite operate *as a group to some effect.* To be sure, we must know the former in order to determine the latter, but we must go on to see how the members of an elite coalesce to make decisions on different issues and what the consequences of these decisions are. It seems not unfair to judge that the study of classes, elites, and power in Canada to date has not seriously attempted this (admittedly extremely difficult) task.

Petty Bourgeoisie

With the progressive development of the capitalist mode of production in Canada beginning in the late nineteenth century, the "old" petty bourgeoisie of independent commodity producers and small businessmen has experienced an almost continuous erosion in numbers and in fortunes. "With their numbers reduced from their numerical and political dominance of the 1850s to a mere 10.9 per cent of income earners in 1968, it is clear that the . . . (old) petite bour-geoisie is reaching the last stages of destruction" (Johnson, 1972:151). Among farmers, the long-term trend has been in the direction of fewer, larger, better-capitalized, and more productive farms. Once an agricultural mainstay, the family farm has become less and less able to compete, and increasing numbers of farmers have had either to leave the land altogether or to supplement their incomes through farm labour (Easterbrook and Aitken, 1956). For, despite large increases in farm productivity, farm incomes have not kept pace with the average. In 1948, average farmers' incomes as a proportion of the average income in Canada stood at about .78; by 1968, it had fallen to .66; and in 1977 it stood at .70. Among independent businessmen, similar processes have been at work, although perhaps to less dramatic effect. Over time, small businesses have faced mounting pressures from their corporate counterparts, with the result that they, too, have found it more and more difficult to compete. In 1948, business operators constituted 6.6 per cent of all income earners in Canada; by 1968, this had declined to 4.1 per cent; and by 1977 to 3.3 per cent. Their incomes also decreased in this period from 1.4 times the average in Canada in 1948 to 1.05 in 1968 to .93 in 1977.

In some contrast to the downward trajectory of the old petty bourgeoisie of independent commodity producers and small businessmen is the growth and prosperity of the new petty bourgeoisie of professionals, including lawyers, physicians, and dentists. As Canada has been transformed from a small-scale, rural, agrarian society to a large-scale, urban, industrial one, the demand for an elite cadre of professionals skilled in the practice of the law has, until very recently, consistently outstripped the supply. And the increasing affluence of Canadians has had a similar effect on the demand for and the supply of medical and dental professionals. These market forces, coupled with the existence of such strong, monopolistic, and self-regulating professional organizations as the Canadian Bar Association, the Canadian Medical Association and their provincial counterparts, have given independent professionals a high degree of autonomy in their work, relative freedom from competition, and generally increasing incomes (e.g., Blishen, 1969:Chapter 6). In 1948, physicians in Canada reported incomes which were 3.6 times the Canadian average; by 1968, this figure had risen to 5.9; and the corresponding figure for 1977 was 4.6. The figures for lawyers in these three years were 3.7, 4.7, and 3.7, while those for dentists were 2.5, 4.0, and 3.8 respectively.

While the autonomy and affluence of the new petty bourgeoisie seem assured in the short run, there are signs that this situation may not continue indefinitely. As the costs of medical care have increasingly been borne by publicly-sponsored schemes of universal medicare, for example, control of the institution of medicine has come more and more to reside in the state, rather than in the medical profession. Physicians are, of course, quite aware of this and very sensitive to the shifting locus of authority, as they have shown in the Saskatchewan doctors' strike of 1962 (Badgley and Wolfe, 1967), and, more recently, in the trend toward withdrawal from participation in public medical insurance programmes. While it is impossible to predict the future trajectory of events in the continuing struggle between the state and the medical profession, much less to say what will happen in the case of the other professional groups, the power and prosperity of the new petty bourgeoisie could well fail to survive the encroachments of big government and big business in the long run, and their futures could lie in some form of public or private employment for a salary or a wage.

Working Class

Unlike most industrialized or industrializing countries, Canada had a fairly large class of landless labourers prior to the advent of industrialization (Teeple, 1972). For, despite the relative abundance of unused land in pre-Confederation Canada, there was no abundance of land available for easy purchase by immigrants and others who might have wanted to start their own farms. Rather, Canada was governed by a ruling group of colonial officials and merchant capitalists who held an effective monopoly over most of the lands of the colonies, and who often retained them for speculative purposes, rather than cultivating or selling them. The substantial numbers of immigrants who came in search of land or employment often found neither, and frequently faced the prospect of unemployment in British North America or emigration to the United States, since failure to develop the land also deterred the development of business and industry.

By the 1860s, the emergence of capitalist forms of production and the factory system could be seen, and the transformation of the class of landless labourers into a capitalist labour market had begun (Pentland, 1960). This, coupled with high levels of immigration and a continuing lack of economic opportunities in the rural areas (MacDougall, 1913, 1973) in the period prior to World War I, made available a large work force for the increasing numbers of low-skill jobs in industry (Kealey, 1973), mining, forestry, railway construction (Bradwin, 1972), and elsewhere. The surplus of labour, however, helped keep wages low and working conditions primitive.

The accumulation and centralization of capital in increasingly large industrial units was felt early on by the skilled craftsmen and artisans. Writing of London, Ontario in the 1860s, Palmer observes that:

> ...the workingman's fight against the impersonalization of the emerging market economy was championed most ardently by the skilled tradesman and his craft union. The International Union of Iron Moulders was the first such organization to come into being in the Forest City (1859), and was soon joined by the Bricklayers Protective Association, founded in 1863. But the most vigorous of early unions was the Typographers, established in the 1860s...(1976:114).

Many of these early craft unionists were British immigrants who had brought their experience in the British labour movement with them across the Atlantic and put it to use in their new home.

The development of the factory system and of mechanized production created new forms of labour involving semi- and unskilled jobs performed under conditions of industrial discipline. The labour market, however, was predominantly composed of rural and immigrant workers, along with increasing numbers of skilled craftsmen and artisans, who were unaccustomed to this kind of regime, and did not take easily to it (Kealey, 1973). When taken together with the low rates of pay and poor working conditions, this contributed importantly to high levels of turnover, considerable labour unrest, and the development of a labour movement in Canada in the latter decades of the nineteenth century.

After an initial surge of organization during the nine-hour movement of 1872, organized labor had been nearly devastated in the depression of the late seventies. Even in those years, though, there was significant working class activity, including a massive general strike on the Grand Trunk Railroad in January 1877, which prefigured the far more famous American railroad strikes of the following summer. In the prosperity of the early eighties, there was a rapid revival of labor organization. The British Amalgamateds, American Internationals, and especially the Knights of Labor all grew quickly. The re-establishment of a Toronto Trades and Labor Council in 1881, a wave of strikes in Toronto in April 1882, and the first Trades and Labor Congress meeting in 1883 were all symbolic of this new resurgence (Kealey, 1973:xxi).

It was an eventful, and sometimes even violent, period in Canadian labour history (Bliss, 1972:180–83).

With the further concentration of capital and mechanization of work in the 1890s and the first two decades of the twentieth century, the demand for semi- and unskilled labour continued to grow. In response to pressures from business-men hopeful of recruiting a cheap and compliant labour force of non-English speakers, the government loosed the gates and immigration reached unprece-dented levels. Despite this, however, union membership rose and labour unrest intensified (Avery, 1975). By 1921, some 16 per cent of the non-agricultural work force in Canada were unionized (see Table 11–3). And a number of strikes reached the point where the civil or military authorities, sometimes reinforced by private police, were called to intervene. "Between 1900 and 1913 no less than 11 strikes across the nation eventuated in the use of regular military forces" (Rine-hart, 1975:41).

Along with growth in the blue-collar labour force came growth in the ranks of the white-collar workers as well. This growth touched all categories of white-collar jobs, but especially the clerical and commercial-financial categories, which saw rapid influxes of women beginning around the turn of the century. White-collar workers, particularly women, have traditionally been slow to unionize, probably because of the historical advantages which white-collar work has enjoyed over blue-collar work and, in the case of women specifically, because of their relatively weaker attachments to the labour force. Consequent-ly, there was little labour unrest amongst white-collar workers in this period, and little motive for union membership.

"Two spectacular workers' movements emerged during the second decade of the Twentieth Century — the One Big Union and the Winnipeg General Strike" (Rinehart, 1975:41). The One Big Union (OBU) was born out of the heightened class hostility in Canada which developed during World War I around issues of inflation and conscription, as well as disaffection among unionists in the western provinces with the eastern-dominated Trades and Labour Congress. Some 250 representatives of official labour organizations met in March 1919 in Calgary to pass, on a unanimous vote, the resolution that:

> Whereas the capitalist class of this country has in the past used every means at its disposal to defeat the workers in their attempt to ameliorate the conditions under which they live; and
>
> Whereas, to successfully conduct a strike, all crafts in an industry must act together; and
>
> Whereas, the present craft union organization which makes it necessary for each craft to secure sanction from its international tends to defeat this object;
>
> Therefore be it resolved that a referendum vote be taken of all affiliated crafts on the following questions:
>
> "Are you in favor of scientifically reorganizing the workers of Canada upon the basis of industrial organization instead of craft unionism?" (Penner, 1973:23–24)

Organized along industrial, rather than craft, lines, the new vehicle for labour would be the OBU. Or so was the hope. But the move to launch the OBU was interrupted by the dramatic events in Winnipeg in May 1919 — the Winnipeg General Strike.

The Winnipeg General Strike (Masters, 1950; Penner, 1973; Bercuson, 1974a, b) was the culmination of over three decades of increasingly bitter labour unrest in a city whose administration was dominated by a local establishment of anti-union businessmen, and whose labour elite numbered among them many who

> ... were immigrants from the industrial heartland of the British Isles and who had received their training in hard-knock schools such as Birmingham, Leeds, the Clydeside or the black mines of Wales. They were fervent believers in the necessity of trade-union organization and many were followers of one socialist school or another... (Bercuson, 1974a:2).

The major issues which lay behind this unhappy history were relatively clear: From the side of business, it was a matter of freedom to build private enterprise unhampered by union organization; from the side of labour, it was a case of the right to form unions and to bargain collectively. From the beginning, however, business had held sway in the city and, often aided by the three levels of government and the courts, had effectively prevented any real erosion of its powers by organized labour.

Against this backdrop, the severe inflation which accompanied World War I (e.g., the Consumer Price Index increased by an estimated 18.2 per cent in 1917 over 1916 — the largest increase recorded to date) further polarized business and labour in an already polarized city. On May 1, three months of negotiations with the Winnipeg Builder's Exchange had come to naught, and the aggregate of unions in the Building Trades Council went out on strike, to be followed the next day by three locals of the Metal Trades Council (Penner, 1973:xxv–xxvi). Four days later, the Building Trades and Metal Councils notified the Winnipeg Trades and Labour Council (TLC) of the employers' refusal to bargain, and the TLC initiated a vote among its affiliated unions on the issue of a general strike. On a vote of 8,667 to 645, a general strike was called for 11:00 A.M., May 15, under the direction of a 300-member Strike Committee, and, when that time arrived, economic activity in the city effectively ceased.

On May 16, the formation of the business-dominated Winnipeg Citizens' Committee of 1,000 to oppose the strike was announced. With essential services paralyzed, the Strike Committee "issued cards reading 'Permitted by authority of Strike Committee' to bakeries, dairies, and other establishments" (Bercuson, 1974a:21), so that food distribution could be resumed without harassment from the strikers. This raised the issue, both within the city and without, of just who was in control — the strikers or the civil authority, and the Strike Committee withdrew the signs four days later. The acting Minister of Justice, the Honourable Arthur Meighen, along with the Minister of Labour, Senator Gideon Robertson, arrived in the city on May 22 to intervene in the strike. Robertson immediately voiced the view that the strike was an OBU-inspired tactic to destroy the international craft unions and to overthrow the government. On May 25, he issued an ultimatum to striking postal workers to return to their jobs and to sign a declaration of divorcement from the TLC or to be dismissed from their jobs, thus initiating a practice which was subsequently used on several other groups, including workers in the provincially-owned telephone system, firemen, and the city police. In most cases, however, the employees refused and were fired.

From the firing of almost the entire city police force on June 9 to the strike's end, Winnipeg was policed by a force of "specials," recruited largely from anti-strike elements in the city, backed up by a newly-assembled militia and the Royal North West Mounted Police. On threat of a strike of train crews which would have completely shut down transcontinental rail service, Robertson pushed the metal trades employers to offer a proposal which, although it allowed for recognition of individual craft unions, did not allow for recognition of the Metal Trades Council. The point was to tempt the moderate union leaders and, thus, to drive a wedge between them and their more radical counterparts. To underscore it, Robertson ordered the early-morning arrests of several "alien" radical strike leaders on June 18, and announced that deportation procedings would begin. A few days later, it was decided to release a number of the arrested radical leaders on bail, with the leaders' agreement to withdraw completely from involvement in the strike, although deportation would have served no real purpose at that point, since the moderate leaders had moved to accept the metal trades employers' offer of June 16. The arrests, along with the resumption of streetcar service, however, had aroused the strikers to mount a protest parade scheduled to start at 2:30 on the afternoon of June 21. At the appointed hour, the crowd moved forward until they encountered a northbound streetcar and attempted unsuccessfully to stop it. When a southbound car then began to push its way through, the crowd pursued it, tried to tip it over, and, failing this, smashed its windows, slashed its seats, and set it afire. With that, a contingent of Mounted Police which had been advancing toward the marchers charged into them twice, and the marchers retaliated with a hail of stones and bottles. Moments after the Mayor had read the Riot Act to the crowd, the officer commanding the Mounted Police, sensing that the situation was out of control, gave the order to fire. One man was killed immediately, and perhaps as many as thirty or more were injured in the melee which followed. On July 25, the strike Committee announced the end of the strike as of 11:00 A.M., June 26.

Not only was the Winnipeg General Strike not an isolated event in the context of the evolution of class relations in Winnipeg, it was not an isolated event in the larger Canadian context. It was partly the consequence of the same social forces which led to the formation of the OBU; and other, if lesser, general strikes occurred in the same period in Calgary, Edmonton, Vancouver, Port Arthur, and Toronto. What made it different was that its scope and duration raised issues which few people had seemed to anticipate beforehand — most importantly, issues of the challenge which a general strike poses to the structure of legitimate authority. In retrospect, it seems clear enough that the Winnipeg General Strike was a step in the direction of establishing the rights of workers to oganize into unions and to bargain collectively, rather than toward revolution. But it did have unanticipated consequences with revolutionary implications and, because of this, it could probably only have failed. Moreover,

> In a very real sense the Winnipeg General Strike marked the end of an era in Winnipeg and western Canada. The Winnipeg strikers had manned the battle lines for their western brothers and their loss seriously undermined the strength of all western labour. The defeat of the strike assured the weakening of those unions and labour leaders who had championed its use and who had called it (Bercuson, 1974a:29–30).

Thus, although the OBU went on to be founded during the days of the strike, and some OBU locals actually survived until the 1950s, the failure of the strike ultimately meant the failure of the OBU as well.

Although the craft mode of production had been largely eliminated in competition with industrial capitalism by the end of World War I, it was not until the 1920s that large-scale capital investment in manufacturing began to occur in Canada. With this investment, productivity rose and wages climbed. And, as part of this,

> It was principally during the 1920s that two significant refinements were brought to bear on the coordination, supervision, and specialization of labour. The application of the principles of "scientific" management to the work process and the advent of mass production techniques, particularly the assembly line, were to have a lasting impact on the organization of work (Rinehart, 1975:43).

These developments were abruptly halted, however, by the onset of the Depression in 1929, and not until the outbreak of World War II did they really resume their pace again.

The failure of the Winnipeg General Strike signalled the beginning of a difficult two decades for the labour movement in Canada (Jamieson, 1973; Williams, 1975). In 1921, union membership stood at 16.0 per cent of the non-agricultural labour force, dropping slightly to 15.3 per cent in 1931, and rising to 18.0 per cent in 1941 (see Table 11-3). The craft unions of the Trades and Labour Congress (TLC) were ill-equipped to absorb the increasing numbers of unskilled and semi-skilled workers and, when the Depression brought rising levels of unemployment and an end to ten years of relative prosperity, "workers wanted jobs, not unions" (Abella, 1974a:xii). In the early years of the Depression, the Communist-led Workers' Unity League attempted to move into the organizational vacuum by forging unions of industrial workers, but its efforts were frustrated by the combined forces of business and government — most notably in the strike of coal miners at Estevan, Saskatchewan in 1931 (Hanson, 1974) and the strike of furniture factory workers in Stratford, Ontario in 1933 (Morton, 1974).

Although efforts at organizing workers along industrial, rather than craft, lines in Canada go back at least as far as the 1880s and the Knights of Labour (Kealey, 1973), the first real breakthrough was made in Oshawa, Ontario in 1937, at the General Motors plant (Abella, 1974b). Following a successful strike in 1928, the plant workers formed a union and applied for a charter from the TLC, only to be directed to disband as a unit and reorganize into several craft unions instead. As a result, the workers were left with no union whatever in the early 1930s. In 1935, the Committee for Industrial Organization (CIO) was formed in the United States, and when the automobile workers walked off the job in protest over a speed-up in the assembly line at the Oshawa plant in 1937, a CIO organizer from the United Automobile Workers of America (UAW) in Detroit arrived to help organize the workers. The strike was bitter, but brief, and pitted the CIO-aided automobile workers against not only General Motors, but also against the Liberal Premier of Ontario, Mitchell Hepburn, who was fearful of incursions of CIO-affiliated unions into other branches of Ontario industry, especially the gold mines. The immediate effect was the establishment of UAW Local 222, although the union was not officially recognized in the actual settlement itself. The larger effect, though, was "the birth of industrial unionism in Canada")Abella, 1974a:121) — if, perhaps, ultimately at the expense of an all-Canadian union movement.

Spurred on by the events in Oshawa, Canadian CIO leaders undertook an ambitious organizing campaign in Ontario, aided by Communist organizers from the now-defunct Workers' Unity League (Abella, 1973). Without financial or organizational support from the United States' parent, however, their efforts could not be sustained and, by the end of 1937, they had largely petered out. At the same time, the American Federation of Labor (AFL) moved to pressure the TLC to keep the CIO out of Canada, and this resulted in the expulsion of all CIO-affiliated unions from the TLC in 1939. Almost immediately, the CIO unions entered into merger discussions with the All-Canadian Congress of Labour (ACCL), an anti-international, anti-communist federation of Canadian unions which was in serious economic and organizational difficulty. Accomplished in September 1940, the merger created the Canadian Congress of Labour (CCL). With the Communist influences in the CIO unions diluted, the CCL's first president and the other five executive officers were either Co-operative Commonwealth Federation (CCF) supporters or, at least, sympathetic to the recently-formed political party.

World War II brought an end to the Depression, and industrialization and prosperity brought new life to the labour movement. Both the TLC and CCL grew in the number and size of their affiliates. By war's end, almost a quarter of all nonagricultural workers in Canada were members of unions, and the labour movement achieved an important victory in the strike of automobile workers at the Ford plant in Windsor, Ontario in 1945, in which the UAW won the right to have union dues deducted from the paycheques of plant employees — members of the union or not — a group medical, hospital, and life insurance plan, and a number of other concessions (Moulton, 1974).

Relations between the TLC and the CCL were generally harmonious throughout the 1940s and early 1950s, although both federations went through periods of bitter internal strife as a consequence of their recent and rapid growth, the anti-communism of the Cold War years, and a shift in communist policy from co-operation with to opposition to the official union leadership (Abella, 1973; Jamieson, 1973). In the CCL — but even more so in the TLC — communists had assumed positions of considerable power and influence during and after World War II. In the CCL, this had been a source of conflict from the very beginning, although the communists were repeatedly prevented from moving into offices on the executive throughout the War and afterward, and the federation continuously endorsed the CCF, beginning in 1943. By contrast, the more conservative TLC was more benignly disposed to the notion of communists in the upper echelons of its organizational hierarchy and in those of its affiliates. The conjunction of the Cold War and the shift toward opposition on the part of the communists brought the issue of communist influence to a head in the late 1940s, however, with the consequence that "the TLC, like the CCL, expelled a number of. . . communist-led affiliates, and aided the international executives of several unions in purging their Canadian branches of communist leaders" (Jamieson, 1973:30).

In 1955, the American Federation of Labor and the Congress of Industrial Organizations came together in the AFL–CIO, thus ending the historic division in the United States' labour movement between the craft and industrial sectors. One year later, their Canadian cunterparts, the TLC, and the CCL, merged to form the Canadian Labour Congress (CLC) and, in that same year, the twelve thousand remaining members of the One Big Union voted to join the CCL, bringing a total of 80 per cent of all organized workers in Canada under the umbrella of the new organization. While many important developments have taken place in Canadian labour since the 1956 merger, including the CLC's affiliation with the New Democratic Party (earlier CCF) in 1961, the organizational structure of the CLC has remained largely unchanged in the interim, and it has more or less maintained its membership at between 75 and 80 per cent of organized Canadian workers.

Alongside the eventful history of the labour movement in English Canada is a distinct, but related, story in Quebec (Jamieson, 1973; Milner and Milner, 1973; Williams, 1975). By mid-century, Quebec had become an urban, industrial province to rival most others, although it has typically lagged behind Ontario, the province most comparable to it in size. And, over time, economic life had come increasingly under the sway of large, industrial enterprises controlled by American or English Canadian capital. Well into the 1950s, however, the social and political life of Quebec remained dominated by the Roman Catholic Church and an indigenous elite of professionals, small businessmen, and intellectuals, whose ideological orientations were quite uniformly Catholic, petty bourgeois, anti-democratic, rural, and nationalistic (i.e., pro-French Canadian). In this atmosphere, capitalistic institutions were regarded as appropriately the preserve of Protestant Anglophones, and the working class were expected to demand only a "living" wage — eschewing the materialism of the Protestant, Anglophone culture and the international unions. As part of this, "'La Confédération des Travailleurs Catholiques du Canada,' (CTCC) was organized by the Church and the nationalist elite who feared that French-Canadian traditions and customs were threatened by the rapid growth of international unions in Quebec" (Milner and Milner, 1973:118).

With the growth of industrial capitalism in Quebec in the 1930s and 1940s, a new class of predominantly urban, industrial workers was created. It was a class to which the Church and the indigenous elite were either unresponsive or sometimes even unsympathetic, and they turned increasingly to the unions as a source of leadership.

> Nature abhors a vacuum and, in the absence of traditional leaders for the industrial working class, the vacuum was easily filled by the unions. This is not to suggest that Quebec's labour unions are of recent date, but rather that their role as leaders and their powerful status are recent. In particular, this is the case for the Catholic unions... (Isbester, 1974:164).

As the ranks of the unions swelled in this period, however, the major labour organizations remained divided among themselves, the major split being between the Catholic unions represented in the CTCC, on the one hand, and the Fédération Provincial du Travail (made up of trade unions affiliated with the Trades and Labour Congress and the American Federation of Labor) and the Congrès Canadien du Travail (composed of industrial unions connected to the CIO), on the other. In general, the Catholic unions made only very modest economic demands, and were concerned to protect the traditional culture in a rapidly industrializing society, while the non-Catholic and international unions worked to bring the economic benefits of industrial workers in Quebec up to the standards of English Canada and the United States (Milner and Milner, 1973:Chapter 7).

As the labour movement in Quebec grew, so, too, did the antipathy of the government and the indigenous elite toward it. One consequence was the forging of ties between the hitherto warring factions in organized labour. These ties were strengthened in 1949 by the common opposition of the several factions to Bill Five, a bill introduced by the Union Nationale government under Premier Maurice Duplessis to establish a comprehensive labour code. And they were further strengthened in the landmark Asbestos strike, in which the CTCC struck the Canadian Johns-Manville asbestos mining operation in Asbestos, Quebec (Trudeau, 1956). While the strike yielded few tangible gains for the miners,

> ... it was at least a psychological victory and it underscored the effect of Quebec's rapidly changing society and economy. Catholic labour not only laid to rest forever its reputation for equivocation and appeasement, but also unified the rest of organized labour in its support. It mobilized the Church in a position that demanded it support the strike; and it exposed the dark underside of the Duplessis government to international attention (Isbester, 1974:188).

In 1957, one year after the founding of the CLC, the Fédération Provincial du Travail and the Congrès Canadien du Travail joined together to create the Fédération des Travailleurs du Quebec (FTQ). By this time, the CTCC had moved off in other directions, however, so that the labour movement in Quebec was once again split. Moreover, "the C.T.C.C. was no longer a tool of the traditional elite, but instead a militant labour union" (Milner and Milner, 1973:154), while the FTQ had developed ties to the Duplessis government. At its convention in 1960, the CTCC finally abandoned its Catholic identity and adopted the name Confédération des Syndicates Nationaux (CSN). The CSN

> ... grew rapidly in size and influence during the 1960s, under the aegis of the Quiet Revolution and a new, more liberal provincial labour code. It made particularly rapid organizational gains among professional and other salaried employees in the public service, as well as winning jurisdiction over six CLC unions with some ten thousand members. Total membership in the confederation more than doubled during the decade, reaching well over two hundred thousand by 1970 (Jamieson, 1973:41).

This period of expansion was accompanied, however, by an internal division in the leadership of the CSN between an older group who had come to power in the Duplessis years, and who had strong federalist and Liberal sympathies, and a newer group who eventually displaced them, and who adopted a more radical, often separatist, orientation. At the same time, similar events were taking place within the FTQ, and the two federations drew closer and closer together during the late 1960s and early 1970s, coming together with the Quebec Teachers' Corporation in 1971 to bargain collectively with the provincial government on behalf of some 200,000 teachers and provincial government employees. When their negotiations failed, the result was an enormous, province-wide strike, in which the leaders of the three organizations were jailed (Milner and Milner, 1973:Chapter 9; Williams, 1975:Chapter 20).

Another important element in the history of Canadian labour has been the increasing importance of governments, that is, the state, as employers of people. The transformation of Canada to industrial capitalism increased the demand for labour, especially in the cities, resulting in large-scale, rural-to-urban migration and unprecedented levels of immigration in the years following World War II. This, coupled with the post-war baby boom and the rapid expansion of the social welfare system (Guest, 1980), produced a real rise in government employment at all levels — municipal, provincial, and federal.

> At the beginning of the Canadian Confederation, the affairs of the federal government, especially its programs within executive departments and agencies, were attended to by fewer than 3,000 civil servants. Now, more than a century later, about 216,000 persons are required to assist the same government. A comparable, although not so phenomenal, growth has occurred at the provincial level (Hodgetts and Dwivedi, 1974:2).

This growth, however, has not been constant and cumulative. Rather, it has occurred largely since World War II. "... for example, in 1901, the Province of Ontario employed just over 600 persons; at the beginning of the post-World War II period there were 9,000; but by 1971 the corresponding figure was nearly 65,000" (Hodgetts and Dwivedi, 1974:2).

Thirty years ago, employment in the state sector involved less than half a million persons; by 1974, this figure had risen to almost two million (Armstrong, 1977:297). In the period 1946–74 when the overall size of the labour force in Canada doubled, the size of the state labour force more than quadrupled, so that today,

> if we add to the list of civil servants (including not only those at the federal but also at provincial and municipal levels) those employed in a vast array of nondepartmental agencies, boards, commissions, enterprises, and teachers and hospital employees, we would find that *at least one in every five* in the labour force in the country is on a public payroll (Hodgetts and Dwivedi, 1974:2, emphasis mine).

Across the three levels of government, the rates of growth in employment have differed considerably. In 1946, the federal government employed over twice as many people as did all of the provincial and municipal governments in Canada combined; by 1974, it employed fewer persons than did either of the two lower levels of government separately (Armstrong, 1977:297). Even at that, however, the rate of increase of employment in the federal government has still been somewhat higher than the corresponding rate of increase for the labour force as a whole.

In general, employees in the state sector have been slow to organize, although the letter carriers came together in a union in 1891 — the first union of public employees in Canada. And, while strikes among state workers were fairly rare in the first half of the twentieth century, they were not entirely unknown, as witness the strike of street railway workers in London, Ontario in 1898–99 (Palmer, 1976), and the strikes of postal workers, policemen, fire-fighters, and other government workers involved in the Winnipeg General Strike, as well as other strikes elsewhere. Rather than coming together in a single, over-arching organization, federal government employees initially tended to form smaller associations, "some based on single occupational groups, such as the Canadian Postal Employees' Association and the Railway Mail Clerks' Federation, and some organized across all occupational groupings, such as the Civil Service Association of Canada and the Civil Service Federation" (Hodgetts and Dwivedi, 1974:62). By contrast, provincial government employees followed the route of a single staff association, beginning in the 1920s in most of the provinces west of Quebec, and in the 1950s and 1960s in Quebec and most of the Atlantic provinces. Typically, however, the staff associations formed in the period before World War II were primarily social or recreational groups, rather than labour unions.

In more recent times, state employees in Canada have become more favourably disposed to membership in labour unions, and they have increasingly engaged in more militant forms of labour activity. In 1959, the British Columbia Government Employees' Association (later Union) staged a short-lived strike after several years of stormy relations with the Social Credit government, and employees of the Quebec Liquor Board walked off the job for several weeks in 1964. In 1965, there was a two-week-long strike of postal carriers and inside workers and, shortly thereafter, St. Lawrence Seaway employees threatened to strike and won a 30 per cent pay rise in arbitration. As part of this heightened level of union activity on the part of state workers, membership in unions at all three levels of government grew rapidly throughout the period of the 1960s, so that,

> by 1970 the Canadian Union of Public Employees, having 136,127 members, mainly workers employed by municipal governments and crown corporations, and the Public Service Alliance, with 119,743 members employed by the federal government, were, respectively, the second and third largest labour organizations in the Country (Jamieson, 1973:46).

The largest was the United Steelworkers of America. By the mid-1970s, however, even the Steelworkers had been eclipsed by the Canadian Union of Public Employees (CUPE), which currently has in excess of 220,000 members.

By 1951, fully 28.4 per cent of the nonagricultural work force in Canada belonged to labour unions, and this figure increased to almost 34 per cent by 1954, where it more or less remained for the rest of the decade. This was a period of relatively slow growth in the labour force, however, and represented a high watermark for the labour union movement which was not to be reached again until the 1970s. When the products of the high birth rates of the mid- and late 1940s began to enter the labour market in the early 1960s, the percentage of workers belonging to unions declined to less than 30, and did not begin to increase again until the latter years of the decade. Much of the recent increase which has resulted in the record levels of union membership, which currently encompass some 37 per cent of the nonagricultural work force, has come from the unionization of workers in the state sector. In the private sector, unionization has proceeded more slowly, and several large industries remain almost wholly unorganized including, most notably, agriculture and finance.

Something of the uneven process of unionization can be seen in the data in Table 11-3, which shows the percentage of workers belonging to labour unions for different industrial sectors. These figures range from a high of 85.5 per cent for fishing and trapping to a low of 0.4 per cent for agriculture, although the broad industrial categories used in the tabulation obscure important variations within many industries, especially manufacturing.

Table 11-3

Workers Unionized by Industry, 1973.

Industry Group	Percentage of Workers Unionized
Fishing and trapping	85.5
Public administration	68.9
Construction	63.5
Transportation, communications, and other utilities	52.5
Mining, including quarries and oil wells	44.2
Manufacturing	43.8
Forestry	37.7
Service industries	21.6
Trade	7.0
Finance	1.3
Agriculture	0.4

Source: Canada (1977: Table 6.24).

Those industries in the monopoly sector with large capital investments and requirements for a skilled and reliable labour force and many primary jobs tend to have high rates of unionization, while industries in the competitive sector with small capital investments and few such labour force requirements do not. The reasons for this lie importantly in the fact that firms in capital-intensive industries with many skilled and experienced workers cannot relocate their operations to a low-wage area or discharge their employees in order to discourage the development of unions without incurring very high costs, either from obtaining new plant facilities or from training new workers, whereas firms in labour-intensive industries with many unskilled workers do not face such costs. At the same time, firms in the monopoly sector are in a better position to pass on to the consumer the additional expenses involved in having a unionized work force, in order to preseve profits. Monopoly firms can, thus, often "afford" labour unions, where competitive firms cannot. Since the state sector resembles the monopoly sector more than it does the competitive sector, especially in its requirements for skilled and reliable workers, it probably tends to have high rates of unionization for much the same reasons that the monopoly sector does.

Relative to most Western, industrialized countries (with the significant exception of the United States), Canada has a relatively low percentage of its workers belonging to labour unions. Overall (i.e., including agricultural workers), about 30 per cent of Canadian workers are unionized. In the United States, about 26 per cent are. By contrast, Sweden's figure is 75 per cent, Austria 65 per cent, Australia 53 per cent, Britain 48 per cent, West Germany 37 per cent, and Japan 36 per cent (Finn, 1977:343). The relatively slow and uneven process of unionization in Canada has provided the basis for a major division in the working class between a relatively advantaged, organized minority and a disadvantaged, unorganized majority. "In industries such as mining, steel, automobiles, and chemicals... labour unions have won high wages" (Johnson, 1972:173).

> Where manufacturing or service industries require low levels of skills and little fixed capital for permanent facilities (such as electronics assembly and clothing manufacturing), or where competition still exists (such as in the textile and furniture industries), workers are forced to accept low wages, or to see their employer either move to a low-wage area or go out of business (Johnson, 1972:173).

Also included in the category of the relatively disadvantaged and unorganized are farm labourers and (especially female) bank employees. The low skill requirements and seasonal character of farm labour give farm workers little bargaining power with employers and this, coupled with their geographical dispersion, makes it difficult for unions to take root and grow among them. Although their work is not seasonal, bank employees have similar problems, since they are concentrated in low-level clerical jobs and scattered across the landscape in a large number of small branches.

Moving On

It is not part of the common culture in Canada to seek interpretations of the trajectory of Canadian society in terms of a (relational) class perspective. Because of this, attempts to do so are made doubly difficult by the apparent strangeness of some of the questions which such a perspective leads us to ask, and by the relative scarcity of information well adapted to answer them. We have seen in the historical record, though, that some set of class concepts can be sensibly applied to the Canadian experience, even if we may be more comfortable speaking of the "economic elite," for example, than of the "big bourgeoisie," and even if an unreconstructed Marxist version of social classes and class relations in capitalism may not illuminate the regions of our history very well. For this reason, it might prove useful to proceed to entertain a number of questions concerning contemporary Canadian society which are central to any class analysis, most particularly questions concerning class consciousness, class and ideology, class and politics, and class and power. The next chapter addresses itself to these questions.

Chapter 12

On Class, Consciousness, and Power in Canada

"'Everyone for himself,' yelled the elephant, as he danced among the chickens" (Tommy Douglas, former Premier of Saskatchewan and leader of the federal New Democratic Party, beginning a political speech).

To the extent that class (still in the relational sense) is an organizing principle of capitalist society, there is awareness of common class membership, a perception of common class interests, and a capacity for class action in pursuit of these interests. To that extent, too, an understanding of class distinctions and relations is important to an identification of the rules which govern the many spheres of social life, especially those of institutional politics (i.e., of political parties and their platforms, sources of funding, electoral support, and the like), the state, and power. Since Canada is fairly counted among the capitalist nations of the world, an assessment of the potential utility of a class analysis of contemporary Canadian society, then, must include answers to such questions as the following. First, how conscious are the members of the several social classes of their common membership? Second, how clearly do they perceive the existence of common class interests? Third, what do they perceive these interests to be? Fourth, how are they organized in pursuit of these interests? Fifth, how do the systems of social class and institutionalized politics relate to one another? Sixth, what is the relationship between the various classes and the state? And seventh, how do the classes stand in relation to one another and to other institutions (most notably the state) in the national system of power? If we were able to answer these questions with confidence, then we would be in an informed position to assess the importance of class as a feature of Canadian society today. This is, however, rather more than we might hope to achieve in the present state of knowledge. But we should proceed in the task as best we can.

Class Consciousness and Ideology

The conditions under which individuals who share a common, objective location in a system of social classes come to perceive the similarity of their position, to view themselves as sharing interests which are in opposition to those of members of other social classes, and to translate these into collective political action on their own behalf are not well specified in existing class theories. Marx was vague

211

on these issues and, although he pointed to this as a particular weakness in the Marxian formulation, Weber was not able to further our understanding of them very much. And subsequent attempts by Giddens and others to identify the mechanisms by which a "class-in-itself" becomes transformed into a "class-for-itself" seem not to have spanned this gap in class theory. Consequently, research on this topic has lacked clear direction, and has tended to be descriptive, rather than designed to test theoretically-informed hypotheses.

Class and Class Consciousness

In Canada, research on the economic elite (e.g., Park and Park, 1973; Porter, 1965; Clement 1975, 1977) has typically proceeded on the assumption that its members are not only well aware of their common class location and shared interests, but often act together in pursuit of these interests. In fact, Clement even goes so far as to say that:

> More than merely elites of position, the economic elites in Canada and the United States are a closely knit group, familiar with each other and each other's business. They take one another into account and frequently enter into joint business ventures ..., in addition to exchanging goods, capital and information with one another (1977:245).

While it could well be true that the Canadian economic elite (or those of Canada *and* the United States) are a class *for* themselves, the evidence at each level — awareness of common class membership, perception of common class interests, and collective action in the common interest — is far from complete. We have a good deal of information on "interlocking directorships, careers in family firms, kinship ties, and class of origin," as well as on "some institutions that serve to draw the elite into common social circles, such as top universities, private schools, and private clubs (Clement, 1977:235). And this information is clearly consistent with the inference that the economic elite are a relatively cohesive and like-minded group who often co-ordinate their efforts to achieve common goals. Still, we lack the fine-grained data on their actual attitudes and ongoing activities, along with the analytical studies of these, which would be required to determine the extent to which and exactly how this is true.

In a rather different approach to the study of class consciousness, a number of investigators have asked people questions in sample surveys about their perceptions of the class structure and their place in it. The results reveal that a substantial minority of Canadians do not believe in the existence of social classes, and that perhaps as many as one-half or more do not see themselves as members of one (Goyder, 1977). At the same time, however, most people will identify themselves as belonging to a particular class when presented with a list of social classes and asked to do so (Goyder and Pineo, 1973; Rinehart and Okraku, 1974). Table 12–1 shows the results of this latter exercise for two samples of Canadians: a national sample, and a sample drawn from London, Ontario.

The two images of the class structure which emerge from the data in Table

Table 12–1

Percentage Distributions of Class Identification in Canada[a] and London, Ontario[b]

Class Identification	Percentage in	
	Canada	London, Ontario
Upper class	2.0%	0.4%
Upper-middle class	12.7	na
Middle class	48.8	43.7
Working class	30.3	39.4
Lower class	2.0	4.1
No such thing, uncertain, no answer	4.2	12.4
Total	100.0	100.0

[a] Calculated from Pineo and Goyder (1973).

[b] Rinehart and Okraku (1974).

12–1 are in some respects quite different from one another. These differences are derived in part from the fact that one is drawn from data on a national sample of Canadians, while the other was constructed from the responses of people in a single Canadian city. Even more obviously, though, they originate in part in differences between the two studies in the nature of the question which was asked. Specifically, the national sample were asked to identify themselves as members of one or another of five classes, whereas the London sample could choose from among only four, the category "upper-middle class" not having been included.

These results are not especially surprising when one considers that the dominant ideology in Canada provides no analysis of society in terms of social classes (Marchak, 1975). There is no clear image in it of a class structure in which a set of social classes stand in certain relation to one another, either in the North American sense of distributively-defined, hierarchical aggregates, or in the European conception of relationally-determined, structural groupings. And there is no well-articulated set of beliefs which would permit individuals to locate themselves in such a structure very readily.

With the likely exception of the economic elite, then, there is little evidence of any thorough-going class consciousness on the part of Canadians today. There both is and has been a good deal of class awareness, as Giddens (1973:Chapter III) refers to it, in which people recognize that they share beliefs, attitudes, and styles of life with others. And, although perhaps as many

Canadians see themselves as members of a class as do not, this overall result may obscure some important differences among certain sub-groups of Canadians, especially between Francophone Quebecers and others. In fact, it appears as if a clear majority of Francophones in Quebec regard themselves as members of a social class, while this is true of only a modest minority of Francophones outside Quebec and of Anglophones generally (Goyder, 1977; Willox, 1979). Too, the brief survey of classes and class relations in Canada presented above revealed a certain amount of conflict consciousness (again, following Giddens's distinctions), in which members of particular classes have come together in the perception that they belong to a class whose interests stand in clear opposition to those of another class. Canadian history shows little recent evidence of revolutionary consciousness (Giddens again), however, in which members of a class have grasped an alternative vision of reality which has led them to strive for a revolutionary re-organization of society. In this respect, the One Big Union (Bercuson, 1977) and (perhaps also) the Front de Libération du Québec (Breton, 1972b) probably represent the major exceptions.

Class and Ideology

In their London, Ontario study, Rinehart and Okraku asked their respondents to choose between the following two descriptions of the power structure in Canada:

1. No one group really runs the government in this country. Instead, important decisions about national policy are made by a lot of different groups, such as labour, religious, and educational groups, and so on. These groups influence all political parties, but no single group can dictate to the others, and each group is strong enough to protect its own interests.

2. Big business really runs the government in this country. The heads of the large corporations dominate the political parties. This means that things in Ottawa go pretty much the way big businessmen want them to (1974:200).

The first description is a simplified version of what is usually referred to as the "pluralist" conception of national power structures (e.g., Riesman, 1953; Dahl, 1961), while the second is more consistent with a Marxist perspective.

Overall, 49.6 per cent of those in the sample endorsed the pluralist alternative, while 46.8 per cent selected the "Marxist" alternative, and the remaining 3.6 per cent were either uncertain or gave no answer. These results are perhaps somewhat surprising, but they should not be simply interpreted to mean that close to one-half of those in the sample were pluralists and just slightly less than that were Marxists. For one thing, each of the two descriptions is a summary package of several statements, rather than a single statement, even though the respondents were asked to select one of the two in its entirety. This means that a respondent may or may not have agreed with any particular statement in a description, even though he or she endorsed it. For another thing, the respondents were constrained to choose one or the other of these two descriptions, even though other descriptions of the national power structure which differ from both of them could have been included. In fact, the authors do mention a third alternative — a power elite model derived from the work of Mills (1956) — only to reject it as inapplicable. While it is true that the particular power elite which Mills identified in the United States has no direct counterpart here, since the Canadian military is not an important locus of power in the same way that the United States' military is, and Mills's power elite model ascribed power at the national level to a triumvirate of business, government, and the military, this does not mean that power elite models as such are inapplicable to the Canadian scene. In fact, Porter (1965) and Clement (1975) have enjoyed success in applying power elite models to Canada. And, finally, to interpret the "Marxian" model as necessarily Marxist is to read rather more into it than many might see, since, although the model does locate effective political power in "big businessmen" or "the heads of the large corporations," this is a view which is not only consistent with Marxism, but with other possible models as well, including a power elite model.

Despite these problems in interpretation, Rinehart and Okraku's findings do suggest that a relatively large number of Canadians may hold conceptions of the national power structure which are at least somewhat at variance with the Canadian, liberal democratic ideal. Moreover, individuals' images of this structures were importantly a function of their occupations. Fully 81.5 per cent of managers, officials, and proprietors (large firms) endorsed the pluralist model, followed by semi-professionals, at 67.7 per cent. Next came professionals, 61.8 per cent of whom selected the pluralist model, followed, in turn, by managers, officials, and proprietors (small firms) (59.0 per cent), clerical and sales workers (55.7 per cent), unskilled workers (38.5 per cent), semi-skilled workers (36.9 per cent), and skilled workers (35.3 per cent). Managers, officials, and proprietors (large firms) thus stood out as being far more likely than members of other occupational categories to endorse the pluralist model of power in Canada. The remaining categories of white-collar workers were rather more divided among themselves on the issue, although a majority in each case adopted the pluralist model. And the three blue-collar categories tended also to be split on the matter, but a clear majority in each case selected the other (i.e., "Marxist") model.

Class Voting

Increasingly, the conclusion which researchers appear to be converging upon after almost twenty years of research on "class" voting in Canada is that levels of class voting can be observed which, while similar to those in the U.S., are measurably lower than those in most of the other Western democratic countries (Ogmundson, 1975; Myles, 1979). This revises the earlier conclusion that, in Canada, there is no observable tendency for persons in like locations in the system of structured social inequality to favour those federal political parties best representing their group interests — a conclusion grounded in the general agreement among students of Canadian politics that the Progressive Conservative and Social Credit/Créditiste parties are essentially "middle class," while the Liberal and New Democratic parties are best seen as "working class" (Alford, 1963, 1967). Ogmundson's research on people's perceptions of the federal political parties at the time of the 1965 general election suggested, however, that "the aggregate view of the citizens places the two major parties, the Liberals and the Progressive Conservatives, together as 'middle class' and the minor third parties together as 'working class'" (1975:508). It is when this system of classification is adopted that both Ogmundson and Myles derive their conclusions about class voting in Canada.

The most recent research on class voting in Canada represents a real step forward in our understanding of this phenomenon. Still, further refinements may prove to be useful, and there remain many questions yet to be answered. First, although the issues in the literature are usually conceptualized in terms of "class" voting, class is generally dealt with in the distributive, socio-economic status sense, rather than in the relational, Marxist sense. Consequently, it might be useful to import a Marxist conception of social class to this tradition of research, and to attempt to assess the relative importance of socio-economic status *and* social class vis à vis one another for voting (see Robinson and Kelley, 1979). Second, Lambert and Hunter (1979) have added the refinement that the Social Credit Party and the Ralliement des Créditistes are perhaps best treated as separate entities, rather than as simply two branches of a single, national party, as Ogmundson and Myles have done. Since the general election of 1963, the two factions have become both progressively isolated from one another and more and more ideologically distinct. And, when their separate identities are recognized, it turns out that Canadians outside Quebec see Social Credit as very close to the Liberals and the Progressive Conservatives in its class orientation, whereas Quebecers see the Créditistes as very much akin to the New Democratic Party in its class orientation. Third, if there is some emergent consensus on issues of class voting at the federal level, there is little such at the level of the provinces. It might be instructive, therefore, to examine provincial class voting in some systematic detail.

In practice, socio-economic status tends to be measured in a wide variety of ways in the literature, including level of educational attainment, occupational standing (Blishen, 1967), amount of annual income, and other ways as well. There is, however, a fairly high degree of agreement (for sociology, anyway) on how it ought to be conceived theoretically, that is, as the relative location of individuals (or families) in a hierarchy of *social valuation* (see Jackson and Curtis, 1968). And it appears as if judgments that people make of the social worth of others are in large measure summary assessments anchored in perceptions of those others' *status characteristics*. For purposes of the present section, therefore, socio-economic status will be measured in terms of a composite index of several status characteristics, including number of years of formal education completed, occupational standing scaled in so-called "Blishen scores" (e.g., Blishen, 1967) and amount of annual income.

As for the Marxist class categories, the difficulties of carrying out empirical research begin with the disagreements over how they ought to be conceptualized theoretically, as outlined in some detail above, and end with the inadequacies of any Canadian data actually to locate people very satisfactorily in some empirically defined set of class categories. Consequently, the present section will rely on a rather simplified and crude division of people into classes which emphasises the distinction between those who own the means of production vs. those who do not and that between those who exercise corporate authority vs. those who do not. This generates a four-fold typology consisting of capitalists, the petty bourgeoisie, managers and others with delegated authority, and white- and blue-collar workers. Finally, given the importance which some sociologists place on the white- vs. blue-collar distinction, these two categories will also be represented separately. This provides some approximation to the class divisions discussed earlier in Chapter 11, although it is hardly a wholly satisfactory representation of them.

In order for significant levels of either socio-economic status or social class voting to occur, certain prior conditions must be satisfied. First, the stratification or class systems (as the case may be) must yield a relatively well-defined socio-economic status hierarchy or set of social classes. Second, people objectively located in these systems must be aware of their positions and aware of how other people are located relative to them. Third, in the context of this awareness, people must feel that they have socio-economic or social class interests to protect. And, fourth, there must be at least a two-party system and some public perception that the parties differ in the socio-economic status or social class interests which they represent.

This brief outline of some of the necessary conditions for socio-economic status or social class voting point to a number of reasons why one might expect these phenomena to be largely absent in Canada. First, there is a good deal of *status inconsistency* (Lenski, 1954; Hope, 1975) in this country, such that people who rank fairly high on one status characteristic (e.g., educational attainment) may rank quite low on another (e.g., occupational standing or income). When this occurs, individuals probably experience real difficulty in locating themselves relative to other people in the hierarchy of socio-economic status, and it is unlikely that there will be (m)any very well-defined socio-economic strata or groups. Second, there are few, if any, sharp breaks in the distributions of status characteristics, which further blurs distinctions among socio-economic strata. Third, the dominant ideology in Canada provides no analysis of society in terms of either socio-economic status or social class but, rather, elaborates the themes of equality of opportunity and individual achievement (Johnstone, 1969; Marchak, 1975). Fourth (as noted above), and perhaps as consequences of this: only a minority of Canadians overall think of themselves as belonging to a "social class"; not all of those who do think of themselves as belonging to one actually identify themselves as members of a particular class; and not all of those who so identify themselves actually feel close to members of their own class (Goyder, 1977). Fifth, and finally, although the federal political parties in Canada do differ somewhat in the socio-economic and/or social class interests which they represent, this is apparently not seen by many (especially lower socio-economic status) persons (Erickson, 1978).

Although the immediate potential for much socio-economic or social class voting in Canada appears to be generally low, there are some segments of the population in which this may not be true. First, it seems as if the level of class consciousness in the upper regions of the capitalist class, or economic elite, is quite high (Porter, 1965; Clement, 1975). Thus, Porter found that the members of his economic elite were about equally split between the Liberal and Progressive Conservative parties, and that there were no supporters among them of either the New Democratic or Social Credit/Créditiste parties. Second, elevated levels of "class" consciousness have been observed among Franco-phone Quebecers (Goyder, 1977; Willox, 1979), although the implications of this for socio-economic or class voting seem not to have been investigated.

While there is some evidence relating to class consciousness that the potential for class voting may be higher among Francophone residents of Quebec than among other segments of the Canadian population, the literature on voting suggests that, at the federal level, "the class-based voting that does occur emerges in particular provinces, being strongest in Ontario and then British Columbia. In contrast, Quebec and the prairie provinces are almost invariably low" (Engelmann and Schwartz, 1975:194). And, these two authors go on to argue, it may also be that:

> ...social class plays a greater role in provincial politics than on the national scene, particularly in the more highly industrialized provinces. Some signs of this are already evident from the greater incidence of class-based voting in Ontario during federal elections. This seems to be the case as well in Ontario provincial elections and those in British Columbia and Saskatchewan. In none of these instances, however, is the evidence overwhelming.... Conversely, class voting has been distinctly low in Alberta during the period of Social Credit dominance, as it has been in Quebec, at least since the 1930s (1975:199).

In the case of provincial voting patterns in Quebec in the period 1935–62, Pinard (1970) points to what he sees as a tendency toward "negative class voting," whereby lower socio-economic status voters were disproportionately drawn to parties of the "right." He suggests, however, that this had less to do with the ideological orientations of the parties involved (the Liberals and the Union Nationale) than with the tendency for the lower socio-economic strata to support protest parties which also happened to be right-wing. And, he notes, "the Quebec pattern of class voting is...negative only for the analyst who perceives ideological differences between the two parties, however limited they may be" (1970:107).

For a more recent period in Quebec history, Hamilton and Pinard (1976) have analysed patterns of party support in the 1970, 1973, and 1976 Quebec provincial elections. And, while their results defy easy summary, it appears as if the social democratic and separatist Parti Québécois (PQ) disproportionately drew its support from among the better-educated, although this pattern was measurably weakened when age was also taken into account, since the young were found to be at once better-educated on the average and more predisposed to vote for the PQ. As for the Créditistes, their support was found disproportionately to come from the less-favoured elements of Francophone society. Since the PQ is some kind of a social democratic party and the Créditistes tend to be seen as a working-class party, the implications for class voting in these results are not easy to see. Moreover, Hamilton and Pinard seem to have been more concerned to describe the social composition of supporters of the several Quebec provincial parties than they were to analyse issues of socio-economic or social class voting. Consequently, their results are not presented in a way which is well-adapted to the latter purpose.

The *1974 Canadian National Election Study* (see Leduc et al., 1974) allows the opportunity to explore issues of socio-economic and social class voting in both federal (for the 1974 general election) and provincial (for the last provincial election in each province prior to the survey) elections (Hunter, 1980b). The study data permit the construction of a socio-economic index — a composite of level of educational attainment, occupational status, and annual income — as well as the operationalization of a set of Marxian class categories (capitalists, petty bourgeoisie, white-collar managers, blue-collar supervisors and foremen, white-collar workers, and blue-collar workers), keeping in mind that the white- vs. blue-collar distinction is employed here as a summary, distributive distinction, rather than as a class distinction. Problems in the data were such, however that the category "petty bourgeoisie" was restricted to farmers, and did not include other segments of this class. With information on both socio-economic status and social class, we will be in a position to assess their importance when considered together for voting.

At the federal level, the "class" positions of the political parties can be identified as in Lambert and Hunter (1979): Liberals, Progressive Conservatives, Social Credit, Créditistes, and New Democrats in order from "for the middle class" to "for the working class." When the socio-economic status and social class locations of individuals were related to the class positions of the parties for which they voted in the 1974 general election, a weak pattern of relationships was revealed for the collection of provinces other than Quebec taken together, but no pattern was found within Quebec itself. The pattern outside Quebec suggested that white-collar workers were most likely to vote for middle-class parties followed, in turn, by capitalists, white-collar managers, farmers, blue-collar supervisors and foremen, and blue-collar workers. And, within each of these categories, the *higher* a person's socio-economic status, the *more* likely that person was to vote for a middle-class party. These results suggest that some combination of socio-economic status and social class may matter for voting for parties representing different socio-economic and class interests, but the overall pattern was too weak to discern very clearly just what this combination might be.

As for provincial elections, the class locations of the several political parties were identified using Lambert and Hunter's criterion again, although the presence of the Parti Québécois and the Union Nationale in Quebec required an independent judgment, since neither of these two parties operates at the federal level. Briefly, the PQ was treated as if it were the class equivalent of the NDP, recognizing that it is not simply a social democratic party. And the Union Nationale was equated with the Progressive Conservative Party in class terms, since these two parties have had close connections in recent times. When the socio-economic and social class locations of voters were related to the class positions of their parties of choice in the most recent provincial election, the only pattern which could be found was within Quebec itself. This pattern was quite pronounced, and showed white-collar managers to be most likely to vote for middle-class parties followed, in turn, by capitalists, white-collar workers, farmers and blue-collar supervisors and foremen (tied), and blue-collar workers. And within each category, the *higher* the socio-economic status of the voter, the *less* likely he or she was to vote for a middle-class party.

The results for the 1973 Quebec provincial election can be seen to reveal both socio-economic status and social class voting, although no easy judgment can be made as to which of these two phenomena is shown the more clearly. This is the case because socio-economic status is apparently represented doubly in the analysis, both in terms of the distinctions between white- and blue-collar workers with managerial or supervisory functions and between white- and blue-collar workers proper, and in terms of the socio-economic status index. The results suggest, though, that ownership of productive private property as such (capitalists and farmers vs. others) does not matter in terms of the class character of the party for which one votes. Participation in authority (white-collar managers vs. white-collar workers, and blue-collar supervisors and foremen vs. blue-collar workers), however, does seem to matter. A puzzle, though, is the tendency for the better-placed *within* each of the categories to be less likely to support middle-class parties, even while those in the white-collar categories (in particular, white-collar workers) were more likely than those in the blue-collar categories (in particular, blue-collar supervisors and foremen and blue-collar workers) to support middle class parties. This could simply be an anomaly in the data attributable to measurement or sampling error, in which case it would not merit sociological interpretation. Perhaps, however, it points to something in the white- vs. blue-collar distinction which goes beyond socio-economic status itself, as Giddens and others have suggested.

In general, the present analysis suggests that, at the federal level, there was at most only some small hint of combination of socio-economic and class voting in the general election of 1974 outside Quebec, but no such hint within Quebec. Conversely, at the provincial level, a pronounced pattern of socio-economic and class voting was found for the 1973 election in Quebec, but no evidence of such could be found outside Quebec for provincial elections. The results obtained for the Quebec election of 1973 were surprising in light of the general view of little or no socio-economic or class voting in that province, although they were broadly in line with what one might have expected from recent studies of class consciousness among Francophone Quebecers. Finally, this analysis points to the potential utility of models of voting behaviour in which explanations in Marxian terms or neo-Marxian notions of social class are entertained and evaluated alongside the more customary conceptions of social stratification. First, simply considering both of these possibilities forces the researcher to conceptualize and measure the variables involved more carefully than has often been the case in the past. Second, by actually including measures of both socio-economic status and social class in the analysis, the influence of each can be assessed independently of the other.

Class and Power

The nature and exercise of power in modern societies are among the most important and least agreed upon phenomena in contemporary social science. The recent renaissance in macrosociological theory and research relating to issues of power in both Canada (begun by Porter's *Vertical Mosaic* (1965)), and the United States (begun by Mills's *Power Elite* (1956)), however, has infused the topic with a vitality which it had lacked since at least the days of Lundberg (1937). It has also contributed importantly to our knowledge of the changing structure and organization of power in each of these countries, as well as of the penetration of the systems of power into Canada (Park and Park, 1973; Grant, 1965; Clement, 1977).

Class and Power in Capitalist Society

In the Marxian version, the matrix of governmental, parliamentary, bureaucratic, judicial, military, and other national, provincial, and municipal institutions which makes up the state in such countries as Canada uses its power in the long-run interest of the bourgeois class (*not,* it should be emphasized, in the short-run interest of particular capitalists). In order to accomplish this, however, the state must have, to use Poulantzas's term, a "relative autonomy" (Miliband, 1973) from the bourgeoisie, so that it can act in the common interest of that class. For "a crude economistic interpretation of the state makes it in fact impossible to understand the real functions the state performs for the capitalist class" (Panitch, 1977:4). In particular, its task is to provide conditions favourable to the accumulation of capital and the maintenance of social order, while avoiding the use of overt coercion (O'Connor, 1973). With the growth and development of capitalism, then, the state must necessarily involve itself more and more in regulating people's lives.

In the Weberian view, the state is a co-ordinating agency with a monopoly over the use of physical force within its own territory. It is responsible for the overall administrative operations of the society, within which a relationship of class domination obtains in the sphere of the economy. "Thus, his criticism of most Marxist contributions is that they fail soberly to distinguish between what is strictly 'economic,' what is 'economically determined,' and what is merely 'economically relevant'" (Gerth and Mills, 1960:47). As capitalism grows, both the public and the private sectors become progressively more bureaucratized, since bureaucratic forms of organization are distinguished from others by their relatively high degree of technical efficiency. Moreover, the development of capitalism requires growth in the state system as a consequence of increased needs for rational administration, so that the question for Weber was whether *any* institution (the economic included) would be able to contain the power of the public bureaucracy in the long run. Rather than increasing economic domination as a consequence of the development of capitalism, then, Weber looked into the future and saw increasing state control and bureaucratic domination.

Contemporary elite theorists (e.g., Porter, 1965) typically favour the idea that there are a variety of different elites in any society. Each of these elites is made up of those people who occupy the leading positions in a particular institutional hierarchy and who, therefore have the power to make decisions in their own institutional domain. One cannot assume the ultimate political dominance of the economic over the political elite, since societies vary over time and differ from one another in the extent to which this is true. So the state elite comprises those who occupy the top political posts in a society, while the economic elite comprises that society's most powerful business figures, and an important task is to determine the extent to which these two hierarchies and their elites are actually separate institutional spheres and groups of people or, in fact, influence one another and overlap in membership.

Class and Power in Canadian Society

In the early history of Canada, the country was dominated by a series of relatively small and cohesive groups — first French, and later British. In the seventeenth, eighteenth, and early ninetheenth centuries, these groups generally took the form of close alliances of merchants and landowners, along with high government officials, professionals, and the leading clergy. The representation of business in the several regional groups varied a good deal, but business people seem everywhere to have been important. In the Family Compact of Upper Canada, business people were prominent members, but "the principal alliance... was political, bureaucratic, religious and professional with a class base in the quasi-aristocracy of Upper Canada" (Clement, 1975:51). By contrast, the Chateau Clique of Lower Canada was perhaps at once the most powerful of these colonial groups, and the most dominated by commercial interests, although its members were clearly subservient to the British investors in whose employ they often were. The Maritime group, finally, was an alliance of important merchant-bankers with strong ties to the British money market, along with administrative and military officials. In each case, economic and political power appear to have been effectively melded into one, and those who exercised political authority were often the same people who wielded economic power.

In the 1840s and 1850s, the westward expansion of the United States posed a clear threat to Canada's control over its vast, thinly populated, and poorly-protected hinterland (Aitken, 1958). The concern to secure the western regions brought the government and Montreal commercial interests together in a protective alliance to build railways to assure the country's interests all the way to the west coast, as well as to ensure the continued importance of the St. Lawrence as the conduit for the staples trade (Fowke, 1957). Railway construction, however, proved far more expensive than initially imagined, and governments at all levels became heavily involved in providing financial aid to the many railroads under construction in this period. As a consequence, the governments incurred responsibility for enormous debts, and "debt was soon to be one of the major forces behind the move to confederation of the provinces" (Clement, 1975:61). Immediately after Confederation, the Conservative government under Macdonald was forced to proceed on its own in order to meet its railway commitments to the provinces. But these efforts were abandoned in 1873 when the Pacific Scandal, in which Macdonald was implicated in a questionable arrangement to grant concessions to a Montreal syndicate calling themselves the Canada (later Canadian) Pacific Railway Company, brought the government down (Myers, 1972:Chapter 12). And it was not until Macdonald's return in 1878 that the Montreal syndicate, with the backing of the Bank of Montreal, signed the contract for a transcontinental railway — but not before the government had granted it large cash subsidies ($25 million to start), tracts of land (25,000,000 acres), a monopoly over all railway construction between the United States' border and its own line, importation of construction materials duty-free, and other major concessions as well.

In the immediate pre- and post-Confederation periods of railway construction, then, the interpenetration of business and government was such that some (e.g., Clement, 1975) have seen it as a period of governance by a "ruling class" — a phrase which Mills describes as "badly loaded," (1956:277), for reasons that it implies political rule by an economic class, although its use in the present context seems intended to convey precisely that thought. At the same time, this interpretation is not universally accepted, and may suggest more internal harmony within these dominant groups than was actually present, at least for some periods. Thus, while it was said at the time, in reference to the alliance between the Conservative Party of Sir John A. Macdonald and the Canadian Pacific Railway that "the day the CPR goes bust, the Conservative party goes bust the day after" (quoted in Laxer (1973:32)), Bliss (1972) points to continuing tensions in the relationship between the two.

With the development of capitalism, and particularly since the turn of the century, the earlier phenomenon of a high degree of overlap in personnel between the state and economic elites has been replaced by a more complex and subtle pattern of relationships.

> there was a... shift in the relationship between these two sectors.... These two institutions were gradually becoming separate but related spheres of activity. Although not exclusively, there was evolving a division of labour between them and a set of norms which prevented the simultaneous holding of political office and key corporate positions (Clement, 1975:86).

Although simultaneous office-holding in the state and economic elites has become rare in recent times, serial office-holding in the two elites has not been altogether unknown. A number of major political figures in recent decades have had their main careers in the economic elite, and there is a fairly well-trodden path from the pinnacles of political power to the boardrooms of the major corporations. Moreover, the incidence of this "elite switching" may have increased somewhat over the past twenty or thirty years. ". . . while only 1.8 per cent. . . of the economic elite in 1951 had their main careers in the political, bureaucratic or military elite; by 1972, this had increased to 5.8 per cent" (Clement, 1975:346; also see Olsen, 1977:208).

In a large-scale capitalist country such as Canada, it is simply impossible for a single group of people to form the state and economic elites, either in the sense of simultaneous or of serial office-holding. Notwithstanding laws which prevent simultaneous office-holding, and with the significant exception of elected politicians, the complexity of modern business and, to a lesser extent, modern government as well, requires that the people who occupy the top positions in these two institutions be well-trained and highly-skilled in what they do, and that they engage in them full-time. Consequently, it is not easy for business and state leaders to exchange places with one another very frequently, much less to perform the two sets of functions at the same time. Moreover, if Poulantzas is correct in his assertion that the state serves capitalism best when it enjoys a relative autonomy from the bourgeois class, then it makes sense from a Marxist point of view that the two elites would overlap very little, if at all, in their membership.

Simultaneous office-holding in the state and economic elites is, then, a phenomenon of the past and, even if serial office-holding may be on the rise in recent times, it is hardly common. If we expand the criterion of elite inter-connectedness to include persons in one elite who have either served in the other, or who have close kin in the other, however, a somewhat different picture may be seen to emerge. Speaking of his 1972 elite, Clement observes that "a total of 39.4 per cent of the current economic elite members either were themselves or had close kin in the state system" (1975:346). And when the criterion is expanded further to include the full range of what Clement (1975:Chapter 6) refers to as "elite forums," such as the Canadian Executive Service Overseas, The Canadian-American Committee, the Ontario Research Foundation and others, in which members of the state, economic, and other elites meet to discuss issues of common interest, it may be that the state and the economy are much better articulated with one another than one might otherwise believe.

The question of the degree of inter-connectedness between the state and the economy is a rather easier one to answer than is that of their influence over one another in the long run. As we have seen, the historical record shows that the Canadian state has frequently operated to protect the institution of private property upon which the existence and power of the bourgeois class are predicated, and there is little evidence that the state has intervened in any real way to effect a significant redistribution of income or wealth over the years. As well, there is a lengthy and deep political tradition in liberal democracies such as Canada which regards what is "good" for private enterprise as being "good" for the country as a whole, or "in the national interest." This is to be expected, of course, in a country where the state has large and increasing requirements for income, and a thriving private sector is a simple and obvious source for obtaining it, even if the percentage of federal government revenues coming from direct taxes levied on the private sector has decreased in recent years (Wolfe, 1977).

While there is a broad similarity of social background between members of the state and economic elites (Olsen, 1977), this, coupled with the state's requirements for income, do not seem sufficient to explain what has been a fairly common government practice in Canada dating to the pre-Confederation period — the extensive government subsidies to the private sector and, sometimes even, of the government's taking over unprofitable private ventures and operating them at public expense. While one need only peruse the story of Canada's railways to illustrate this amply enough, the entire transportation network in this country — beginning with many of the early canals — has in large part either been constructed by private business with government aid or built entirely by government itself (Easterbrook and Aitken, 1956). Moreover, there is good evidence in much of this that the impetus has often originated in the economic elite, and that the profits have just as often been returned to them (see, for example, Myers, 1972). On the other hand, examples of the state's taking over profitable private businesses in Canada are comparatively rare, although they do exist, as in the British columbia government's takeover of the B.C. Electric Company in 1959 and the more recent Saskatchewan government's nationalization of the potash industry in that province.

The suggestion, then, is that, on balance, it is probably more accurate to describe the state and its elite as subordinate to the economy and its elite than the other way around. This was Porter's (1965) conclusion and, while a thorough-going replication of his research remains yet to be done, there would seem to be little reason to expect that things have changed very much in recent decades. But why should this be so? Unfortunately, it is not yet possible to evaluate in detail the Marxist contention that such a situation is inherent in the very nature of capitalism itself. But some of the major reasons seem clear enough.

First, it is likely that the economic elite in Canada have a considerable capacity for collective action in their common interest, as a consequence of their social homogeneity and interconnectedness, among other things. By contrast, the state elite consists at the highest levels of one federal and ten provincial elites. Not only is the state elite much more heterogeneous socially than is the economic elite, but the several elites which it comprises are seriously divided on the question of federal-provincial distribution of powers, to mention but one. And contributing further to the weakness of the state system is the fact that "our federal (and provincial) political elites are characterized by an avocational career pattern such that most members have had minimal previous experience" (Ogmundson, 1975:201). This contributes, Ogmundson argues, citing Porter (1965), to an excessive reliance on the part of politicians on advice from highly-placed civil servants. Second, the two major federal political parties in Canada, the Liberals and the Progressive Conservatives, are almost exclusively funded by big business. These two parties currently (as of 1980) hold power in two of the four western provinces, along with Ontario and all of the Atlantic provinces. The Social Credit party, which is currently in power in British Columbia, is similarly indebted to big business as a source of funding, making a total of eight of the ten provinces governed by parties which are dependent largely upon the economic elite for funds. Third, any successful political party in Canada must necessarily depend upon the mass media for support in gaining and maintaining power, and the mass media — with the significant exception of the Canadian Broadcasting Corporation — are in large measure owned and controlled by big business (Clement, 1975; but see Baldwin, 1977). Finally, although this by no means exhausts the important reasons which might be mentioned, large fractions of the economic elite in Canada are in the employ of foreign-controlled corporations in which the important decisions are made beyond the political boundaries of this country. While all companies doing business in this country must, of course, obey the laws of the land, it is much more difficult to supervise the activities of those which are controlled from abroad, and this can only weaken the authority of the state system in the long run. And, related to this problem, the division of powers between the federal and provincial governments means that corporations — especially foreign-controlled ones — can often achieve their aims through dealings with weaker, provincial governments anxious for economic development, rather than with the more powerful, federal government. Under such circumstances, it can only be expected that the state system in Canada has and will continue to be responsive to the needs of the economic system, especially its wealthiest and most powerful sectors.

As for the other elites in Canada, there would appear to be only one whose interests and relative autonomy might at some point place it in clear opposition to the economic elite, and that is the labour elite. It overlaps very little with any of the other elites, and it is the most representative in terms of its social composition. The power of organized labour in Canada, however, is seriously circumscribed by the fact that only a minority of workers belong to a labour union in the first place. Moreover, the labour elite is importantly divided along regional, ethnic, and other lines, and the conflict-ridden history of the labour movement in Canada suggests only a very limited potential for collective political action. As well, about two-thirds of all union members in Canada belong to United States-based international unions which have followed Samuel Gompers tradition of eschewing partisan political activity, preferring to concentrate upon a relatively narrow range of economic issues in dealing with governments and employers. Consequently, organized labour's political arm — the New Democratic Party — is at once relatively weak and rather conservative. It is a social democratic party in something akin to the European tradition of such parties, and not at all an anti-capitalist one.

Summing Up

Among the several classes in Canadian society, only the big bourgeoisie or economic elite display evidence of any very thorough-going class consciousness, in which they are aware of their common class membership, perceive common class interests, and are capable of collective action in pursuit of those interests. And this seems to have been true historically, as well as today. To be sure, there is a fairly widespread belief, especially within the lower echelons of the working class, that Canada does not represent the liberal democratic ideal of a society of competing interest groups with counterbalancing power and influence, but only a minority of this class are even nominal members of working class organizations, and the most prominent of these organizations — the labour unions — are quite docile politically, preferring to concentrate their efforts on a relatively narrow range of economic issues. At the level of institutional politics, the two largest parties — the Liberals and the Progressive Conservatives — represent political alternatives which the economic elite as a class appear to find congenial enough, while the New Democratic Party is a labour party, but a social democratic, rather than a strictly socialist, one. The absence of any parties with a strong working-class platform, coupled with the relatively low levels of class consciousness and organization in the working class, makes it fairly easy to understand how it is that levels of class (in either the distributive or relational senses of the term) voting in Canada are so low as to be barely detectable, with the apparent exception of contemporary Quebec. Finally, the economic elite in Canada are a fairly cohesive group of like-minded people whose congealed power appears to prevail in the long run, with the state playing the crucial role of umpire to settle disputes within and between classes so that the game might go on.

Part V

Class Tells

Chapter 13

Class Tells

"Class tells" (comment by the late John F. Kennedy upon seeing Richard M. Nixon on television during the 1960 U.S. presidential campaign).[1]

At the end of Part I of this book (see Chapter 4), an attempt was made to point to certain critical areas of contact among social theories in the form of identifying a number of "outstanding issues." This list, which was presented in no particular order and was in no way intended to be exhaustive even of "important" issues, contained the following:

1. The momemtum of meritocracy, or the extent to which societies such as Canada could be seen to move in the direction of reward for merit and away from reward for qualities unrelated to performance;
2. The changing class structure, or the growth and decline of the several classes in relation to one another, along with whatever changes there might be in the defining criteria of class;
3. Class, stratum, and consciousness, or the extent to which members of social classes or strata (not the same thing) appeared to recognize their common location, perceive the existence of common interests, and act together in the common interest;
4. The state and the economy, or how the state and the several social classes relate to one another in the overall structure of power; and
5. Sources of social order, or the relative importance of a harmony of social values and the mechanisms of force and coercion for the maintenance of social order.

It should be clear by now that no definitive resolutions of these issues are available for a number of reasons. First, each issue is in itself very subtle and complex, so that no simple resolution might be expected in any case. Second, the relative scarcity, especially in Canada, of empirical social research relating to these issues means that, even if the issues were simple and well-defined, the present state of knowledge in the discipline would probably be inadequate to resolve them. Third, information relating to a single country (in this case, Canada) is generally not sufficient to provide tests of theoretical propositions, since it is usually of a "one-shot," case study kind, even though an effort has been made here to give a historical dimension to the analysis wherever possible. At the same time, it is hardly an act of great theoretical courage simply to say that

---

[1] The late President Kennedy's father, Joseph P. Kennedy, made his initial fortune in bootlegging during Prohibition and was later U.S. Ambassador to the Court of St. James (U.K.).

the questions asked are difficult and the information available inadequate to answer them. Some summary judgments, however tentative, on each of the above issues, then, might be a useful way to end this voyage and to suggest to others where they might begin to explore further.

On the Issues

Momentum of Meritocracy

Contrary to the dicta of the functional theory of stratification and of human capital theory, no relatively straightforward, meritocratic interpretation of the distribution of rewards seems to apply. People do not seem to be rewarded in proportion to their capacities to produce, and no simple, technical connection appears to exist between their formal training, on the one hand, and their occupations and incomes, on the other. In addition, there is evidence that the distribution of available income is becoming somewhat less equal over time, at least in recent years, with more of it going to the highest income earners (most notably the big bourgeoisie and certain favoured fractions of the petty bourgeoisie, such as independent professionals), and less of it to middle- and low-income earners (including most of those who work for a wage or a salary, and certain disfavoured fractions of the petty bourgeoisie, including small businessmen, independent commodity producers, and others). Although there has been a decline in gender and ethnic inequalities overall, certain of the latter (especially those involving Indians and the Inuit) will persist for decades at least, and these declines could just as well signify a general levelling of incomes and related rewards within the working class than any clear movement in the direction of reward for merit. Although the data on wealth are inadequate to support any generalizations with regard to changes over time, information on dividend income shows increasing inequalities over the years, and at least a plausible inference is that this, when considered alongside increasing inequalities in the distribution of income, can be at least partly understood in terms of the changing relationships among the several social classes, with the bourgeoisie generally advancing at the expense of the rest. Finally, while it is impossible to say with confidence that levels of social inheritance have increased or decreased over time independently of changes in the structure of opportunity (especially in the occupational sphere), there is a measurable tendency for people to inherit the social positions earlier occupied by their parents, and the mechanism of the inheritance of wealth guarantees that major inequalities in one generation are reproduced in the next — in particular, those inequalities associated with class. Only those with entrepreneurial talent and extraordinary luck ever earn great wealth, and only those with parents of this kind ever inherit it.

What seems most likely to happen in the future is a relatively simple projection of what has happened in the past, that is, slowing increasing inequalities in income and (probably as well) wealth. In capitalist systems still expanding in economic growth, this can probably occur in the absence of any profound class cleavages and conflicts. In a western industrial world faced with the imminent prospect of the depletion of a number of critical, nonrenewable natural resources, such as petroleum, and in a country which has an industrial base which is largely owned from without its borders, this seems unlikely. If industrial growth in Canada continues at its slow pace or, indeed, slows still further, and no fairly cheap alternatives to oil and gas are developed quickly, there will be less and less income and wealth to distribute, especially as the branch plants of U.S. industries reduce or cease their activities altogether. And one consequence is likely to be heightened conflicts among classes over the distribution of the available income and wealth, coupled with increasing rates of under- and unemployment. At least initially, this conflict is likely to take the form of increasing militancy on the part of organized labour, with the short-run effect that the relatively well-paid among the working class will gain at the expense of the rest.

Changing Class Structure

As in the case of the momentum to meritocracy, many of the changes which have been wrought in the class structure of Canada in the period of the present century have been at once subtle and slow. Some, however, as in the case of the decline of the independent commodity producers and small businessmen, have not. Where once the self-employed were a numerical majority of the labour force, now they form an almost insignificant minority. And, as their numbers have fallen, so have their economic and political fortunes, although independent professionals (e.g., most physicians, lawyers, and dentists) appear to stand as something of an exception to this, at least up to now. As for the mass of those who are employed for a salary or a wage, it seems clear that some overall process of de-skilling has occurred over the past fifty years or so, although this has probably been more pronounced among skilled and semi-skilled workers than among others, and there are some categories of workers who seem to have experienced a real upgrading in knowledge and skill. This latter phenomenon seems evident, for example, in the still ever-increasing application of science to such activities as industrial production, economic planning (both private and public), agriculture, mining, forestry and fisheries management, transportation, communications, and others at the impetus and under the direction of people who can only be described as true technical experts in command of the most advanced theoretical knowledge of their day. As for the bourgeoisie, finally, it would appear as if the processes of the centralization and accumulation of capital have strengthened the hand of the larger in competition with the smaller and that the emergence of the joint-stock corporation has both given them more capital to work with and permitted them effective control over many businesses in which they are neither complete owners nor even majority stockholders. The separation of ownership and control and the consequent creation of a category of functionaries without capital has tended to remove those who own or control productive private property from the day-to-day or, even, week-to-week operations of their businesses, but this has not been obviously accompanied by any real diminution of their powers.

Again, recognizing that one cannot predict the future but, rather, can only project present trends into what seems like the most probable future, we can speculate on what seems likely to happen in the years to come. First, as the destruction of the agricultural and small-business fractions of the petty bourgeoisie is now almost complete, little more needs to be said about it. As for the independent professionals, however, their collective fate remains to be determined. It may not be long, however, before this is done. Increasingly, the autonomy of fee-charging, independent professionals seems to be being eroded by the forces of the state and big business. Government regulation of their activities, for example, has increased markedly over the years, and most self-employed physicians in Canada now rely upon provincial medical plans for the collection of their fees. Indeed, the fee schedules which most physicians now use are acually fixed in negotiations between the several provincial medical associations and their provincial governments. And, beyond this, increasing numbers of persons who would once have "hung out their shingle" or joined some group medical, legal, or other practice now find themselves in the employ of either the state or of private business. This process of the subordination of the free professions, which was greatly accelerated by the events of the doctors' strike in Saskatchewan almost twenty years ago, seems likely to continue in the decades ahead. Second, the process of the de-skilling of skilled and semi-skilled workers seems likely to increase which, when coupled with the anticipated continuing decrease in workers' real incomes, should put an end to any movement in the direction of embourgeoisement, although evidence of this latter phenomenon was equivocal even in the period beginning after World War II and ending in the mid-1970s when the real incomes of workers were on the incline. At the same time, the economic fortunes of the cadre of true technical experts are likely to increase as the problems of the state and big business escalate, and this will set them more and more apart from the bulk of employed workers, although it does not appear as if their political power will assume the proportions which were anticipated by the post-industrial society theorists, for example. They will remain paid employees — well-remunerated for their expertise, to be sure, but working at the command of their employers. Third, businesses in the Canadian-controlled monopoly sector (transportation, banking, etc.) will probably continue to do relatively well, even as the economic importance of the western countries declines over time, thus guaranteeing the presence of an indigenous Canadian elite, while those in the foreign-controlled monopoly sector (especially those involved in the manufacture of such consumer durables as automobiles) can be expected to cut back their branch plant operations in the face of a prolonged economic recession, reducing the profile of the comprador elite. As for the largely Canadian-controlled competitive sector of the economy, it is likely to be hardest hit by the kind of long-term economic difficulties which one might expect to accompany the transition from a heavy dependence upon petroleum to a reliance on other forms of energy, as it was in the Great Depression of the 1930s.

Class, Stratum, and Consciousness

One fact which seems quite clear in the analysis of structured social inequality in Canada is that there is very little consciousness of class among the bulk of those who work for a salary or a wage in Canada. A substantial minority of the working class do not appear even to recognize the existence of classes, much less to locate themselves as members of one. Among those who do perceive the existence of social classes, there is little evidence that they have any clear conception of common class interests. And what collective action in pursuit of shared interests there appears to be among the working class largely takes the form of trade union efforts to work within the system with the goals of improved working conditions and financial benefits. At the same time, there is some suggestion of heightened levels of class consciousness among certain segments of the working class in Quebec, at least in the recent past. This situation may be slightly different among some fractions of the petty bourgeoisie, judging from the actions of such groups as the various farmers' organizations, professional associations, and small-business organization but, even if their influence sometimes seems inordinate in relation to their size, the petty bourgeoisie as a whole is a small and shrinking group fighting a rear-guard battle. Among the bourgeoisie, finally, it seems likely that levels of class consciousness exist at the level of the big bourgeoisie or economic elite. Of the several social classes, it is they who appear to be the exception. Numerically small, they are an enormously powerful collection of people who seem quite aware that they belong to a particular social class with distinctive class interests, and the evidence is that they frequently act in concert in pursuit of these interests.

Given the fact that material and symbolic rewards are continuously distributed among the population all the way from those who enjoy much to those who have little, there is little basis in the distributive system for the development of social strata. Consequently, social strata in Canada do not appear to provide any real foundation for consciousness and collective action. Among certain status groups, however, most notably Indians and certain other ethnic groups, there is evidence of consciousness of common group membership, perception of common interests, and collective action in pursuit of these interests.

Past trends, even if they are not well documented, provide little hint that the present situation is likely to change very much in the near future. With the obvious exception of the economic elite and the possible exception of the working class in Quebec, class neither provides nor shows promise of providing a basis for mobilizing people. And, if the experience of the Great Depression is any guide, the period of declining working class and petty bourgeoisie fortunes which we appear to be heading into is not likely to change this very much, although some elevation in levels of trade union consciousness can probably be expected as unions seek to minimize the impact of economic recession on their members. Finally, it is simply impossible to anticipate what will happen in the case of the many different status groups in Canada, since their interests are so varied, except that the continued economic development of the northern regions will probably guarantee increased resistance on the part of the Indians and the Inuit, and that land claims issues will figure prominently in this.

State and Economy

Approaching the issue from an elite theory perspective, Porter (1965) advanced the argument — never seriously disputed — that the economic elite were the best-organized and most powerful group in Canadian society, and a good deal of the subsequent commentary on this analysis has taken the form of suggesting that Porter did not go far enough. For Porter, this seems more or less to have just "happened," while many Marxists (e.g., Park and Park, 1973) tend to see it as an inevitable consequence of capitalism, where a small number of people are able to co-ordinate enormous economic resources and act together to use the state system to their own advantage. At the least, it is probably a fair enough criticism of Porter that he did not sufficiently seek to locate the sources of the power of the economic elite or big bourgeoisie, even if it remains arguable that the situation which he described is an unavoidable result in the kind of economic system in which we live.

From the above analysis, it follows that no clear threat to the class domination of the big bourgeoisie by some other class is imminent. If some version of the scenario of the gradual economic decline of the western industrial countries should be realized in the decades immediately ahead, however, some realignment of the relationship between the big bourgeoisie and the state is not altogether unlikely. In particular, it was suggested earlier that this decline might be expected to have a kind of double impact on Canada, involving both the contraction of the Canadian-controlled monopoly and competitive sectors of the economy and the withdrawal of foreign- (largely U.S.-) controlled branch plants. If this occurs, then the position of the economic elite in the overall power structure of Canada can only be eroded, and one likely beneficiary would be the state. Moreover, if (as seems probable) this decline has importantly to do with a difficult transition from a heavy dependence upon oil and gas as sources of energy to (nuclear-generated) electricity, the hand of the state would seem to be strengthened further, since the electrical utility is largely controlled by branches of the state in the form of provincially-owned corporations.

Sources of Social Order

Perhaps of the issues considered here the most difficult to define and pronounce upon has to do with the extent to which societies can be said to cohere as a consequence of some kind of voluntary process of consensus, as opposed to an order imposed upon the weak and many by the powerful and few. While there has been scant research and discussion on this issue as it relates specifically to Canada, there are commentators on other liberal democracies who emphasize one or the other of these two possibilities, and there are those, such as Dahrendorf (1959), who regard the two as complementary aspects of the same reality, rather than as alternatives to one another.

That there is a good deal of dissensus at the level of values in Canada seems clear but, at the same time, this is hardly a completely ordered society, so that observations of value dissensus might be expected in any case. If one is to argue effectively that an underlying consensus on values does not provide the basis for social order, he or she must show that those levels of consensus which can be observed are insufficient to guarantee the social order which obtains, and this remains to be done (but see Mann, 1971). But, beyond this, it is entirely possible that social order is underwritten by consensus, but that this consensus is itself imposed from above by a dominant class whose powers enable it to impose it upon those subordinated to them. Where once social order may have been enforced through some relatively direct use of power, now it may be guaranteed through the dissemination of a dominant ideology promulgated by a dominant class. In order to establish this argument, however, some detailed historical scholarship not yet seriously attempted in this country would seem to be required.

If no definitive answers to the questions raised by this issue can be provided here, there are some clues which still might be useful. First, that the big bourgeoisie form the single most powerful group in Canada seems indisputable. Second, that this group is characterized by a high degree of consensus in values appears to be clear enough, especially when they are compared in this regard to the mass of the working class. Third, with the significant exception of the state-controlled Canadian Broadcasting Corporation, the mass media of communication in Canada, including the newspapers, television, and radio, are largely owned and controlled by members of the economic elite (Clement, 1975), and almost all we know about the world beyond our immediate experience is gained, first- or second-hand, from the mass media. Taken together, these facts suggest that some version of an argument of order-through-coercion does not seem implausible. There is one class, the big bourgeoisie or economic elite, which is at once highly class-conscious and possessed of the means to disseminate its ideology to the population virtually without competition. And all that social order may require is that the powerful be organized and the carriers of a coherent ideology and the weak be disorganized and without a counter-ideology of their own.

Summing Up

This has been a highly selected, introductory analysis of structured social inequality in Canada. It has touched upon only some issues, and upon many of them only lightly. At the same time, it has sought to organize, present, and interpret the materials with which it has dealt in a way which is at least occasionally original, in the hope that some real contributions to knowledge would be made. Future research will determine if this has been so.

Bibliography

Abella, Irving M. *Nationalism, Communism, and Canadian Labour.* Toronto: University of Toronto Press, 1973.

Abella, Irving M. (ed.) *On Strike.* Toronto:Lorimer, 1974a.

Abella, Irving M. "Oshawa 1937." in Irving M. Abella (ed.), *On Strike.* Toronto: Lorimer, 1974b, 93–128.

Aberle, David F., Albert K. Cohen, Arthur K. Davis, Marion J. Levy, Jr., and Francis X. Sutton. "The Functional Prerequisites of a Society." *Ethics,* 60(1950):100–111.

Acheson, T.W. "Changing Social Origins of the Canadian Industrial Elite, 1880–1910." *Business History Review,* XLVII (1973).

Adams, Ian, William Cameron, Brian Hill, and Peter Penz. *The Real Poverty Report.* Edmonton:Hurtig, 1971.

Agger, Ben. *Western Marxism: An Introduction.* Santa Monica:Goodyear, 1979.

Aitken, H.G.J. "Defensive Expansion: The State and Economic Growth in Canada." in H. G. J. Aitken (ed.), *The State and Economic Growth.* New York:Social Science Research Council, 1959, 79–114.

Alexander, Karl L., Bruce K. Ekland, and Larry J. Griffin. "The Wisconsin Model of Socio-Economic Achievement: A Replication." *American Journal of Sociology,* 81(1975):324–42.

Alford, Robert R. *Party and Society.* Chicago:Rand McNally, 1963.

Alves, Wayne M. and Peter H. Rossi. "Who Should Get What? Fairness Judgments of the Distribution of Earnings." *American Journal of Sociology,* 84(1978):541–64.

Ambert, Anne-Marie. *Sex Structure.* 2nd ed. Don Mills:Longman, 1976.

Anderson, Charles H. *The Political Economy of Social Class.* New York: Prentice-Hall, 1974.

Archibald, W. Peter. *Social Psychology as Political Economy.* Toronto: McGraw-Hill Ryerson, 1978.

Armstrong, Hugh and Pat Armstrong. "The Segregated Participation of Women in the Canadian Labour Force, 1941–71." *Canadian Review of Sociology and Anthropology,* 12(1975):370–84.

Armstrong, Pat and Hugh Armstrong. *The Double Ghetto.* Toronto:McClelland and Stewart, 1978.

Armstrong, Hugh. "The Labour Force and State Workers in Canada." in Leo Panitch (ed.), *The Canadian State.* Toronto:University of Toronto Press, 1977, 289–310.

Armstrong, Donald E. "Education and Economic Achievement." *Documents of the Royal Commission on Bilingualism and Biculturalism.* Ottawa:Information Canada, 1970.

Aronowitz, Stanley. *False Promises: The Shaping of American Working Class Consciousness.* New York:McGraw-Hill, 1973.

Atkinson, A. B. *The Economics of Inequality.* London:Oxford University Press, 1975.

Ausubel, David P. *Educational Psychology.* New York:Holt, Rinehart and Winston, 1968.

Averitt, Robert T. *The Dual Economy: The Dynamics of American Industry Structure.* New York:Norton, 1968.

Avery, Donald. "Continental European Workers in Canada 1896–1919: From 'Stalwart Peasants' to Radical Proletariat." *Canadian Review of Sociology and Anthropology,* 12(1975):53–64.

Badgley, Robin F. and Samuel Wolfe. *Doctors' Strike.* Toronto:Macmillan, 1967.

Baker, Paul Morgan. "On the Use of Psychophysical Methods in the Study of Social Status: A Replication and Some Theoretical Problems." *Social Forces,* 55(1977):898–920.

Baldwin, Elizabeth. "On Methodological and Theoretical 'Muddles' in Clement's Media Study." *Canadian Journal of Sociology,* 2(1977):215–22.

Banfield, E. *Political Influence.* New York:Free Press, 1961.

Beattie, Christopher. *Minority Men in a Majority Setting.* Toronto:McClelland and Stewart, 1975.

Beck, E. M., P. M. Horan, and C. M Tolbert. "Stratification in a Dual Economy: A Sectoral Model of Earnings Determination."*American Sociological Review,* 43(1978):704–20.

Becker, Gary S. *Human Capital.* Chicago:University of Chicago Press, 1964.

Bell, Daniel. *The Coming of Post-Industrial Society.* New York:Basic Books, 1973.

Bendix, Reinhard and Seymour Martin Lipset (eds.), *Class, Status, and Power.* 2nd ed. New York:Free Press, 1966.

Benedict, Ruth. *Patterns of Culture.* New York:Mentor, 1959.

Bercuson, David Jay. "The Winnipeg General Strike." in Irving M. Abella (ed.), *On Strike.* Toronto:Lorimer, 1974a, 1–32.

Bercuson, David Jay. *Confrontation at Winnipeg.* Montreal:McGill-Queen's Press, 1974b.

Bercuson, David Jay (ed.), *Canada and the Burden of Unity.* Toronto:Macmillan, 1977.

Bercuson, David Jay. *Fools and Wise Men: The Rise and Fall of the One Big Union.* Toronto:McGraw-Hill Ryerson, 1978.

Berg, Ivar. *Education and Jobs: The Great Training Robbery.* Boston:Beacon Press, 1970.

Berger, Peter L. and Thomas Luckmann. *The Social Construction of Reality.* New York:Doubleday, 1966.

Berle, A. A. and G. Means. *The Modern Corporation and Private Property.* New York:Harcourt, Brace, and World, 1932.

Bernstein, Basil (ed.), *Class, Codes, and Control.* Vol. 1. London:Routledge and Kegan-Paul, 1971.

Bibb, Robert, and William H. Form. "The Effects of Industrial, Occupational, and Sex Stratification on Wages in Blue-Collar Markets." *Social Forces,* 55(1977):974–96.

Bienvenue, Rita M. "Intergroup Relations: Ethnicity in Canada." in G. N. Ramu and Stuart D. Johnson (eds.),*Introduction to Canadian Society.* Toronto:Macmillan, 1976, 212–51.

Black, George F. *The Surnames of Scotland.* New York:The New York Public Library, 1946.

Blackburn, R. M. and Michael Mann. *The Working Class in the Labour Market.* Cambridge Studies in Sociology. London:Macmillan, 1979.

Blau, Peter M. and Otis Dudley Duncan. *The American Occupational Structure.* New York:Wiley, 1967.

Blaxall, Martha and Barbara Reagan (eds.), *Women and the Workplace.* Chicago:University of Chicago Press, 1976.

Blishen, Bernard R. "A Socio-Economic Index for Occupations in Canada." *Canadian Review of Sociology and Anthropology,* 4(1967):41–53.

Blishen, Bernard R. *Doctors and Doctrines.* Toronto:University of Toronto Press, 1969.

Blishen, Bernard R. "Social Class and Opportunity in Canada." *Canadian Review of Sociology and Anthropology,* 7(1970):110–27.

Blishen, Bernard and Hugh A. McRoberts. "A Revised Socio-Economic Index for Occupations in Canada." *Canadian Review of Sociology and Anthropology,* 13(1976):71–79.

Bliss, Michael. "Dyspepsia of the Mind: The Canadian Businessman and His Enemies, 1880–1914." in David S. Macmillan (ed.), *Canadian Business History.* Toronto:McClelland and Stewart, 1972, 175–91.

Bluestone, Barry. The Tripartite Economy: Labor Markets and the Working Poor." *Poverty and Human Resources Abstracts,* 5(1970):15–35.

Bottomore, T. B. *Elites and Society.* Middlesex:Penguin, 1964.

Bourgault, Pierre. *Innovation and the Structure of Canadian Industry,* Ottawa: Science Council of Canada, 1972.

Bowles, Roy T. and Prudence Craib. "Canada: Economy Opportunity and Class." In John Allan Fry (ed.), *Economy, Class and Social Reality.* Toronto:Butterworths, 1979.

Bowles, Samuel and Herbert Gintis. *Schooling in Capitalist America.* New York:Basic Books, 1976.

Bradwin, Edmund W. *The Bunkhouse Man.* Toronto:University of Toronto Press, 1928, 1972.

Braverman, Harry. *Labor and Monopoly Capital: The Degradation of Work in the Twentieth Century.* New York:Monthly Review Press, 1974.

Brazeau, E. Jacques. "Language Differences and Occupational Experience." in Marcel Rioux and Yves Martin (eds.), *French-Canadian Society*. Vol. I. Toronto:McClelland and Stewart, 1965, 296–307.

Breton, Raymond. "The Socio-Political Dynamics of the October Events." *Canadian Review of Sociology and Anthropology*, 9(1972):33–56.

Breton, Raymond. *Social and Academic Factors in the Career Decisions of Canadian Youth*. Ottawa:Information Canada, 1972b.

Buckley, Walter. "Social Stratification and Social Differentiation." *American Sociological Review*, 23(1958):369–75.

Burawoy, Michael. "Contemporary Currents in Marxist Theory." *The American Sociologist*, 13(1978):50–64.

Canada. *Report of the Royal Commission on Bilingualism and Biculturalism*. Vol. 2. Ottawa:Queen's Printer, 1968.

Canada. *Report of the Royal Commission on Bilingualism and Biculturalism*. Vol. 3. Ottawa:Queen's Printer, 1969.

Canada. *Income Distribution By Size*. Ottawa:Dominion Bureau of Statistics, 1970.

Canada. *Education in Canada's Northland*. Ottawa:Information Canada, 1972a.

Canada. *Foreign Direct Investment in Canada*. Ottawa:Queen's Printer, 1972b.

Canada. *Perspective Canada*. Ottawa:Information Canada, 1974a.

Canada. *Immigration Policy Perspectives*. Ottawa:Information Canada, 1974b.

Canada. *Perspective Canada II*.Ottawa:Statistics Canada, 1977.

Canada. *Income Distributions by Size*. Ottawa:Statistics Canada, 1978a

Canada. *Report of the Royal Commission on Corporate Concentration*. Ottawa:Ministry of Supply and Services, 1978b.

Canada. *The Distribution of Income and Wealth in Canada*. Ottawa:Statistics Canada, 1979.

Canada. *Taxation Statistics*. Ottawa:Ministry of Supply and Services. Annual.

Chodos, Robert. *The CPR*. Toronto:James Lewis and Samuel, 1973.

Clark, Burton. *Educating the Expert Society*. San Francisco:Chandler, 1962.

Clark, Harold F., and Harold S. Sloan. *Classrooms on Main Street*. New York:Teachers' College Press, 1966.

Clark, S.D. *Canadian Society in Historical Perspective*. Toronto:McGraw-Hill Ryerson, 1976.

Clement, Wallace. *The Canadian Corporate Elite*. Toronto:McClelland and Stewart, 1975.

Clement, Wallace. *Continental Corporate Power*. Toronto:McClelland and Stewart, 1977.

Clement, Wallace and Daniel Drache. *A Practical Guide to Canadian Political Economy*. Toronto:Lorimer, 1978.

Clinard, Marshall B. "The Theoretical Implications of Anomie and Deviant Behavior." In Marshall B. Clinard (ed.), *Anomie and Deviant Behavior*. Glencoe:Free Press, 1964, 1–56.

Collins, Randall. "Functional and Conflict Theories of Educational Stratification." *American Sociological Review*, 36(1971):1002–19.

Collins, Randall. *Conflict Sociology.* New York:Academic Press, 1975.

Coser, Lewis A. "Presidential Address: Two Methods in Search of a Substance." *American Sociological Review,* 40(1975):691-700.

Cottle, Basil. *The Penguin Dictionary of Surnames.* London:Penguin Books, 1978.

Crawford, Craig. "Social Status, General Personal Orientations, and Social Participation: A Comparison of Canadian and American Survey Data." Unpublished M.A. thesis, University of Waterloo, 1975.

Creighton, Donald. *The Empire of the St. Lawrence.* Toronto:Macmillan, 1937, 1956.

Crompton, Rosemary and Jon Gubbay. *Economy and Class Structure.* London:Macmillan, 1977.

Crozier, Michel. *The World of the Office Worker.* New York:Schocken, 1965.

Cuneo, Carl J. "A Class Perspective on Regionalism." in D. Glenday, H. Guindon, and A. Turowetz (eds.), *Modernization and the Canadian State.* Toronto:Macmillan, 1978, 132-56.

Cuneo, Carl J. and James E. Curtis. "Social Ascription in the Educational and Occupational Status Attainment of Urban Canadians." *Canadian Review of Sociology and Anthropology,* 12(1975):6-24.

Dahl, Robert. *Who Governs?* New Haven:Yale University Press, 1961.

Dahrendorf, Ralf. *Class and Class Conflict in Industrial Society.* Stanford: Stanford University Press, 1959.

Dahrendorf, Ralf. "On the Origin of Inequality Among Men." in Andre Beteille (ed.), *Social Inequality.* Middlesex:Penguin, 1969, 16-44.

Danziger, K. "Differences in Acculturation and Patterns of Socialization Among Italian Immigrant Families." in Robert M. Pike and Elia Zureik (eds.), *Socialization and Values in Canadian Society.* Vol. II. Toronto: McClelland and Stewart, 1975, 129-57.

Darroch, Gordon. "Another Look at Ethnicity, Stratification, and Mobility in Canada." *Canadian Journal of Sociology,* 4(1979):1-25.

Davis, Allison. *Social-Class Influences Upon Learning.* Cambridge:Harvard University Press, 1948.

Davis, Arthur K. "Canadian Society as Hinterland Versus Metropolis." in Richard J. Ossenberg (ed.), *Canadian Society: Pluralism, Change, and Conflict.* Scarborough:Prentice-Hall, 1971, 6-32,

Davis, Kingsley and Wilbert E. Moore. "Some Principles of Stratification." *American Sociological Review,* 10(1945):242-49.

Davis, Kingsley. *Human Society.* New York:Macmillan, 1948.

Davis, Kingsley. "Reply to Tumin." *American Sociological Review,* 18(1953): 349-97.

Davis, Kingsley. "The Myth of Functional Analysis as a Special Method in Sociology and Anthropology." *American Sociological Review,* 24(1959): 757-72.

Denis, Ann B. "CEGEP Students: Varieties in Socialization Experience." in Robert M. Pike and Elia Zureik (eds.), *Socialization and Values in Canadian Society.* Vol. II. Toronto:McClelland and Stewart, 1975, 209-36.

Denton, Margaret A. and Alfred A. Hunter. "The Experience of Female Candidates in the 1979 and 1980 Canadian General Elections." Unpublished manuscript, Department of Sociology, McMaster University, 1980.

Doctor X. [pseud.], *The Intern*. New York:Harper and Row, 1965.

Doeringer, Peter and Michael Piore. *Internal Labour Markets and Manpower Analysis*. Lexington:Heath, 1971.

Dofny, J. and M. Rioux. "Social Class in French Canada." in M. Rioux and Y. Martin (eds.), *French-Canadian Society*. Toronto:McClelland and Stewart, 1964.

Drache, Daniel. "Canadian Capitalism: Sticking with Staples." *This Magazine*, 9(1975):7–10.

Drache, Daniel. "Rediscovering Canadian Political Economy." In Wallace Clement and Daniel Drache (eds.), *A Practical Guide to Canadial Political Economy*. Toronto:Lorimer, 1978, 1–53.

Dreeben, Robert. *On What Is Learned In School*. Reading:Addison-Wesley, 1968.

Dubnoff, Steven. "Inter-Occupational Shifts and Changes in the Quality of Work in the American Economy." Paper presented at the annual meeting of the Society for the Study of Social Problems, San Francisco, 1978.

Duncan, Beverly. "Dropouts and the Unemployed." *Journal of Political Economy*, 73(1964):121–34.

Duncan, Otis D. "A Socio-Economic Index for all Occupations." in Albert J. Reiss (ed.), *Occupations and Social Status*. New York:Free Press, 1961, 109–38.

Duncan, Otis D., D. C. Featherman, and Beverly Duncan. *Socio-economic Background and Achievement*. New York:Seminar, 1972.

Durkheim, Emile. *The Division of Labor in Society*. Glencoe:Free Press, 1964.

Durkheim, Emile. *Suicide*. Translated by John A. Spaulding and George Simpson. Glencoe:Free Press, 1966.

Easterbrook, W. T. and H. G. H. Aitken. *Canadian Economic History*. Toronto:Macmillan, 1956.

Easterbrook, W. T. and M. H. Watkins (eds.), *Approaches to Canadian Economic History*. Toronto:McClelland and Stewart, 1967.

Economic Council of Canada. *Fifth Annual Review*. Ottawa:Queen's Printer, 1968.

Economic Council of Canada. *Living Together: A Study of Regional Disparities*. Ottawa:Ministry of Supply and Services, 1977.

Edwards, Richard C., Michael Reich, and David M. Gordon. *Labor Market Segmentation*. Lexington:Heath, 1975.

Engelmann, F. C. and M. A. Schwartz. *Canadian Political Parties: Origin, Character, Impact*. Scarborough:Prentice-Hall, 1975.

Engels, Friedrich. *Herr Eugen Duhring's Revolution in Science*. New York: International Publishers, 1885.

Engels, Friedrich. *The Origin of the Family, Private Property and the State*.

K. Marx and F. Engels, *Selected Works,* Vol. II. Moscow: Foreign Languages Publishing House, 1955.

Engels, Friedrich. "Why There is No Large Socialist Party in America." in Lewis S. Feuer (ed.), *Marx and Engels, Basic Writings on Politics and Philosophy.* Garden City:Anchor, 1959, 457–58.

Esterlin, Richard. "Does Money Buy Happiness?" *The Public Interest,* 30(1973): 3–10.

Fearn, Gordon F. N. *Canadian Social Organization.* Toronto:Holt, Rinehart and Winston, 1973.

Finn, Ed. "Deterrents to Unionization." *Labour Gazette,* 77(1977):341–46.

Fisher, L. A. and J. A. Cheyne. *Biological and Cultural Interactions as Found in Social Studies Research and Educational Media.* Toronto:Ontario Ministry of Education, 1978.

Folger, John K. and Charles B. Nam. "Trends in Education in Relation to the Occupational Structure." *Sociology of Education,* 38(1964):19–33.

Fowke, V. C. *The National Policy and the Wheat Economy.* Toronto:University of Toronto Press, 1957.

Frank, A. C. *Capitalism and Underdevelopment in Latin America.* New York: Monthly Review Press, 1969.

Gaskell, Jane. "The Sex-Role Ideology of Working Class Girls." *Canadian Review of Sociology and Anthropology,* 12(1)(1975):453–61.

Geer, Blanche. "Teaching." in B. R. Cosin, I. R. Dale, G. M. Esland, D. MacKinnon, and D. F. Swift (eds.), *School and Society.* London:Routledge and Kegan-Paul, 1977, 5–10.

Genovese, Eugene. *The Political Economy of Slavery.* New York:Pantheon Books, 1965.

Gerth, Hans H. and C. Wright Mills (eds.), *From Max Weber.* New York: Free Press, 1960.

Giddens, Anthony. *The Class Structure of the Advanced Societies.* London: Hutchinson, 1973.

Giddens, Anthony. "Elites in the British Class Structure." in Philip Stanworth, and Anthony Giddens (eds.), *Elites and Power in British Society.* London: Cambridge University Press, 1974, 1–21.

Gilbert, Sid. "The Selection of Educational Aspirations." in R. A. Carlton, L.A. Colley, and N.J. MacKinnon (eds.), *Education, Change, and Society.* Toronto:Gage, 1977, 281–97.

Glenn, Evelyn Nakano and Roslyn L. Feldberg. "Degraded and Deskilled: The Proletarianization of Clerical Work." *Social Problems,* 25(1977):52–64.

Goldthorpe, John H. "Class, Status and Party in Modern Britain." *European Journal of Sociology,* 13(1972):342–72.

Goldthorpe, J. H. and K. Hope. *The Social Grading of Occupations: A New Approach and Scale.* Oxford:Clarendon Press, 1974.

Gordon, David M. *Theories of Poverty and Unemployment.* Lexington:Heath, 1972.

Gorz, Andre. *Strategy for Labor.* Boston:Beacon, 1964, 1968.

Gouldner, Alvin. *The Coming Crisis of Western Sociology*. New York: Basic Books, 1971.

Goyder, John C. "Income Differences Between the Sexes: Findings From a National Survey." *Canadian Review of Sociology and Anthropology*, in press.

Goyder, John C. and James E. Curtis. "Occupational Mobility in Canada Over Four Generations." *Canadian Review of Sociology and Anthropology*, 14(1977):303–19.

Grant, George. *Lament For A Nation*. Toronto:McClelland and Stewart, 1965.

Greenbaum, Joan. "Division of Labor in the Computer Field." *Monthly Review*, 28(1976):40–55.

Guest, Dennis. *The Emergence of Social Security in Canada*. Vancouver:University of British Columbia Press, 1980.

Gunderson, Morley. "Work Patterns." in Gail C. A. Cook (ed.), *Opportunity for Choice*. Ottawa:Information Canada, 1976, 93–142.

Hall, Oswald and Richard Carlton. *Basic Skills at School and Work: The Study of Albertown, an Ontario Community*. Toronto:Ontario Economic Council, Occasional Paper I, 1977.

Hamblin, Robert L. "Mathematical Experimentation and Sociological Theory: A Critical Analysis." *Sociometry*, 34(1971):423–52.

Hamblin, Robert L. "Social Attitudes: Magnitude Measurement and Theory." in Hubert M. Blalock, Jr. (ed.), *Measurement in the Social Sciences*. Chicago:Aldine, 1974, 61–120.

Hamilton, Richard and Maurice Pinard. "The Basis of Parti Quebecois Support in Recent Quebec Elections." *Canadian Journal of Political Science*, 9(1976):3–26.

Hamilton, Richard and Maurice Pinard. "Poverty in Canada: Illusion and Reality." *Canadian Review of Sociology and Anthropology*, 14(1977): 247–52.

Hanson, S.D. "Estevan 1931." in Irving M. Abella (ed.), *On Strike*. Toronto: Lorimer, 1974, 33–78.

Harp, John and John R. Hofley (eds.), *Structured Inequality in Canada*. Scarborough:Prentice-Hall, 1980.

Harvey, Edward. *Educational Systems and the Labour Market*. Don Mills: Longman, 1974.

Hauser, Robert M., Peter J. Dickinson, Harry P. Travis, and John N. Koffel. "Structural Changes in Occupational Mobility Among Men in the United States." *American Sociological Review*, 40(1975):585–98.

Hayward, Lynda Mary. "Ethnicity and Home Ownership in Metropolitan Toronto." Unpublished M. A. thesis, University of Waterloo, 1980.

Heller, Celia S. (ed.), *Structured Social Inequality*. New York:Macmillan, 1969.

Hempel, Carl. "The Logic of Functional Analysis." in L. Gross (ed.), *Symposium on Sociological Theory*. Evanston:Row-Peterson, 1959, 271–307.

Henderson, D. W. and J. C. R. Rowley. "The Distribution and Evolution of

Canadian Family Incomes." Discussion Paper No. 91. Ottawa:Economic Council of Canada, 1977.

Henderson, D. W. and J. C. R. Rowley. "Decomposition of an Aggregate Measure of Income Distribution." Discussion Paper No. 107. Ottawa: Economic Council of Canada, 1978a.

Henderson, D. W. and J. C. R. Rowley. "Structural Changes and the Distribution of Canadian Family Incomes, 1965–1975." Discussion Paper No. 118. Ottawa:Economic Council of Canada, 1978b.

Henretta, John C. and Richard T. Campbell. "Net Worth as an Aspect of Status." *American Journal of Sociology*, 83(1978):1204–23.

Hewitt, Christopher. "The Effect of Political Democracy on Equality in Industrial Societies: A Cross-National Comparison." *American Sociological Review*, 42(1977):450–64.

Himelfarb, Alexander and C. James Richardson. *People, Power, and Process.* Toronto:McGraw-Hill Ryerson, 1979.

Hodge, R., P. Siegel, and P. Rossi. "Occupational Prestige in the United States 1925–1963." in R. Bendix and S. M. Lipset (eds.), *Class, Status and Power.* 2nd ed. New York:Free Press, 1966, 322–34.

Hodgetts, J. E. and O. P. Dwivedi. *Provincial Governments as Employers.* Montreal:McGill-Queen's Press, 1974.

Hollingshead, August B. *Elmtown's Youth.* New York:Wiley, 1949.

Hollingshead, A. B. and F. C. Redlich. *Social Class and Mental Illness.* New York:Wiley, 1958.

Homans, George C. "Contemporary Theory in Sociology." in Robert E. L. Faris (ed.), *Handbook of Modern Sociology.* Chicago:Rand-McNally, 1964, 951–77.

Hope, Keith. "Models of Status Inconsistency and Social Mobility Effects." *American Sociological Review*, 40(1975):322–43.

Horan, Patrick M. "Is Status Attainment Research Atheoretical?" *American Sociological Review*, 43(1978):534–41.

Horowitz, Irving Louis. *Three Worlds of Development: The Theory and Practice of International Stratification.* New York:Oxford, 1966.

Horowitz, Morris and Irwin Herrenstadt. "Changes in Skill Requirements of Occupations in Selected Industries." in National Commission on Technology, Automation, and Economic Progress, *The Employment Impact of Technological Change.* Appendix, Vol. II to *Technology and the American Economy.* Washington, D. C.:U. S. Government Printing Office, 1966b, 223–87.

House, James S. "Facets and Flaws of Hope's Diamond Model." *American Sociological Review*, 43(1978):439–42.

Hughes, Everett C. *French Canada in Transition.* Chicago:University of Chicago Press, 1943.

Hunter, Alfred A. "A Comparative Analysis of Anglophone-Francophone Occupational Prestige Structures in Canada." *Canadian Journal of Sociology*, 2(1977):179–93.

Hunter, Alfred A. "Gender, Incomes, and the Task Requirements of Occupations" (working title). Unpublished manuscript, Department of Sociology, University of Waterloo, 1980a.

Hunter, Alfred A. "On Class, Status, and Voting in Canada." Unpublished manuscript, Department of Sociology, University of Waterloo, 1980b.

Isbester, Fraser. "Asbestos 1949." in Irving M. Abella (ed.), *On Strike*. Toronto: Lorimer, 1974, 163-96.

Jackson, Elton F. and Richard F. Curtis. "Conceptualization and Measurement in the Study of Social Stratification." in Hubert M. Blalock, Jr. and Ann B. Blalock (eds.), *Methodology in Social Research*. New York: McGraw-Hill, 1968, 112-49.

Jamieson, Stuart M. *Times of Trouble: Labour Unrest and Industrial Conflict in Canada, 1900-1966*. Task Force on Labour Relations, Study No. 22. Ottawa:Ministry of Supply and Services, 1968.

Jamieson, Stuart M. *Industrial Relations in Canada*. 2nd ed. Toronto:Macmillan, 1973.

Jasso, Guillermina and Peter H. Rossi. "Distributive Justice and Earned Income." *American Sociological Review*, 42(1977):639-51.

Jencks, Christopher, Marshall Smith, Henry Acland, Mary Jo Bane, David Cohen, Herbert Gintis, Barbara Heyns, and Stephen Michelson. *Inequality: A Reassessment of the Effect of Family and Schooling in America*. New York:Harper and Row, 1972.

de Jocas, Y. and G. Rocher. "Inter-Generation Mobility in the Province of Quebec." *Canadian Journal of Economics and Political Science*, 23(1957): 58-66.

Johnson, Leo A. "The Development of Class in Canada in the Twentieth Century." in Gary Teeple (ed.), *Capitalism and the National Question in Canada*. Toronto:University of Toronto Press, 1972, 141-83.

Johnson, Leo A. *Poverty in Wealth*. 2nd ed. Toronto:New Hogtown Press, 1974.

Johnson, Leo A. "Illusions or Realities: Hamilton and Pinard's Approach to Poverty." *Canadian Review of Sociology and Anthropology*, 14(1977): 341-46.

Johnstone, John C. *Young People's Images of Canadian Society*. Studies of the Royal Commission on Bilingualism and Biculturalism. Ottawa:Queen's Printer, 1969.

Joy, Richard J. *Languages in Conflict*. Toronto:McClelland and Stewart, 1972.

Kagan, Jerome. "What is Intelligence?" in Alan Gartner, Colin Greer, and Frank Riessman (eds.), *The New Assault on Equality*. New York:Harper and Row, 1974, 114-30.

Kahl, Joseph. *The American Class Structure*. New York:Holt, Rinehart and Winston, 1957.

Kalbach, Warren E. and Wayne W. McVey. *The Demographic Bases of Canadian Society*. Toronto:McGraw-Hill, 1971.

Kealey, G. (ed.) *Canada Investigates Industrialism*. Toronto:University of Toronto Press, 1973.

Kemper, Theodore David. "On the Nature and Purpose of Ascription." *American Sociological Review,* 39(1974):844–53.

Kemper, Theodore David. "Marxist and Functionalist Theories in the Study of Stratification." *Social Forces,* 54(1976):559–78.

Kerr, Clark, John T. Dunlop, Frederick Harbison, and Charles A. Myers. *Industrialism and Industrial Man.* New York:Oxford University Press, 1960.

Kilbourn, William. *Canada: A Guide to the Peaceable Kingdom.* Toronto: Macmillan, 1970.

Krueger, Cynthia. "Prairie Protest: The Medicare Conflict in Saskatchewan." in Seymour Martin Lipset, *Agrarian Socialism.* Berkeley:Anchor, 1971, 405–34.

Kubat, Daniel and David Thornton. *A Statistical Profile of Canadian Society.* Toronto:McGraw-Hill Ryerson, 1974.

Lambert, Ronald D. and Alfred A. Hunter. "Social Stratification, Voting Behaviour, and the Images of Canadian Federal Political Parties." *Canadian Review of Sociology and Anthropology,* 16(1979):287–304.

Lane, David. *The End of Inequality? Stratification Under State Socialism.* Middlesex:Penguin, 1971.

Lanphier, C. Michael and Raymond N. Morris. "Structural Aspects of Differences in Incomes Between Anglophones and Francophones." *Canadian Review of Sociology and Anthropology,* 11(1974):53–66.

Lasswell, Harold and Abraham Kaplan. *Power and Society: A Framework for Political Inquiry.* New Haven:Yale University Press, 1950.

Lautard, Hugh. "Occupational Segregation by Sex and Industrialization in Canada:1891–1971." Paper presented at the Annual Meetings of the Canadian Sociology and Anthropology Association, Fredericton, New Brunswick, 1977.

Laxer, Jim. "Introduction to the Political Economy of Canada." in Robert M. Laxer (ed.), *(Canada) Ltd. The Political Economy of Dependency.* Toronto:McClelland and Stewart, 1973, 26–41.

Leduc, Lawrence, Harold Clarke, Jane Jenson, and Jon Pammet. "A National Sample Design." *Canadian Journal of Political Science,* 7(1974):701–5.

Leggett, John. *Class, Race, and Labor.* New York:Oxford, 1968.

Lenski, Gerhard. "Status Crystallization: A Non-Vertical Dimension of Social Status." *American Sociological Review,* 19(1954):405–13.

Lenski, Gerhard. *Power and Privilege.* New York:McGraw-Hill, 1966.

Levitt, Kari. *Silent Surrender: The Multinational Corporation in Canada.* Toronto:Macmillan, 1970.

Lewis, Oscar. *The Children of Sanchez.* New York:Random House, 1961.

Linton, Ralph. *The Study of Man.* New York:Appleton-Century, 1936.

Lipset, Seymour M. *Agrarian Socialism.* Berkeley:University of California Press, 1950.

Lipset, Seymour M. "Value Differences, Absolute or Relative: The English-Speaking Democracies." in Bernard R. Blishen, Frank E. Jones, Kaspar

D. Naegele, and John Porter (eds.), *Canadian Society*. 2nd ed. Toronto: Macmillan, 1964, 478–93.

Lipset, S. M. and R. Bendix. *Social Mobility in Industrial Society*. Berkeley: University of California Press, 1959.

Lockwood, David. *The Blackcoated Worker*. London:Allen and Unwin, 1958.

Lopreato, J. and L. Lewis. "An Analysis of Variables in the Functional Theory of Stratification." *Sociological Quarterly*, 4(1963):301–10.

Love, Roger and Michael C. Wolfson. *Income Inequality: Statistical Methodology and Canadian Illustrations*. Ottawa:Statistics Canada, 1976.

Lowe, Graham. "Trends in the Development of Clerical Occupations in Canada." Paper presented at the Annual Meetings of the Canadian Sociology and Anthropology Association, Fredericton, New Brunswick, 1977.

Lundberg, Ferdinand. *America's 60 Families*. New York:Vanguard, 1938.

Maccoby, Eleanor and Carol Jacklin. *The Psychology of Sex Differences*. Stanford:Stanford University Press, 1974.

MacDougall, John. *Rural Life in Canada*. Toronto:University of Toronto Press, 1913, 1973.

MacKinnon, Neil J. and Paul Anisef. "Self-Assessment in the Early Educational Attainment Process." *Canadian Review of Sociology and Anthropology*, 16(1979):305–19.

MacLysaght, Edward. *Irish Families*. New York:Crown, 1972.

Malinowski, B. "Anthropology." in *Encyclopaedia Britannica*. First Supplementary Volume. London and New York, 1926, 132–33.

Malinowski, B. "The Group and the Individual in Functional Analysis." *American Journal of Sociology*, 44(1939):938–64.

Mallet, Serge. *La Nouvelle Classe Ouvriere*. Paris:Editions du Seuil, 1969.

Mann, Michael. "The Social Cohesion of Liberal Democracy." *American Sociological Review*, 35(1971):423–39.

Mann, Michael. *Consciousness and Action Among the Western Working Class*. London:Macmillan, 1973.

Mandel, Ernest. *Marxist Economic Theory*. New York:Monthly Review, 1968.

Manley, Michael and Alfred A. Hunter. "The Task Requirements of Occupations" (working title). Unpublished manuscript. Department of Sociology, University of Waterloo, 1980.

Manzer, Ronald. *Canada: A Socio-Political Report*. Toronto:McGraw-Hill Ryerson, 1974.

Marchak, M. Patricia. *Ideological Perspectives on Canada*. Toronto: McGraw-Hill Ryerson, 1975.

Marfels, Christian. *Concentration Levels and Trends in the Canadian Economy*. Royal Commission on Corporate Concentration, Study No. 31. Ottawa:Ministry of Supply and Services, 1976.

Martin, W. B. W. and A. J. Macdonell. *Canadian Education: A Sociological Analysis*. Scarborough:Prentice-Hall, 1978.

Marx, Karl. *Capital*. Vol. I. New York:International Publishers, 1967.

Marx, Karl. *Value, Price and Profit.* New York:International Publishers, 1935.

Marx, Karl and Friedrich Engels. *Basic Writings on Politics and Philosophy.* Edited by Lewis S. Feuer. Garden City:Anchor, 1959.

Marx, Karl and Friedrich Engels. *The German Ideology.* Moscow:Foreign Language Publishing House, 1965.

Marx, Karl. *Selected Works.* Vol. I. Moscow:Progress Publishers, 1969.

Maslove, Allan. *The Pattern of Taxation in Canada.* Ottawa:Information Canada, 1972.

Masters, D. C. *The Winnipeg General Strike.* Toronto:University of Toronto Press, 1950.

Mayhew, Leon. "Ascription in Modern Societies." *Sociological Inquiry,* 38(1968):105–20.

McDougall, J. Lorne. *Canadian Pacific: A Brief History.* Montreal:McGill-Queen's Press, 1968.

McLaughlin, Steven D. "Occupational Sex Identification and the Assessment of Male and Female Earnings Inequality." *American Sociological Review,* 43(1978):909–21.

McRoberts, Hugh A., John Porter, Monica Boyd, John Goyder, Frank E. Jones, and Peter C. Pineo. "Differences dans la Mobilite Professionnelle des Francophones et des Anglophones." *Sociologie et Sociétés,* 8(1976):61–79.

Meltz, Noah M. "Manpower in Canada, 1931–1961." *Historical Statistics of the Canadian Labour Force.* Ottawa:Queen's Printer, 1969.

Meltz, Noah M. and David Stager. *The Occupational Structure of Earnings in Canada, 1931–1971.* Ottawa:Anti-Inflation Board, 1977.

Merton, Robert K. *Social Theory and Social Structure.* Rev. ed. Glencoe: Free Press, 1957.

Miliband, Ralph. *The State in Capitalist Society.* London:Quartet Books, 1969.

Miliband, Ralph. "Poulantzas and the Capitalist State." *New Left Review,* 82(1973).

Miller, George. "Professionals in Bureaucracy: Alienation Among Industrial Scientists and Engineers." *American Sociological Review,* 32(1967): 755–67.

Mills, C. Wright. *The Power Elite.* New York:Oxford University Press, 1956.

Mills, C. Wright. *The Sociological Imagination.* New York:Grove, 1959.

Mills, C. Wright. *The Marxists.* New York:Dell, 1968.

Mills, C. Wright. "Comment on Criticism." in G. William Domhoff and Hoyt B. Ballard (eds.), *C. Wright Mills and the Power Elite,* Boston:Beacon, 1968, 229–50.

Milner, S. H. and H. Milner. *The Decolonization of Quebec.* Toronto:McClelland and Stewart, 1973.

Morris, Raymond N. and C. Michael Lanphier. "Response." *Canadian Review of Sociology and Anthropology,* 12(1975):228.

Morris, Raymond N. and C. Michael Lanphier. *Three Scales of Inequality: Perspectives on French-English Relations.* Don Mills:Longman, 1977.

Morton, Desmond. "Aid to the Civil Power: The Stratford Strike of 1933." in Irving M. Abella (ed.), *On Strike*. Toronto:Lorimer, 1974, 79–92.

Moulton, David. "Ford Windsor 1945." in Irving M. Abella (ed.), *On Strike*. Toronto:Lorimer, 1974, 129–62.

Murphy, Raymond. *Sociological Theories of Education*. Toronto:McGraw-Hill Ryerson, 1979.

Myers, Gustavus. *A History of Canadian Wealth*. Toronto:James Lewis and Samuel, 1914, 1972.

Myles, John F. "Differences in the Canadian and American Class Vote: Fact or Pseudofact?" *American Journal of Sociology*, 84(1979):1232–37.

Naegele, Kaspar D. "Canadian Society: Further Reflections." in Bernard R. Blishen, Frank E. Jones, Kaspar D. Naegele, and John Porter (eds.), *Canadian Society*. 2nd ed. Toronto:Macmillan, 1964, 497–522.

Nagel, Ernest. *Logic Without Metaphysics*. Glencoe:Free Press, 1956.

Nagel, Ernest. *The Structure of Science*. New York:Harcourt, Brace and World, 1961.

National Opinion Research Centre. "Jobs and Occupations: A Popular Evaluation." *Opinion News*, XI(1947):3–13.

Naylor, R. T. "The Rise and Fall of the Third Commercial Empire of the St. Lawrence." in Gary Teeple (ed.), *Capitalism and the National Question in Canada*. Toronto:University of Toronto Press, 1972, 1–41.

Naylor, R. T. *The History of Canadian Business, 1867–1914*. Two volumes. Toronto:Lorimer, 1975.

Newman, Peter C. *The Canadian Establishment*. Volume I, Revised and Updated. Toronto:McClelland and Stewart-Bantam, 1975, 1979.

Newman, Peter C. *Bronfman Dynasty*. Toronto:McClelland and Stewart-Bantam, 1978.

Nisbet, Robert A. *Community and Power*. New York:Oxford University Press, 1962.

O'Connor, James. *The Fiscal Crisis of the State*. New York:St. Martin's, 1973.

Ogmundson, Rick. "Party Images and the Class Vote in Canada." *American Sociological Review*, 40(1975a):506–12.

Ogmundson, Rick. "The Sociology of Power and Politics: An Introduction to the Canadian Polity." in G. N. Ramu and Stuart D. Johnson (eds.), *Introduction to Canadian Society*. Toronto:Macmillan, 1976, 157–211.

Olsen, Dennis. "The State Elites." in Leo Panitch (ed.), *The Canadian State: Political Economy and Political Power*. Toronto:University of Toronto Press, 1977, 199–224.

Ostry, Sylvia. *The Occupational Composition of the Canadian Labour Force*. Ottawa:Dominion Bureau of Statistics, 1967.

Ostry, Sylvia. *The Female Worker in Canada*. Ottawa:Dominion Bureau of Statistics, 1968.

Palmer, Bryan D. "Give Us the Road and We Will Run It: The Social and Cultural Matrix of an Emerging Labour Movement." in G. S. Kealey and P. Warrian (eds.), *Essays in Canadian Working Class History*. Toronto: McClelland and Stewart, 1976, 106–24.

Panitch, Leo. "The Role and Nature of the Canadian State." in Leo Panitch (ed.), *The Canadian State: Political Economy and Political Power.* Toronto:University of Toronto Press, 1977, 3-27.

Park, Libbie and Frank Park. *Anatomy of Big Business.* Toronto:James Lewis and Samuel, 1962, 1973.

Parkin, Frank. *Class, Inequality, and Political Order.* London:Paladin, 1972.

Parsons, Talcott. *The Structure of Social Action.* New York:McGraw-Hill, 1937.

Parsons, Talcott. "An Analytical Approach to the Theory of Social Stratification." *American Journal of Sociology,* 45(1940):841-62.

Parsons, Talcott. *The Social System.* Glencoe:Free Press, 1951.

Parsons, Talcott. "A Revised Analytical Approach to the Theory of Social Stratification." in Reinhard Bendix and Seymour M. Lipset (eds.), *Class, Status and Power: A Reader in Social Stratification.* Glencoe:Free Press, 1953, 92-128.

Penner, Norman (ed.), *Winnipeg 1919.* Toronto:James Lewis and Samuel, 1973.

Pentland, H. C. "Labour and the Development of Industrial Capitalism in Canada." Unpublished Ph.D. thesis, University of Toronto, 1960.

Perry, Robert L. *Galt, U. S. A.* Toronto:Maclean-Hunter, 1971.

Phillips, Paul. *Regional Disparities.* Toronto:Lorimer, 1978.

Pinard, Maurice. "Working Class Politics: An Interpretation of the Quebec Case." *Canadian Review of Sociology and Anthropology,* 7(1970):87-109.

Pinard, Maurice and Richard Hamilton. "The Parti Quebecois Comes to Power: An Analysis of the 1976 Quebec Election." *Canadian Journal of Political Science,* 11(1978):739-75.

Pineo, Peter C. and John C. Goyder. "Social Class Identification of National Sub-Groups." in James E. Curtis and William C. Scott (eds.), *Social Stratification: Canada.* Scarborough:Prentice-Hall, 1973, 187-96.

Pineo, Peter C. and John Porter. "Occupational Prestige in Canada." *Canadian Review of Sociology and Anthropology,* 4(1967):24-40.

Piore, Michael J. "Notes for a Theory of Labour Market Stratification." in David Gordon et al. (eds.), *Labor Market Segmentation.* Lexington: Heath, 1975, 125-50.

Pipes, Sally C. and Michael Walker. *Tax Facts: The Canadian Tax Index and You.* Vancouver:Fraser Institute, 1979.

Podoluk, Jenny R. *Incomes of Canadians.* Ottawa:Dominion Bureau of Statistics, 1968.

Porter, John. *The Vertical Mosaic.* Toronto:University of Toronto Press, 1965.

Porter, John. *Canadian Social Structure: A Statistical Profile.* Toronto:McClelland and Stewart, 1967.

Porter, Marion R. John Porter, and Bernard R. Blishen. *Does Money Matter?* Downsview:Institute for Behavioural Research, 1973.

Poulantzas, Nicos. *Classes in Contemporary Capitalism.* London:New Left Books, 1975.

Prentice, Alison. *The School Promoters.* Toronto:McClelland and Stewart, 1977.

Projector, Dorothy S. "Survey of Financial Characteristics of Consumers." *Federal Reserve Bulletin,* 50(1964):285.

Quebec. *Report on the Royal Commission of Inquiry on Education in the Province of Quebec.* Printer for the Government of the Province of Quebec, 1966.

Radcliffe-Brown, A. R. "On the Concept of Function in Social Science." *American Anthropologist,* 37(1935):395-96.

Radcliffe-Brown, A. R. *A Natural Science of Society.*Glencoe:Free Press, 1948a.

Radcliffe-Brown, A. R. *The Andaman Islanders.* Glencoe:Free Press, 1948b.

Rainwater, Lee. "Poverty, Living Standards and Family Well-Being." Working Paper No. 10. Cambridge:Joint Centre for Urban Studies of M.I.T. and Harvard, 1972.

Rawls, John. *A Theory of Justice.* Cambridge:Harvard University Press, 1971.

Raynauld, A., G. Marion, and R. Beland. "La Repartition des Revenues Selon, les Groupes Ethnic au Canada." Rapport Final. Unpublished manuscript, 1967. Cited in Lanphier, C. Michael and Raymond N. Morris. "Structural Aspects of Differences in Incomes Between Anglophones and Francophones." *Canadian Review of Sociology and Anthropology,* 11(1974):53-66.

Raynauld, A., G. Marion, and R. Beland. "Structural Aspects of Differences in Income Between Anglophones and Francophones." *Canadian Review of Sociology and Anthropology,* 12(1975):221-27.

Reaney, P. H. *A Dictionary of British Surnames.* London:Routledge and Kegan-Paul, 1958.

Reiss, Albert J., Jr. (ed.), *Occupations and Social Status.* New York:Free Press, 1961.

Reiter, Rayna Rapp. "Review of Steven Goldberg, *The Inevitability of Patriarchy.*" *Contemporary Sociology,* 6(1977):91-92.

Reynolds, Lloyd G. *The Control of Competition in Canada.* Cambridge: Harvard University Press, 1940.

Richmond, Anthony H. *Post-War Immigrants in Canada.* Toronto:University of Toronto Press, 1967.

Richmond, Anthony H. *Ethnic Residential Segregation in Metropolitan Toronto.* Toronto:Institute for Behavioural Research, York University, 1972.

Riesman, David. *The Lonely Crowd.* New York:Doubleday, 1953.

Rinehart, James W. and Ishmael O. Okraku. "A Study of Class Consciousness." *Canadian Review of Sociology and Anthropology,* 11(1974):197-213.

Rinehart, James W. *The Tyranny of Work.* Don Mills:Longman, 1975.

Robb, A. Leslie and Byron G. Spencer. "Education: Enrolment and Attainment." in Gail C.A. Cook (ed.), *Opportunity for Choice.* Ottawa:Information Canada, 1976, 53-92.

Robinson, Robert V. and Jonathan Kelley. "Class as Conceived by Marx and Dahrendorf: Effects on Income Inequality and Politics in the United States and Great Britain." *American Sociological Review,* 44(1979):38–58.

Robinson, R. A. H. and M. Lapointe. *A Comparison of Men's and Women's Salaries and Employment Fringe Benefits in the Academic Profession.* Royal Commission on the Status of Women in Canada. Ottawa:Queen's Printer, 1971.

Rodriguez, Orlando. "Occupational Shifts and Educational Upgrading in the American Labour Force Between 1950 and 1970." Paper read at the Annual Meetings of the American Sociological Association, New York City, 1976.

Rowntree, B. S. *Poverty — A Study of Town Life.* London:Macmillan, 1901.

Rudner, Richard S. *Philosophy of Social Science.* Englewood Cliffs:Prentice-Hall, 1966.

Runciman, W. G. *Relative Deprivation and Social Justice.* London:Routledge and Kegan-Paul, 1966.

Ryan, William. *Blaming the Victim,* New York:Random House, 1971.

Ryerson, Stanley. *Unequal Union.* Toronto:Progress, 1968.

Ryerson, Stanley. "Who's Looking After Business: A Review." *This Magazine,* 10(1976):41–46.

Schecter, Stephen. "Capitalism, Class, and Educational Reform in Canada." in Leo Panitch (ed.), *The Canadian State: Political Economy and Political Power.* Toronto:University of Toronto Press, 1977, 373–416.

Schmitt, David R. "Magnitude Measures of Economic and Educational Status." *Sociological Quarterly,* 6(1965):387–91.

Seccombe, W. "The Housewife and Her Labour Under Capitalism." *New Left Review,* 83(1973):3–24.

Sharlin, Allan. "From the Study of Social Mobility to the Study of Society." *American Journal of Sociology,* 85(1979):338–60.

Shepard, Jon M. *Automation and Alienation: A Study of Office and Factory Workers.* Cambridge:MIT Press, 1971.

Silverstein, S. "Occupational Class and Voting Behaviour: Electoral Support of a Left-Wing Protest Movement in a Period of Prosperity." in Seymour M. Lipset, *Agrarian Socialism,* Berkeley:University of California Press, 1971, 435–79.

Smith, Adam. *An Inquiry into the Nature and Causes of the Wealth of Nations.* New York:Modern Library, 1776, 1937.

Sorenson, Aage B. "A Model and a Metric for the Analysis of the Intragenerational Status Attainment Process." *American Journal of Sociology,* 85(1979):361–84.

Special Senate Committee on Poverty. *Poverty in Canada.* Report of the Special Senate Committee on Poverty. Ottawa:Information Canada, 1971.

Spence, A. M. *Market Signaling.* Cambridge:Harvard University Press, 1974.

Spenner, Kenneth I. "Temporal Changes in Work Content." *American Sociological Review,* 44(1979):968–75.

Squires, Gregory D. "Education, Jobs, and Inequality: Functional and Conflict Models of Social Stratification in the United States." *Social Problems,* 24(1977):436–50.

Stacey, Judith, Susan Bereaud, and Dennis C. Featherstone (eds.), *And Jill Came Tumbling After.* New York:Dell, 1974.

Stanworth, Philip and Anthony Giddens. *Elites and Power in British Society.* London:Cambridge University Press, 1974.

Stirling, Robert and Denise Kouri. "Unemployment Indexes — The Canadian Context." in John Allan Fry (ed.), *Economy, Class, and Social Reality.* Toronto:Butterworths, 1979, 169–205.

Stolzenberg, Ross M. "Education, Occupation, and Wage Differences Between Black and White Men." *American Journal of Sociology,* 81(1975):299–323

Svalastoga, Kaare. *Social Differentiation.* New York:McKay, 1965.

Synge, J. "The Sex Factor in Social Selection Processes in Canadian Education." in R.A. Carlton, L.A. Colley, and N.J. MacKinnon (eds.), *Education, Change, and Society: A Sociology of Canadian Education.* Toronto: Gage, 1977, 289–310.

Taylor, Norman W. "The French-Canadian Industrial Entrepreneur and His Environment." in M. Rioux and Y. Martin (eds.), *French-Canadian Society.* Volume I. Toronto:McClelland and Stewart, 1964, 271–95.

Teeple, Gary. "Land, Labour, and Capital in Pre-Confederation Canada." in Gary Teeple (ed.), *Capitalism and the National Question in Canada.* Toronto:University of Toronto Press, 1972, 43–66.

Tepperman, Lorne. *Social Mobility in Canada.* Toronto:McGraw-Hill, 1975.

Thurow, Lester. *Poverty and Discrimination.* Washington:The Brookings Institute, 1969.

Thurow, Lester. *Generating Inequality.* New York:Basic Books, 1975.

Tolbert, Charles, Patrick M. Horan, and E.M. Beck. "The Structure of Economic Segmentation: A Dual Economy Approach." *American Journal of Sociology, 85(1980):1095*–1116.

Touraine, Alain. *The Post-Industrial Society: Tomorrow's Social History: Classes, Conflicts and Culture in the Programmed Society.* New York: Random House, 1971.

Trudeau, P.E. *La Grève de l'amiante.* Montréal:Cité Libre, 1956.

Truman, Tom. "A Critique of Seymour Martin Lipset's Article, 'Value Differences, Absolute or Relative: The English-Speaking Democracies.'" *Canadian Journal of Political Science, 4(1971):497*–525.

Tumin, Melvin M. "Some Principles of Stratification: A Critical Analysis." *American Sociological Review,* 18(1953a):387–93.

Tumin, Melvin M. "Reply to Kingsley Davis." *American Sociological Review,* 18(1953b):672–73.

Tumin, Melvin M. *Social Stratification.* Englewood Cliffs:Prentice-Hall, 1967.

Turrittin, Anton H. "Social Mobility in Canada: A Comparison of Three Provincial Studies and Some Methodological Questions." *Canadian Review of Sociology and Anthropology, Special Issue (1974):163–86.*

United States. *Estimates of Worker Trait Requirements for 4,000 Jobs.* Department of Labor. Washington:General Printing Office, 1956.

Urquhart, M.C. and K.A.H. Buckley (eds.), *Historical Statistics of Canada.* Toronto:Macmillan, 1965.

Walker, Charles R. and Robert H. Guest. *The Man on the Assembly Line.* Cambridge:Harvard University Press, 1952.

Warner, W. Lloyd, Marcia Meeker, and Kenneth Eells. *Social Class in America.* New York:Harper and Row, 1960.

Warner, W. Lloyd, J.O. Low, Paul S. Lunt, and Leo Srole. *Yankee City.* One volume abridged edition. New Haven:Yale University Press, 1963.

Watkins, Mel. "Ryerson on Naylor: The Usefulness of Book Reviews." *This Magazine,* 11(1977):34.

Weber, Max. *From Max Weber: Essays in Sociology.* Edited and translated by Hans H. Gerth and C. Wright Mills. New York:Oxford, 1946.

Weber, Max. *The Theory of Social and Economic Organization.* Translated by A.M. Henderson and Talcott Parsons. Glencoe:Free Press, 1964.

Wesolowski, W. "Some Notes on the Functional Theory of Stratification." *Polish Sociological Bulletin,* 3–4(1962):28–38.

Westley, M.A. and M.W. Westley. *The Emerging Worker.* Montreal:McGill-Queen's Press, 1971.

Williams, Jack. *The Story of Unions in Canada.* Toronto:Dent, 1975.

Williams, Trevor. "Education and Biosocial Processes." in R.A. Carlton, L.A. Colley, and N.J. MacKinnon (eds.), *Education, Change, and Society.* Toronto:Gage, 1977, 248–80.

Willox, Paul. "Quebec Labour and the Rise of Working Class Consciousness." in John Allan Fry (ed.), *Economy, Class and Social Reality.* Toronto: Butterworths, 1979, 263–82.

Wiseman, Nelson and K.W. Taylor. "Ethnic vs. Class Voting: The Case of Winnipeg, 1945." *Canadian Journal of Political Science,* 7(1974):314–28.

Wolfe, David. "The State and Economic Policy in Canada, 1968–1975." in Leo Panitch (ed.), *The Canadian State: Political Economy and Political Power.* Toronto:University of Toronto Press, 1977, 251–88.

Wolfson, M.C. and R. Love. *Income Inequality: Statistical Methodology and Canadian Illustrations.* Ottawa:Statistics Canada, 1976.

Wright, Eric O. "Class Boundaries in Advanced Capitalist Societies." *New Left Review,* 98(1976):3–41.

Wright, Eric O. *Class, Crisis and the State.* London:New Left Books, 1978.

Wrong, Dennis. "The Oversocialized Conception of Man in Modern Sociology." *American Sociological Review,* 26(1961):183–93.

Young, Michael. *The Rise of the Meritocracy.* Penguin:Harmondsworth, 1961.

Zeeman, E.C. "Catastrophe Theory." *Scientific American,* 234(1976):65–83.

Index

257